Maldevelopment

THE UNITED NATIONS UNIVERSITY/THIRD WORLD FORUM

STUDIES IN AFRICAN POLITICAL ECONOMY
General Editor: Samir Amin

The United Nations University's (UNU) Project on the Third World and World Development aims to study contemporary global developments from the perspective of the South: ongoing trends and structural changes in the world-system are analysed in terms of their consequences for the different regions of the third world and their implications for development strategies and policy options that the developing countries can pursue, singly and collectively through South-South co-operation. Through an interdisciplinary and global comparative framework, the Project integrates the UNU's previous research work on the regional perspectives of Africa, Asia, and Latin America—research which has been undertaken over the last decade and has involved, worldwide, hundreds of researchers organized into regional networks. (The Studies in African Political Economy series grew out of the work of the African regional network as part of an earlier UNU project, Transnationalization or Nation-Building in Africa.) The comparative research into the different regions' experiences of the 1980s provides a basis for comprehending their expectations for the 1990s and for formulating development strategies that would be fully cognizant of the changes that have occurred at all levels of the global system. Those changes have been analysed in this Project through five main themes: the process of transnationalization, the crisis of states, the emergence of social movements, the cultural dimension of contemporary developments, and conflicts and the possibilities of co-operation in the third world.

TITLES IN THIS SERIES

M.L. Gakou
The Crisis in African Agriculture
1987

Peter Anyang' Nyong'o (editor)
Popular Struggles for Democracy in Africa
1987

Samir Amin, Derrick Chitala, Ibbo Mandaza (editors)
SADCC: Prospects for Disengagement and Development in Southern Africa
1987

Faysal Yachir
The World Steel Industry Today
1988

Faysal Yachir
Mining in Africa Today: Strategies and Prospects
1988

Faysal Yachir
The Mediterranean: Between Autonomy and Dependency
1989

Azzam Mahjoub (editor)
Adjustment or Delinking? The African Experience
1990

Hamid Ait Amara, Bernard Founou-Tchuigoua (editors)
African Agriculture: The Critical Choices
1990

Samir Amin
Maldevelopment: Anatomy of A Global Failure
1990

Fawzy Mansour
The Arab World: Nation, State and Democracy
1990

THE UNITED NATIONS UNIVERSITY/THIRD WORLD FORUM

STUDIES IN AFRICAN POLITICAL ECONOMY

Maldevelopment

Anatomy of a Global Failure

Samir Amin

United Nations University Press
Tokyo

Zed Books Ltd.
London and New Jersey

Maldevelopment: Anatomy of a Global Failure
was first published in 1990
by:
Zed Books Ltd., 57 Caledonian Road, London N1 9BU, UK, and
171 First Avenue, Atlantic Highlands, New Jersey 07716, USA
and:
United Nations University Press, The United Nations University,
Toho Seimei Building, 15–1 Shibuya 2-chome, Shibuya-ku, Tokyo 150, Japan
in co-operation with
The Third World Forum, B.P. 3501, Dakar, Senegal.

Copyright © The United Nations University, 1990.

Translation by Michael Wolfers
Cover designed by Andrew Corbett.
Typeset by EMS Photosetters, Rochford, Essex.
Printed and bound in the United Kingdom
by Biddles Ltd, Guildford and King's Lynn.

British Library Cataloguing in Publication data

Amin, Samir 1931
    Maldevelopment: anatomy of a global failure. – (The United Nations
University/Third World Forum Studies in African Political Economy).
    1. Economic development. Sociopolitical Aspects
    I. Title II. Series
    330.9

    ISBN 0-86232-930-2
    ISBN 0-86232-931-0 pbk

Library of Congress Cataloging-in-Publication Data

Amin, Samir.
    Maldevelopment: anatomy of a global failure / Samir Amin;
translated from the French by Michael Wolfers.
        p.   cm.
    ISBN 0-86232-930-2. — ISBN 0-86232-931-0 (pbk.)
    1. Developing countries—Economic policy. 2. Africa—Economic
conditions—1960- 3. Economic history—1971- I. Title.
HC59.7.A7777   1990
338.9′009172′4—dc20   89-70607
                                                                 CIP

Contents

Introduction: why a political analysis?

If the 1960s were characterized by the great hope of seeing an irreversible process of development launched throughout what came to be called the Third World, and in Africa particularly, the present age is one of disillusionment. Development has broken down, its theory is in crisis, its ideology the subject of doubt. Agreement on failure in Africa is sadly general. Opinions are more varied in regard to Asia and Latin America. Some emphasize the economic successes of the newly industrializing countries, such as South Korea, Brazil and India, and conclude that the only possible development is one that intelligently succumbs to the increasing worldwide expansion of all economies on the earth. These examples should be followed, and the illusions of alternative paths to the transnational model abandoned, since, in the meantime, socialism is itself in crisis in the countries of the East, and the Third World countries who look to them for inspiration, and the socialist countries themselves are obliged to yield to a harrowing revisionism and are seeking reintegration in the expansion of a world economy.

In this book it is proposed to analyse this failure of development from a political stand-point, for discussion of the options in the framework of macro-economic schema provides no more than commonplace and foreseeable findings. We must aim higher and integrate in the discussion all the economic, political, social and cultural facets of the problem and at the same time fit them into a local framework that takes account of interaction on a world scale.

We acknowledge that this aim comes up against major theoretical difficulties. Social reality as a whole has three facets: economic, political and cultural. The economic aspect is perhaps the best known. In this field, conventional economics has forged tools of immediate analysis and with greater or lesser success of management of an advanced capitalist society. Historical materialism has sought to plunge deeper and has often succeeded in illuminating the character and extent of social struggles underlying the economic choices.

The field of power and politics is relatively less known; and eclecticism in the theories advanced shows the inadequate scientific mastery of the reality. Functional political thought, like its former or recent ingredients (geopolitics, systems analysis, etc.) may sometimes be of immediate use in shaping strategies but remains conceptually impoverished and does not warrant the status of a critical theory. It is true that historical materialism provides a hypothesis as to the organic relationship between the material base and the political superstructure, and the hypothesis is fruitful if it is not too crudely interpreted. The Marxist schools, however, have not conceptualized the issue of power and politics (modes of domination) as they have the economic categories (modes of production). The propositions in this direction, by Freudian Marxists for example, have the undoubted merit of drawing attention to neglected aspects of the issue but have not yet produced an overall conceptual system. The field of politics lies virtually fallow.

It is not by chance that the first chapter of Volume One of *Capital* includes the section entitled 'The Fetishism of Commodities and the Secret thereof'. Marx intends to unveil the mysteries of capitalist society, and the reason why it appears to us as directly governed by economics, in the forefront of the social scene and the determinant of the other social dimensions that seem then to accommodate to its demands. Economic alienation thus defines the essence of the ideology of capitalism. Conversely, pre-capitalist class societies are governed by politics, which takes the forefront of the stage and provide the constraints that other aspects of the social reality – including economic life – seem bound to obey. If a theory of these societies were to be written, the work would be entitled 'Power' (instead of capital for the capitalist mode) and the opening chapter would deal with 'the fetishism of power' (instead of the fetishism of commodities).

But no such work has been written. There is nothing analogous to the clockwork precision with which the economic operation of capitalism has been described. Marxism has not provided a theory of politics for pre-capitalist society (and hence a theory of politics in general) as it has provided a theory of capitalist economics. At best there are concrete analyses of the relationship of politics and economics in such and such a capitalist society (in Marx's political writings devoted particularly to the vicissitudes of France) highlighting the degree of the autonomy of politics in these circumstances and especially the conflict that may arise between the logic of power and that of capitalist management.

As for the cultural dimension, it is an even more complex mystery, as empirical observation of this aspect of reality (of religious faiths for example) has so far yielded no more than intuitive forays. This explains why discussion of the cultural dimensions of history remains imbued with culturalism, meaning the tendency to treat cultural characteristics as trans-historical constants. Furthermore, culture has no generally accepted boundaries, since their definition depends precisely on the underlying theory of social dynamic that is being followed. According to the observer's interest in a pursuit of common ingredients in the social evolution of all peoples or conversely a rejection of such inquiry, emphasis will be placed on the analogous and shared characteristics of seemingly diverse cultures or alternatively on the particular and specific.

Finally, in such circumstances the mode of articulation of these three dimensions of the overall social reality remains a virtual unknown in regard to its operative dynamic as soon as the search goes beyond an a posteriori explanation or too broad an abstraction (such as an assertion of a determination 'in the last analysis' by the material base or the 'decisive' force of macro-economic strategic models). Furthermore so long as there is no significant advance in this area, the debate will continue to be encumbered by emotional responses, romantic visions and scholastic prejudices.

The analysis of the failure of development offered here must, therefore, explain the hypotheses on which it is based, particularly those concerning the theory of state and nation, the theory of inter-state system, and so on. Similarly, it must add historical profundity and a cultural dimension to the consideration of the contemporary crisis of development.

The first four chapters examine the various dimensions of this crisis of development: an economic survey, the drift of the 1975–85 decade; the crisis of state and society; Africa's vulnerability. Africa's backwardness has its deep origin in the fact that the continent as a whole has not yet begun what might be called the 'agricultural revolution' – an essential precondition. Other aspects of backwardness flow from this initial one, especially the backwardness of an industry that is virtually blocked (except for the mineral exports sector) at a stage too elementary to warrant description as interwoven industry and industrialization. In such circumstances demographic growth and accelerated urbanization without industrialization take dramatic forms and accentuate the fragility of states and societies.

For reasons arising both in the history of the peoples of the continent and in the more recent patterns of their integration in the modern capitalist world system, the 'national question', that is, the complex ensemble of relations between state, nation and ethnicity, and civil society, takes particular shape in Africa that must be studied just as much as the shape of transnationalization and development strategies. So long as adequate political responses have not been found for these problems little enduring progress can be made in economic development.

The continent's fragility leads to more direct forms of external intervention being taken here than elsewhere. Such interventions, largely determined by the geo-strategic concerns of the superpowers and Europe, are a heavy burden on the options of the African states.

However, and perhaps even owing to the tragic effects of the fragility of the continent's states, Africa reveals numerous attempts to 'escape the rut', whether through national policies that are or were intended to be radical, or through regional co-operation. These attempts have scored only limited results, of a mediocre kind, or have simply failed.

The 1975–85 decade may be seen as one of drift from a plan of semi-autocentric development, conceived in the context of a readjustment of the world system to a perspective less unpromising for Africa and the Third World. At the end of the decade, the continent's states, weaker than ever, made desperate and disparate attempts to 'adjust' to demands that subordinated and marginalized them even more.

The second four chapters offer some ingredients for a response to the challenge of history. We are here putting forward a thesis with a political basis.

The thesis is that 'alternative development' (alternative that is to a simple adjustment to the demands of the expansion of the world system) is not only necessary for the great majority of the Third World peoples, but also possible, including from a 'technical' point of view. This 'alternative development' is neither statism nor liberalization. The fact that statism yields only mediocre results (and we shall make an uncompromising critical analysis elsewhere) does not mean that liberalization offers a solution to the problem of development. Experience has repeatedly shown some things that should never be forgotten: that intervention in 'money supply', dubious enough in the developed capitalist economies, verges on the grotesque when transposed to most Third World economies; that high interest rates associated with unfettered international transfers encourage the flight of capital from the poor countries to the rich; that liberalization of prices substitutes artificial and damaging 'world market' prices (incorporating all the subsidies practised in the developed world) for the so-called 'controlled' prices that are often nearer to the 'truth' (balance of local supply and demand) than the former; that the 'real' exchange rate is not that shown in transactions on a frequently marginal parallel market; that devaluation has little effect on balance of payments; that reduction of the social expenditure of the state is an ineffective substitute for reform in its mode of intervention; that wages cuts accentuate distortions in income distribution and resource allocation; that the 'open door' and removal of protection lead to de-industrialization and collapse of the first steps forward; that finally, 'adjustment' imposed in this way leads at best to a regressive and stagnant 'equilibrium'.

The content and internal political and social conditions for this 'alternative development', that we describe as national and popular, will be examined in order to foresee the external conditions that would favour its implementation, through South–South co-operation and through gradual evolution of the world system towards a better balanced political and economic polycentrism.

The political plan is precisely one for a polycentric world, not restricted to five 'great powers' (United States, Soviet Union, Europe, Japan, China) replacing the duopoly of two superpowers and continuing to marginalize the Third World, but a genuinely polycentric world providing Asia, Africa and Latin America with real scope for development. The profound differences between these regions, stemming certainly from their unequal economic development but also from their social options ('capitalism' or 'socialism') and their cultural roots, entail a variety of paths of development, complementary in character but not reducible to a 'universal remedy'. This vision of the future demands the establishment of regional spaces founded on close co-operation between national economies that are individually autocentric, and articulated on a relationship where adjustment is no longer seen in a one-way direction in which the weak surrender to the demands of the strong, but as interdependent in the true meaning of the word. This plan is the only prospective means of resolving the 'development issue' and ensuring world peace and security.

This book deals with problems specific to the Third World. Yet the very existence of the global system into which the South is integrated compels consideration not only of the predominant South–West relations, but also of the 'East' (Eastern Europe, the USSR, China), which is an actor in international affairs and has also appeared as a historical experience inspiring national liberation movements in the Third World. But this book was written in 1988 (and published in French early in 1989), before the extraordinary acceleration of events in Eastern Europe. Yet reading again the references to the East made in the book, I do not feel that they are mistaken.

The thesis I have explicitly developed for several years, which is reflected in this book, is rather confirmed by the recent evolutions. The thesis is based on two closely related views. The first view is that the so-called socialist regimes have in fact been the product of national popular revolutions (not socialist ones) directed against the effects of polarization and peripheralization produced by the global expansion of actually existing capitalism. Therefore the conflict between capitalism and socialism continued to operate within these societies throughout their history. This objective contradiction should have been managed through political democracy and a mixed economy. Instead it was managed through statism, thus reflecting the reconstitution of privileged class interests. The outcome of the continuing social struggles will determine whether these class interests will get rid of the popular dimension of the systems and opt openly for capitalism or whether, on the contrary, this dimension will, through democracy, be reinforced.[1] The second view is that actually existing capitalist expansion generates a polarization at the global level which it cannot overcome and that this contradiction – which has been overlooked, including by orthodox marxism – has been, and will remain for the foreseeable future, most explosive. It is this contradiction that is already responsible for both the 'socialist' revolutions and the national liberation movements. This contradiction not only remains in the forefront of the modern world, but is continuously growing more acute: the more the economic system globalizes, the more it generates frustrations in the peripheralized areas, thus constantly reanimating violent nationalistic responses, including, as we see now, in the countries of Eastern Europe and in the USSR.[2]

Of course if the book were to be written now, these theses, which remain correct, would be expressed slightly differently. I refer particularly here to two sets of problems. The first set deals with changes in the balance of international forces, particularly within Europe;[3] the second set deals with the resolution of those 'regional conflicts' that, to a certain extent, might be facilitated by the USSR–USA *rapprochement*.[4] Yet I maintain the view that polycentrism remains the only response which allows the necessary room for autonomy in the further development of progressive forces on a world scale.[5]

This book owes much to the discussions over five years in the context of two programmes 'African regional perspectives' and 'The Third World and world development' conducted in close co-operation by the United Nations University (UNU), the Third World Forum (FTM) and the United Nations Research Institute for Social Development (UNRISD), with generous financial support from SAREC (Sweden) and Italian co-operation.

More than 200 African intellectuals and researchers, pondering ten main themes (for example, the crisis of agricultural modernization; industrialization and urbanization; state and democracy; the international and geo-strategical dimension; the challenge of South Africa; South–South co-operation; the Mediterranean in the world; the cultural dimension of the challenge) have participated in these discussions that have resulted in the publication of 15 books (listed in an appendix). This book, however, is not a 'summary' of the others, but offers a three-way discussion (Asia, Africa, Latin America) of the five 'themes' in the programme on 'The Third World and world development': the challenge of worldwide economic expansion, the crisis of state, the social movement, the cultural dimension of the challenge, conflicts and regional and world security.

Notes

1. Cf. particularly chapter 6 section 2 on the national popular content of 'actually existing socialism'; also section 3 (the democratic issue) and 4 (the role of the intelligentsia). Cf. also chapter 5, section 2, on the delinking issue.

2. Cf. particularly chapter 8. The recent evolutions strengthen rather than weaken the thesis I had expressed long ago on this relation between class and nation (Cf. *Class and Nation, historically and in the current crisis*, Monthly Review Press, New York, 1980). I refer here also to chapter 3 section 1, on the Nation State (the 'Russian Empire' saved – for a while perhaps – by bolshevism, and the russification which had little to do with socialism); chapter 3, nationalism in the Eastern countries, the 'roll back' strategy of the West.

3. Therefore, referring to chapter 8 (ref. above), I maintain the view expressed that the contradiction centre/peripheries remains fundamental (it is even more obvious now than at the time the book was written!), while additions should be considered with respect to intra-European relations and their various possible futures. On this last point I have expressed these new additional points in *L'avenir du socialisme*, forthcoming in the French–European socialist journal, *L'évènement européen*.

4. Cf. on the issue of conflicts, chapter 4 section 2, in which, of course with respect to the Middle East issue (as well as other issues of conflicts in the Third World) we should today consider the effects of the changes in the USSR–USA relations, as well as the adjustment that they command at the level of local actors. Yet some of these conflicts (Nicaragua, South Africa, Palestine) are certainly not the 'product' of the former East–West conflict, but are deeply rooted in the unequal North–South relation, which remains.

5. Cf. Chapter 2 section 2 on the end of the Bandung era and the need for polycentrism; and Chapter 8 on the North–South relations in the crisis.

1.   Africa's Economic Backwardness

Sources and methods for the analysis

South of the Sahara

It has long been known that Africa's development has broken down.[1] During the 1960s the annual per capita growth rate in GDP did not exceed 1.3%, before falling to 0.8% in the 1970s, and to almost nil during the first half of the 1980s, while the annual per capita growth rate in agricultural production became negative, –1%. Furthermore, these lamentable results seemed general in the continent. The best results in the countries often cited as exemplary were, in fact, modest. The record annual per capita growth rates in GDP in the 20 years, 1960–80, lie between 2.5% and 4% for the non-mining countries (Côte d'Ivoire, Kenya, etc.) and went no higher than 6% to 7% for the mining and oil-producer countries (Gabon, Nigeria, etc.) The best annual growth rates in agricultural production in the ten years 1970–79 were no higher than 3%. Industrial growth rates were also modest, despite the extremely low starting point: 3.3% a year for the 1970s as a median of Sub-Saharan Africa as against 1.8% for agriculture and 4.2% for services.

At the same time the current deficit on the external balance rose from $1.5 billion in 1970 to $8 billion in 1980 and nearly $25 billion in 1985, while foreign debt-servicing in 1985 took 30% of foreign earnings, as compared with 12% in 1980 and 6% in 1970. From 1985, debt-servicing was soaking up 123% of earnings from the export of primary products, the principal element in Africa's exports. The net contribution of foreign capital, which was positive until 1975, has since become negative and increasingly so: the surplus of debt-servicing ($15 billion in 1981, $21 billion in 1985) over the contribution in new loans rose from $5 billion to $22 billion in the same period. The total debt – in 1980 – was $130 billion.

Public finance has moved into a negative position, with a higher rate of growth in current public expenditure than in fiscal and related earnings everywhere (except for the few years of OPEC boom in the oil-exporting countries). Since 1985 in two-thirds of the African countries, state finances not only no longer contribute to any investment effort (as is the case in four-fifths of the countries!) but do not even provide for routine public services to the level that was maintained in the 1960s. In three-quarters of the African countries the only means of maintaining investments at a level to insure nil growth (implying a fall in per capita consumption) and essential imports (equipment and food) is reliance on foreign aid. This explains why Africa's foreign debt is mostly 'public', whereas 'private' indebtedness of firms takes first place in Africa and Latin America. Whenever the foreign contribution goes down, inflation removes any benefit from the change.

Social indicators are even more shattering. With a population growth rate higher than 2.5% a year, and still rising, with urban growth rate ranging from 5% to 9.1% a year, it is estimated that half the potentially active, male, urban population has no steady income and constitutes a reserve of unemployed and semi-employed that cannot be taken up. The situation in the rural areas is no better since, as everyone knows, Africa has become the famine continent, taking over from Asia.

The crisis is staggering and to varying degrees widespread. But it is nothing new. All the negative factors that have been explosive in the drama of the 1970s and 1980s date back to the 1960s or earlier decades.

The ultimate reason for the failure of 'development', more striking in this region than in any other, is that Africa has not begun its agricultural revolution, without which any development is unimaginable. Agricultural revolution means a complex range of transformations capable of positive growth in agricultural and food production per inhabitant (of the order of at least 1%) over a substantial period (several decades at least), and an even healthier growth in agricultural production per rural family (of the order of 2% to 3%). Only by dint of this are industrialization, urbanization and social development possible.

In Africa, however, production and productivity per rural family has remained stagnant or even declined in some regions. In such circumstances rural emigration is not the result of relative over-population created by successful albeit socially unbalanced agricultural advance, but the opposite, a desperate flight of populations seeking an escape from famine. This kind of emigration causes monstrous urbanization without any prospect of industrialization being able to absorb the flow, and without generating any source of finance for new activities. Elsewhere, in Latin America and Asia, some steps have been taken on the path to agricultural revolution even if it has taken a chaotic and often tragic form from the national and popular stand-point.

The failure has deep pre-colonial and colonial roots. Unhappily little has been done since colonialism to reverse the trends.

The priority task of the agricultural revolution, and one that will remain for several decades to come, is obviously complex and multi-faceted. It has a technological aspect: what kinds of equipment and inputs (water supply, fertilizers, and so on) could bring an improvement in productivity per cultivator and per acre. These technical choices bring in their train the appropriate economic policies of support: for example, options as to prices and income structures to encourage behaviour in accordance with the aims, the industrial policies and appropriate patterns of financing. In turn these economic policies have social and political implications: what kinds of rural social administration (organization of property and its utilization, ground rents and agricultural wages, marketing, credit or producer co-operatives, among others) can help movement in the desired direction, or by contrast obstruct it; how the modes of social administration in effect, produced by historical social relations (particularly between the state and the peasantry) can be an obstacle to change; what kinds of social administration of trade and industry (state holding, co-operation, local and foreign private capital, and so on) may be combined with those required by agricultural progress.

On none of these questions, still less their interlocking relationships, can the experience of the developed regions of the West and East or of Asia and Latin America be transferred as it is. There are many reasons for this: availability of land, pre-capitalist modes of social organization and levels of productivity, too great a diversity of established industrial technology.

Because it is an entirely new task and a complex challenge, the 'remedies' proposed by the development agencies are open to question. Many of them have failed the test of experience. Hence the flood of fashions. Some people, in the name of instant efficiency, refuse to acknowledge our profound ignorance of what 'has to be done' and think it enough to invoke litanies either in praise of the virtues of the 'market' (as if a few price changes could bring the necessary incentives) or of state intervention (in disregard of the historical, political and cultural content that has shaped it) and there are, alas, too many of them to be cited here.

The origins of Africa's agricultural failure

Explanations for Africa's agricultural failure tend to be partial and contradictory.[2] The remote past – pre-colonial Africa – is partly to blame. If there is one 'special characteristic' – apart from huge variety – of the modes of rural organization in the greater part of Africa, it is perhaps that the still scarcely begun communal or tribute-paying forms implied extensive occupation of the soil. This allowed for much greater food self-sufficiency than is commonly imagined, thanks to relatively high productivity of labour (as a complement to extremely low return to the acre). Higher production per head entails moving to intensive modes requiring a much greater overall quantity of labour in the year. This increase of production per head is accompanied by a reduced productivity of labour (of physical output per working 'day') but also by an improved return per acre. This move to intensive agriculture, as a precondition to any development worth the name, is the challenge that the African peoples must take up.[3]

But the challenge has not yet been taken up. Colonization did not only fail to do so; it was not even its aim. Colonialism found it easier to take an immediate superprofit without cost (without investment) by forcing the African peasants into unpaid – or poorly paid – surplus labour through forms of indirect control. Slightly higher output per head at the cost of a greater labour contribution, without equipment or modern inputs (but to the destruction of Africa's land capital), combined with a worsening of peasant living standards, was enough to provide an appreciable margin for capital dominating the global system. Colonization thus continued the ancient tradition of the slave trade: exploitation by pillage that made no provision for reproduction of the labour force over the long term or of the natural conditions for production.

Independence brought no change to this mode of integration in the world capitalist system. Change has come in response to the demands of the new phase in the worldwide expansion of capital (the European construct and United States hegemony) and not in response to the problem of the African peasant. Moreover the prosperity of the 1960s in the West has brought a new enthusiasm in Africa for the 'extraverted system'. And if René Dumont, always sensitive to the peasant question, has lucidly and courageously denounced the 'false start in Africa',[4] the World Bank, which is nowadays concerned about the peasants' fate (while the IMF forces the most wretched to pay the price of the failure) gave its enthusiastic support to the policies that were to lead, ten years later, to disaster.

The crisis of the 1970s was the result of a conjunction between the super-exploitation of land, men and women, reaching a level difficult to relieve and the crisis striking the capitalist system as a whole. In the face of this crisis the proposals raining down on Africa at an increasing rate are no more than a manifestation of a 'quest for palliatives'.

If it is no more than a matter of palliatives, then the media's talk 'in favour of agriculture' is shown as a contrast to a supposed 'preference for industrialization' that was at the origin of the failure. But any meaningful quest for greater output per cultivator is precisely to allow increased urbanization; and urbanization without industrialization can only be parasitic and disastrous. In turn, industry (but not unselectively) is necessary to permit greater output from agriculture for which it must supply equipment and to which it must offer a growing market. Here lies the option for an autocentric popular and national strategy. If this option is rejected in favour of a systematic integration in worldwide expansion, talk of 'priority for agriculture' becomes hollow and essentially demagogic. The contradictions in the other 'proposals' are manifest: export industry supposes low salaries and consequently low prices for food crops, at the same time as it urges price rises as an incentive to the peasants to produce more.

The populist garb some have given the proposals do not change their meaning despite talk of basic needs and the strategy of 'petty family production'. Meanwhile, such rhetoric has never prevented the Western 'aid' bodies from showing a preference, in fact, to support for agro-business and kulaks – in the name of efficiency. That these policies continue to be advanced is evidence at bottom of the scant seriousness with which Africa is treated. For Africa, in the imperialist view of the world, is above all a source of mineral resources for the West; neither its industrialization nor its agricultural development are genuinely considered.

There is nothing natural about the wretchedness of African agriculture.

Undoubtedly underpopulation of tropical Africa, compared with the dense population of tropical Asia, has been an obstacle to intensifying what is described as significant internal migration; and whatever may be said, the Sahel is not irrevocably doomed. There is water there (a group of rivers whose flow matches that of the Nile, extraordinary underground and fossil lakes, if confidential studies are to be believed),[5] sources of energy – what about uranium? and the sun and the oil at less than 1,000 metres? – serviceable soils, populations. A social system that claims to be incapable of co-ordinating these 'factors' into a satisfactory plan able to nourish the populations in question can scarcely be regarded as rational, so let us admit that the capitalist system is not rational since it does not necessarily ensure the reproduction of the labour force in each of its segments. Here in the Sahel, for capitalism *per se*, it is the existence of the Sahelian peoples that is 'irrational'. Since for this capitalism, it would be more appealing if the Sahel had only uranium and not useless Sahelians . . . Such is the logic of this world system for which Africa is still exclusively a source of minerals. By highlighting the campaigns for emergency 'relief' distribution, the Western institutions have created a belief that the Sahel was irrevocably doomed. Hence it is accepted as if it were natural that the uranium was not intended for the 'natives', and Sahelians must be taught better ways of gathering the blades of grass in the desert and not waste them in their ovens! Africa must adapt to the West's wastage! Is there a better illustration of the vocation as a mineral resource that imperialism consecrates to the continent, and of the subjection of all the so-called development programmes to this essential logic than this ingenuous call to the 'imperatives' of the export of the regions's energy resources? But why not the reverse: let Africa regain control and use of its resources and Europe make the adjustment.

Capitalism's capacity in the abstract to 'solve the problem of African development' could be endlessly discussed. Not only has concrete capitalism, as it exists, that is, with worldwide expansion, failed to 'solve' – but rather created – the problem over the past 150 years (or even the four centuries since the start of the slave trade) but also has nothing in mind for the next 50 years. The challenge will, therefore, be taken up only by the African peoples, on the day when the necessary popular alliances enable them to delink their development from the demands of transnationalization.

Analysing the exploitation of peasants

If Africa as a whole has not even begun its agricultural revolution, this is essentially because the entire system in which it is integrated is based on super-exploitation of the African peasants' labour, and this is beneficial both to the system of dominant capitalism and to the local classes who act as its relay. The system of super-exploitation of the countryside, established by colonialism, has not been challenged by the neo-colonial system that faithfully carries on the tradition.

We are inadequately equipped to provide a theoretical analysis of this super-exploitation[6] because the great majority of African peasants are petty producers and consequently there are no obvious direct exploiters, such as the great landowners are or have been elsewhere. Conventional economic theory, almost on principle, ignores the phenomenon of labour exploitation. By virtue of its emphasis on market mechanisms it remains a prisoner of the prejudice it feeds on, that of 'pure and perfect competition'. At most it allows itself to note in passing the gap between this model and the reality of capitalist production. It is particularly the case of Third World peasant production, which far from being independent, is subject to this exploitation by capital.

There are varying forms of integration of this peasantry in the world capitalist system: typified in very broad terms, by the integration of petty peasant production in the world commodity market. The essential here is not as it might at first seem: monopoly of colonial houses, mediated through state bodies in some circumstances, and such monopoly allowing super-profits from circulation, but at a more profound level, namely, direct interference by capital in the organization of production. Obviously such interference will not be perceived if the field of economics is separated from politics, for it operates precisely through political, administrative and technical incorporation of the petty peasantry. It is through such incorporation that the peasants are obliged to specialize in certain crops, to buy the inputs these need and finally to rely on the income of their apparent sale. The peasant's formal ownership of the land and the means of production is maintained but emptied of its genuine content: the peasants lost control over economic decision-making and organization of the production process and is no longer genuinely a 'free petty producer'. Thus, behind the apparent sale of the output is concealed a sale of his labour power. Hence the peasant is integrated in capitalist production relations invisible on the scale of the peasant production unit, but perfectly visible at the level of the global system in which he is integrated. It is just as difficult to understand the failure to see the system of exploitation, of which Marx in *Capital* provided a masterly and recognized example, in the system of 'putting out' work.

Clearly, forms of exploitation of the peasant economy have themselves evolved in various ways. Sometimes integration in capitalist exchange has provoked appreciable differences in appropriation of the soil and the instruments of production. In such a case, the rich peasants' ('kulak') direct exploitation of agricultural labourers, or of share-croppers, is superimposed by exploitation of the collective commodity production by monopoly capital. In other cases, administrative, colonial or neo-colonial incorporation is associated with primary native social control that for want of a better term may be described as parastatal, semi-feudal. Obviously the class that battens on this 'incorporation' does not directly appropriate the soil or the means of production, which is left in the peasants' hands, but it still levies its tithe – the output of the peasant's surplus labour – in one way or another. Here, too, the exploitation of the peasant in these apparently pre-capitalist systems – apparent only (as they are the product of capitalist integration) – must not obscure the fact that the systems are integrated in global capitalist exploitation.

Obviously there are additional forms of superimposing relations of capitalist exploitation on pre-capitalist relations, whether themselves based on super-exploitation or not, just as there is an extremely varied range of forms of articulation between pre-capitalist and capitalist relations. In the case of Sub-Saharan Africa, we have noted three classifications: the 'trading economy', the 'reserve economy' and the 'concessionary companies economy'. All these forms of exploitation must be studied concretely; no abstract theory deduced a priori from some general principles can take the place of concrete analyses.

In analysing these forms of extraction of surplus it would be helpful to raise in general terms the issue of the law of value, which in the end implicitly governs the validity of the thesis. To make it possible to discuss exploitation the comparison of the values and costs of the labour power of the peasant in question and of the labourer – whose labour is embodied in the goods sold to that peasant – must have some meaning, as obviously the goods exchanged have values and costs that can meaningfully be compared. That is to say that the thesis assumes a worldwide value category of commodities and a worldwide value category of labour power. Even if the first of these theses has won general acceptance, the second has not. The sixth chapter of *Capital* [first published in 1933] however, showed that Marx already had some sense of the problem. Marx suggests in effect how difficult it is to grasp the value at the level of the basic unit of production. He raises consideration of the concept of 'collective labourer' and suggests that this tends to include all the workers in an increasingly broader area, comprising various production units. The contents of this chapter, remarkably in advance of its time and not known to Bukharin, were, however, implicitly taken on board by the latter in his view of a capitalist development that taken to its logical conclusion would lead to a 'sole ownership' of the means of production: by the state. The value category would then apparently have vanished; although it would still be there . . . Bukharin perhaps had partly in mind a possible evolution of the USSR. But above all he had in mind the profound tendency of capitalism whereby without reaching the stage of 'sole ownership' we have by now reached the stage where the dominance of capitalism spreads well beyond the production units that form its base. It is on such theoretical foundations that we have shaped our thesis that labour power tends to have a unique value on a world scale although it retains differential costs, above or below this value. The precise measure of this tendency to a differentiation of the costs of labour power can be gauged, albeit crudely, by 'double factorial terms of trade', or the relationship between gross terms of trade and the index of comparative productivities of labour.

An analysis of exploitation in these circumstances calls for a complementary analysis of the overall political economy of the colonial and neo-colonial system. In fact the increasing exploitation of peasant labour is the main source of the typical distortions of peripheral capitalist development. To go further in this field it is necessary to make a concrete case by case examination of how income distribution and the resulting demand have shaped industrial patterns. It is then necessary to make a concrete examination of how the increasing exploitation integrates the societies of peripheral capitalism in the international division of labour in such a way as to reproduce and intensify the increasing exploitation of labour. Obviously these patterns of development and the increasing contradictions they have provoked are at the origin of the crisis in the imperialist system and of the responses to it by the national liberation movement. The character of the compromises that have invested the independence of Third World states and hence the character of the reforms on which they embarked (such as replacement of the former colonial companies by state bodies) must be considered in this perspective.

We should argue that the current crisis of Third World agriculture reflects the partial character of these reforms, inadequate to free the peasants and the country from imperialist exploitation. We should further argue that peasant super-exploitation has reached a degree that endangers not only reproduction of the peasant producers themselves (through famine, rural exodus, and so on) but industrial development too, in the sense that agriculture gradually loses its capability of ensuring acceptable prices for food crops, essential in turn for exploitation of the working class. As is well known, the response of monopoly capital to this crisis is to envisage a series of technical innovations known as the 'green revolution'. These innovations are certainly intended in part to raise the productivity of peasant labour, but also and principally to integrate in the more intensive relations dominated by agro-business transnationals. A counterposing definition must be established as to the social, economic and technical changes necessary to sustain a national and popular programme capable of raising the living standards of the peasants and workers, and broadening the material and social base of the essential development of the forces of production.

The 'green revolution' of our day is undoubtedly different from the 'agricultural revolution' that preceded the industrial revolution in 18th century Western Europe but both these 'revolutions' lie within the same overall perspective: that of making agriculture capable of supplying the urban proletariat with the means of reproducing their labour power. The 'agricultural revolution' of mercantilist and physiocratic Europe fulfilled this essential role by disaggregating feudal relations and transforming them into agrarian capitalist relations. The methods of this transformation are peculiar to their time: there were as yet no industries; the production of inputs for the new agriculture was supplied by the labour of peasants and rural artisans; the surplus food crops sold by the peasants and capitalist farmers to the towns were delivered in their raw states without significant processing.

The 'green revolution' of our day surfaced in regions integrated in a global system already dominated by industry: that of the manufacture of agricultural inputs (farm machinery, fertilizers, sprays, for example) and of food industries offering urban consumers processed foods, with a reduction of the artisanal or domestic labour to prepare them in usable form. This 'revolution' certainly presupposes the abolition of certain pre-capitalist relations that had become too serious a handicap to agricultural modernization. Agrarian reforms fulfilled this preliminary role in most of the Third World during the three decades after the Second World War. Once this step had been taken the 'green revolution' was on the agenda. It encouraged – peasant or farming capitalist (kulak) – agriculture to integrate in the upstream industries (supplying agricultural inputs) and downstream industries (food processing). Who would control this agro-industrial integration? That was the issue.

Capitalism's 'classic' solution is to operate this integration through subjection of the farmers to industry, that is to the monopolies of the agro-business. This evolution, which had its early beginning in the United States and Canada and spread to the whole of Western Europe in the aftermath of the Second World War, is now proposed for the Third World countries. It would have the effect not only of transferring the benefit of peasant surplus labour to the monopolies but also of worsening the overall national dependence of peripherally capitalist societies on these monopolies, and further accentuating the distortions of accumulation in these societies.

In the early 1960s and in the excitement of independence, there began to develop in agriculture a sometimes rather impetuous movement of modern petty commodity producers whenever favourable conditions arose. We have suggested this to be the case where rural population density was 'optimum' (of the order of 30 inhabitants to the square kilometre) and where it was possible to attract wage labour by the immigration of outsiders to the ethnic group of the area. This movement encouraged the hope of the launch of an agricultural revolution, reproducing, *mutatis mutandis*, a model common in 19th century Europe. But the movement was soon smothered and had results only on the scale of limited micro-regions (in the south of Côte d'Ivoire and in Kenya for example) to the extent that on a continental scale or even within the beneficiary countries the overall results remained mediocre.[7] The reason for this smothering is related to the fact that this agriculture of 'modern farmers' is super-exploited by the upstream industries (foreign in this instance) supplying inputs and by the world market imposing real price cuts on these export crops (the World Bank systematically encouraged over-production for this purpose).

The second solution is to subject agriculture to the state – one whose historical origins and class structure are integrated in various ways in the world system. It might be a Soviet-type state, contemptuous of the peasants, which sees the countryside as no more than a manpower reserve for industrialization and the provider of foodstuffs for the towns. It 'collectivizes' and 'modernizes' by obliging the peasants to resort to mechanization, while retaining control of the machinery – this was the formula of the Soviet machine and tractor stations – just as it retains ownership and management of the agricultural produce processing industries. But it might also be a peripherally bourgeois state, one unable (for various particular historical reasons in this or that instance) to base its overall power on an alliance with an agrarian bourgeoisie, that becomes the peasant's 'partner', or in fact his master. This form allows exploitation of peasant labour to be subjected to the demands of industrial accumulation.

The third solution, which is still being sought, would entail a genuine popular alliance with the peasants as genuine partners. In this dispensation the sphere of activities controlled by the peasantry could be extended to the upstream and downstream industries. In other words the 'shearing' from prices unfavourable to the rural community could be avoided by collective negotiation of the relative prices of industry and agriculture. Maoism adopted this principle, in intention at least. It was said of the Chinese commune, created in 1957–58, that it was based on equality between the town and countryside. The commune, as is well known, operated on three levels: the team (the natural village) handling simple means of production (draught equipment, hand tools), which – at China's level of development of the forces of production – are still the mainstay of agricultural production; the brigade handling modern equipment utilized by several teams (machinery, transport vehicles, improvements in the irrigation system, and so on); and finally the commune handling some minor upstream industries (for example, tool manufacture, workshops, rural building) and downstream (simple processing: rice mills, shelling, grain mills, among others). Peasant control in principle over these three levels, in marked contrast with the Soviet machine and tractor stations, bore witness to the reliance the authorities claimed to place on the peasantry and reflected the reality of the worker and peasant alliance that gave substance to this authority. The commune, moreover, in integrating social services (health, education, and so on) and administrative powers into its management system paved the way for an eventual integration of political power and economic management. Undoubtedly the 'industries' managed by the commune were still, at the current stage of the country's development, rather elementary: and team output accounted for some 80% to 85% in value of the output of all three levels. In addition, some – the most modern – of the inputs were provided for agriculture by industry properly speaking, that is collectives of urban workers (or the state).

Obviously the challenge to the system after the Mao Zedong's death raises a question mark over the reality of the system as it was operating in the 1960s and 1970s, but this goes beyond the scope of this study. It has been argued that control of the communes really remained in the hands of the party bureaucracy who imposed prices less favourable than supposed. Deng Xiaoping relied on this argument in order to dissolve the communes, 'decollectivize' and allow the 'market' to operate to the peasants' advantage, and thus correct the terms of trade in a favourable direction, if not for the entire rural community at least for the segments that succeeded in securing a strong foothold in the new market for foodstuffs.[8]

It is impossible to define the exact forms of organization and implementation of economic management and national and popular politics formulated from a priori abstractions divorced from the actual dialectic of relations between state, peasants and workers. The principles emerging in this schema of the three outline models do, however, merit systematic consideration.

Finally, an analysis of exploitation of peasant labour power inevitably entails the closest examination of the organization of commodity and non-commodity labour within the peasant family. Obviously, the prices paid for peasants' labour decrease as they correspond to an increase in the quantity of 'unpaid' labour, that is the non-commodity labour by the peasant man, and much more often of the peasant woman.

For want of the means, it is rare to find a precise measurement of the quantity and character of the total labour supplied by the entire peasant family. A comparison of this overall quantity of labour and that supplied by the entire family of the worker under capitalist industry would provide a measurement of the real gap between the price of labour power at the periphery and at the centre of the system. We argue that this gap would be even more massive than that indicated solely by the double factorial terms of trade, which takes into account only the comparative amounts of direct labour producing goods.

North Africa and the Arab world: from statism to comprador capitalism

Economic performance, assessed in conventional terms, is not as disastrous as in Sub-Saharan Africa.[9] The average real annual growth rate in the three decades (1955–85) turned out – according to the calculations of the Economic Commission for Western Africa – at about 5%, with industry accounting for 7% (as compared with less than 3% for Sub-Saharan Africa where the starting point was much lower), agriculture for 2% (only slightly higher than that of Sub-Saharan Africa), and the tertiary sector for 8% (4% in Sub-Saharan Africa). In fact these performances are mediocre, despite the better rates of industrialization: the spread of the tertiary sector, prematurely and too speedily, is a handicap north and south of the Sahara, and is the effect of a crisis in society and state development, employment and urbanization, and not a response to the crisis. Agriculture remained fairly stagnant, contributing, with the heavy urbanization of the region (where the urban population has since 1985 exceeded half the population total) a food deficit which also represents more than half the nation's basic food consumption. In other words, as a rule the countrysides do not feed the towns, even if they – just about – manage to ensure their own subsistence. If there are not the chronic famines of the Sahel, with a regressive depopulation of the countryside (and a collapse of agricultural production), migration from the countryside to the towns is no longer, as it was in the West's dual agricultural and industrial revolution, the social effect, of this revolution, combined with a significant increase in agricultural output.

Faysal Yachir, in his synthesis of the economic modernization of the Arab world, suggests that:

> beyond national particularities, the countries of the region have evolved within the framework of a unique economic model, whereby the state takes responsibility for the development of capitalism in close relationship with the system of the world economy.

He distinguishes the variant of 'overt state capitalism' (Morocco and Tunisia and the Gulf states in the Mashreq) whereby 'the state supplies the conditions for the emergence of national capital within the narrow framework enjoined by the international division of labour' from the variant of 'populist state capitalism' (Nasser's Egypt, and Algeria, Syria and Iraq) whereby 'the state seeks to build an autonomous public economic by turning its back on the international division of labour'. The distinction is the effect of specific class alliances of the national liberation movement, more clearly bourgeois in the first variant, or by contrast aimed against at least some sections of the bourgeoisie in the second. In both cases, however, state intervention remains decisive, since it accounts for 40% to 70% of investment and controls 40% to 60% of industrial output.

On the credit side of the model is its acceleration of the rate of industrialization. In the 'open' variant, however, the fragmented character of this industrialization makes it impossible as yet to describe the countries in question as 'semi-industrialized', whereas Egypt and Algeria have reached this stage (to be found nowhere else in Africa except South Africa). But despite this positive aspect, the model has fairly speedily reached the end of its historical possibilities, owing to the following handicaps:

(i) industrialization does not necessarily entail a breach of the rules of the international division of labour, especially when, as Yaçhir notes in regard to the Arab world, the economy remains 'strongly dependent on external outlets, products, technology and financial flows'. This industry is more an appendix to the world economy than the basis of a national economy;

(ii) consumption and investment have remained largely dependent on transfers from abroad (oil revenue, migrants' transfers, private capital, public aid or loans on the international finance market). The model's vulnerability to the fluctuations of the world conjuncture is not reduced but on the contrary accentuated;

(iii) 'the agrarian structures have not been transformed in a direction that allows decisive improvements in returns' (Yachir).

These three handicaps combined have permitted the 1970–80 offensive, with the aim of 'driving back statism for the benefit of capitalism increasing the integration in the international division of labour' (Yaçhir). The half-statist, half-commodity character of the rationality of the statist model encouraged this apparent fluctuation in strategy and language. The obvious pressure mobilized by the IMF and exerted on the countries in the region because of their foreign debt ($35 billion for Egypt and Algeria, $15 billion for Morocco and $8 billion for Tunisia) had much the same effect.

Despite the liberalization measures, the results have been very disappointing. Foreign capital was in no rush to replace the state's disengagement, except in the form of sub-contracting companies who,

> buy practically nothing in the country, do their repairs in Europe, use obsolete and second-hand equipment and personnel with absolutely no skill and enjoy no autonomy in the conception of the product and its marketing. (Yachir)

Foreign capital spurns Egypt for political motives (to which we shall return in

and faced inflation, foreign debt and a deficit in the balance of payments. The form of conjunction between international capital and the Turkish dictatorship is well known: a total opening to the exterior (fluid exchange rates, dismantling of exchange and import controls) combined with an offensive on the mass of the people and even on the middle strata who were officially required to restructure 'industry with a view to export competitiveness'. The theology – the private sector offers the universal panacea – only thinly veils the plan for subordination to the strategy of redeployment of international capital, theoretically assigning Turkey to labour-intensive industry – cheap labour obviously – for the benefit of the Western consumer! But in the light of the industrial structure inherited from Kemalism the crisis resulted in de-industrialization, and consequently in widespread unemployment and spiralling instability, rather than any restructuring.

How is it possible to ignore the analogy with the Arab world and the currently fashionable *infitah*? The comparison must be modified country by country. In the countries of so-called 'liberal' capitalism, where statist intervention is nonetheless essential (Morocco, Tunisia, Saudi Arabia) the upsurge of the 1960s is more reminiscent of the model of the Turkey of the Democratic Party than that of Kemal Ataturk and Inonu. Conversely, in the countries of radical state capitalism (Egypt, Syria, Iraq, Algeria) the populist note is certainly more marked than in Kemalist Turkey, for the reasons indicated earlier. But countries of both kinds were deep in crisis from the middle of the 1970s; a crisis merely reduced, concealed or delayed in the oil-producer countries (Iraq, Algeria, Saudia Arabia). As for the options followed by the local authorities and preached by the same external forces (IMF and so on) the maximum openness was to the detriment of the standards of living of the poorest section of the community – above all those in modern Turkey.

The history of contemporary modern Turkey presents strong analogies with that of the Arab countries. This history is a chapter in that of the Third World (of the systems of peripheral capitalism in our opinion) and not Europe (of systems of central capitalism).

For some 65 years or more, however, Turkey has proclaimed its 'Europeanness' and consciously cut loose the ties that bound it to the waters of the Orient. The Kemalist option had no hesitation in forcing the issue and maintaining a distance from Islam that no other Muslim country dared match. Furthermore, in order to establish the new Turkish nation on an ideological basis divorced from the Arab and Persian Muslim Orient, Kemalism invented an entire Turanian, non-Persian, non-Semitic mythology. But, after such efforts, was Europe ready to accept Turkey? Was Turkey offered any corner in its councils? Not at all. Nowadays is there anything more than the reality, and even more daunting prospect, of a lumpen-Europeanization of Turkey? If, with an easy conscience, Europe can blame the 'failure' of modernization among the Arabs on attachment to Islam, is the argument abandoned when it comes to the fate Western capitalism reserves for a Turkey that did try to break with its past? Is it not time to realize that the myth of 'European assimilation' is finished?

The history of contemporary Turkey concerns the Arabs in two issues of the national and cultural dimension of development options: First in regard to a necessary consideration of the political and ideological options of the preceding generations. The option of the break-up of the Ottoman Empire, in the name of the principle of nationalities that had become sacrosanct, was neither unavoidable nor prevalent in the Arab Orient of the end of the 19th century. Secondly, in regard to a consideration of the tragic prospects that surrender to the imperatives of capitalist expansion offers the Arab, and the Turkish people. For the model of 'lumpen-Europeanization' is not exclusive to the Turks. Western strategy for the Arab world is clear: to destroy Eyypt in order to remove any hope of a revival of the Arab nation, then, on this basis, to isolate the Maghreb from it in order to subject it to collective European 're-colonization' (as a continuation of the prior French colonization) through the mirage of 'integration' in the building of Europe. The dominant classes in the Maghreb are not immune to the nods and winks in this direction, as so many mundane facts and even political statements testify (cf. Chapters 4 and 8).

Finally, it may be helpful to broaden the discussion at least by raising questions.

Is the fate of the Arab world, in the foreseeable future at least, namely the reinforcement of its subordination through a greater integration in the transnational capitalist system, a special case in the general trend on the scale of the Third World as a whole? Is this sad prospect a passing retreat, to be replaced sooner or later by a new attempt to establish bourgeois national states as more equal partners in the world system? Or is it the end of a long period and an indicator of an irreversible failure of bourgeois national plans in the region in particular and the Third World in general? Can this failure be blamed exclusively on internal factors not conducive to the achievement of such a bourgeois national plan, as these factors missed out on the 'opportunities' provided by integration in the worldwide capitalist expansion? Or is this integration itself a significantly and perhaps decisively unfavourable factor that makes the bourgeois national plan impossible in our age?

It will be shown later (cf. Chapter 3) that as regards the Arab world, the prolonged phase of the Nahda (meaning the renaissance from the start of the 19th century with Mohamed Ali's attempt in Egypt to the 1970s when *infitah* was adopted) is a closed book. This Nahda embodied in various forms the renewed attempt of the Arab bourgeoisie (and the Egyptian in particular) to take its place as autonomous partner in the worldwide capitalist system. Kemalism was also a form – Turkish in this instance – of a similar approach, to be found in other guises in other regions of the periphery. These plans probably have no future.

These remarks will be developed in the discussion on the political and cultural dimensions of development and apply not only to the Mashreq and Egypt but also to the Maghreb, if only by reason of Egypt's cultural and ideological leadership and the particular problematic of the Arab nation. They are today of more consequence than the heritage of French colonization in

North Africa, although the latter had a strong impact on the social character and the options of the national liberation movement in the three countries. Without repeating what we said of the national movement in *The Maghreb in the Modern World*, let us recall one of its conclusions:

> [T]he history of the national movements in the Maghreb countries was, until very recently, very different. And as will be seen, the time factor helps to explain the lags and differences . . . In Algeria, more than a century passed between the time of Abdel Kader and the 1954 insurrection. Algeria's past was distant; a long, dead period elapsed between the old nationalism and the new. In Tunisia the transition was more rapid. Modern nationalism was formed by a direct breach with the old nationalism. The break came between the two wars, and it was a break between men who knew one another personally. In Morocco, the Protectorate was of such recent date that the old nationalist generation has survived almost up to the present day, and the break was delayed until after independence. Nor can the device of the Protectorate be regarded as wholly irrelevant to the issue, since it enabled old structures to survive, even though they had long outlived their function. Examples of these were the Makhzen of the Bey of Tunis and the Sultan of Morocco, which lingered on long after the Makhzen of Abdel Kader had been entirely destroyed and forgotten. Moreover, the social structures which lay behind these social forms were not in every case identical. The Algerian landed aristocracy had long disappeared – indeed, Abdel Kader himself did more to destroy it than did colonization – while in Morocco this class was actually reinforced by colonization. The situation in Tunisia lay somewhere between these two extremes. Even though these structures are today gradually losing their importance in the face of the rapidly rising tide of the petty bourgeoisie – a phenomenon common to all three countries – they did for a long time condition the nature of the national movement. Last but not least, the difference in legal status was to condition the French attitude towards the Maghreb countries in the last period before independence.[10]

The national movements in the three countries of French North Africa were faced by a range of similar problems: (1) the almost total absence of local industries, as colonization was in the hands of Malthusian metropolitan interests who imposed an exclusively agricultural and mining specialization (there is nothing in French North Africa comparable to the private Misr industrial Egyptian group that emerged in the 1920s); (2) the implantation of settler colonialism in significant numbers and their expropriation of 'settler land'. This problem found a *de facto* solution in the emigration of the settlers, the devolution of settler land to self-managing collectives in Algeria, and to the rural bourgeoisie in the other two countries; (3) the attempt to 'Frenchify' the society (with particular violence in Algeria).

Nevertheless, in the space of two decades the Maghreb succeeded in hoisting itself to the level of semi-industrialized countries, or the verge thereof; it was able without great disaster to fill the gap left by the exodus of the majority of technical, or even semi-skilled, personnel; it embarked, with success varying from country to country, on a process of re-Arabization. This is a body of achievement that was remarkably difficult in the circumstances it inherited. By contrast the legacy of agrarian duality from colonization has not really been overcome. In Algeria the denuding of the countryside embarked upon in the colonial era was considerably speeded up during the prolonged Algerian war (by the policy of 'regrouping' enforced by the French army). Any judgement of the mediocre results of agricultural modernization in the independent Maghreb must be tempered with these disastrous effects of the colonial inheritance.

False analyses, false solutions

Conceptions of Africa's agricultural development: a critique

The example of the Sahel's CILSS

Africa has been and is a trial ground in agricultural development to the point that some would argue 'everything ventured, nothing gained'. This is possibly because almost all these experiments have remained trapped in the old colonial (and racist!) prejudice that Africa was not ready either for industry, or for serious modernization of its agriculture and that from the outset an extensive approach is the only one possible. A paternalist conception of 'aid' as supposedly capable of sustaining pursuit of extensive development rounds off the picture.

This viewpoint may be illustrated by the case of the Sahel countries.[11] As is well known, not until the wave of drought in the mid-1970s did the world become aware of the dramatic situation in the region. Drought and famine reduced food crops by at least one-third and cost hundreds of thousands of lives. The CILSS (Permanent Interstate Committee for Drought Control in the Sahel) formed in 1973, and the Sahel Club were finally persuaded that the priority for the strategic development aim for the region should be food self-sufficiency. But in what circumstances was this aim feasible? Could the strategy laid down by the donors in the Sahel Club (OECD and international bodies) achieve it?

A brief summary of the character and structure of the Sahel's economic and social development over the past half-century would run as follows: a modest rate of growth in rural output, due entirely to extensive methods, under conditions increasingly damaging to the region's ecological balance; an absence of industrialization, especially for support to agricultural growth; a continual worsening of the double factorial terms of trade reflecting the decline of reward for peasant labour in the international division of labour; a continual worsening of the exaction from peasant income by the expansion of the administration and the tertiary sector.

The Sahel Club was well aware of the modest and extensive character of rural development; but it failed to note other characteristics of global development and thereby condemned itself to remaining bound by the apparent causes of the situation.

The facts about the extensive character of the region's rural development are well known. Despite the extension of areas sown with cereals from 1,570,00 hectares in 1955 to 3,430,000 in 1978, the yield per hectare fell from 500 to 400 kilos. Areas enjoying regular supplies of water, accounted for only 1% of cultivated land and were being increased very slowly – 5,000 hectares a year – which scarcely replaced the areas that had deteriorated due to poor maintenance. Moreover, even in the irrigated holdings, the methods were mainly extensive: the yields were scarcely more than two tonnes to the hectare (instead of the potential five or six tonnes) and double cropping was never, or almost never, practised. Costs of mechanization, spraying and maintenance were such that either the holdings had to be heavily subsidized, or the remaining income to reward the peasants was grossly inadequate. As for stock-raising, since in the previous period (1950–70) the herds were increasing at a high rate (of 3% to 5% annually) thanks to the multiplication of watering points and to the vaccination campaigns, but as the extensive methods were unchanged, the result was serious over-grazing. Drought under these circumstances ravaged the herds and wiped out the quantitative advances made in the previous twenty years.

Continual expansion of extensive agriculture and stock-raising must of necessity reach a limit. Arguing that 'the disaster is due to the destruction of landed capital' is no explanation but a tautological repetition that growth is extensive. Furthermore, in this extension of area the responsibility of export crops is undeniable, at least in Senegal and some regions of the interior. As groundnuts and cotton took up a not inconsiderable area in these regions and to the extent that the 'profitability' of these crops requires the peasants to look elsewhere for their own subsistence, the development of these crops substantially increased the area under cultivation. This has been shown in studies of the gradual desertification of the groundnut basin of Senegal.

The same is true of 'over-grazing', which is not the 'cause' but the effect of the extensive option for stock-raising. But the option has reasons: it permitted an increase of production of relatively cheap meat (at the risk of the future) both for the internal market and for export. The Sahel in particular, by supplying meat relatively cheaply in comparison with the coast's prices, made its contribution to the development of the regions where foreign financed companies operate.

Deforestation must be explained in the same way. If the African peasants sought their sources of energy in this way it was because they had no choice. The world economic system has therefore benefited from a 'hidden subsidy' corresponding to the 'free energy' available to the peasants of the Sahel. This ingredient, like the others, has made its contribution to the maintenance of incredibly low real rates of reward for peasant labour and hence the attractive prices for the beneficiaries of the agricultural output exported by the Sahel.

In short, the option for extensive rural development arises from the very logic of the unequal international division of labour. Extensive agricultural development is in fact the only way open to the countries of the Sahel to supply an 'exportable' output by drawing on the value of their peasants' labour. If the labour can be rewarded at rates as low as it is (these rates can be calculated by dividing the return on the marketed harvest by the number of days of labour required to produce it) it is because the peasants procure their subsistence (in, for example, cereals, firewood) through their labour unrewarded by the system. The world system therefore benefits from a 'negative rent', corresponding to the value consumed by the productive system that 'eats' its landed capital.

The system of an unequal international division of labour can, of course, operate only where there is a system of local relay runners with an interest in implementing it. The Sahel peasants would not have become integrated of their own accord, on the contrary, their prime concern has been and continues to be to remain outside it. Peasant autarky had to be smashed in order to bring the 'modern system' into play. There were only two ways to do this: (1) to authorize and promote differentiation within the peasantry, allowing private appropriation of the soil by a minority and compelling the majority to sell their labour or to rent land; or (2) to maintain the rural communities and impose on them a statist authority charged with their 'incorporation', that is to impose a 'progress' of which they would not be the beneficiaries. In the Sahel region the colonial system chose the second way, and the colonial administration played this role and bequeathed it to the states.

The amount of public aid granted the Sahel countries rose from $755 million to $1.7 billion between 1974 and 1979, a 50% growth in real terms, provided principally by the contribution of Arab countries alongside the Western countries and international bodies (Arab countries' share rose from 5% to 25% during the past 15 years). The aid itself increased between 1975 and 1978 from 3.9% to 5% of the total public aid to the Third World. It takes pride of place in public investment budgets and even current budgets, as it accounts for a not inconsiderable proportion of GDP (on average about 20%). Aid is, therefore, vital for the daily survival of states in the region. Doubtless comparison of the amounts of aid with those of local public expenditure and gross domestic product must be made with caution. This is because payments for foreign inputs, that constitute a large proportion of the counterpart of this aid, are hardly comparable with those of local inputs, as a counterpart of the GDP and local public expenditure: hence for example a foreign technical assistant may cost many times more than the equivalent local official.

About one-third of this so-called 'non project' aid is a direct consumer subsidy to state and private budgets. Such aid in fact comprises: (a) pure and simple budgetary support granted by France and the Arab countries; (b) balance of payments support supplied by the Arab countries and additionally by the EEC Stabex fund, in the shape of free delivery of goods – or as a counterpart cancellation of foreign debt; (c) emergency relief and food aid; (d) technical assistance support for research and training. The remaining two-thirds of aid are assigned to development programmes: (1) 40% to rural development; (2) 38% to infrastructure; (3) 18% to human resources (education, health, and so on). As industry (including tourism) receives only 4% of the aid, it might seem exaggerated to draw the conclusion, as the World Bank has, of 'distortion in favour of industry to the detriment of agriculture'!

The Sahel Club's strategy is aimed at achieving food self-sufficiency by the year 2000, which means doubling the output and tripling that of meat. This strategy is furthermore intended to achieve this while maintaining a high rate of rural employment, namely by modernizing so-called traditional agriculture and not by concentrating efforts on a highly capital intensive modern sector.

With this outlook, the CILSS strategy is essentially one of extending the areas of dry farming at the rate of 100,000 hectares a year. What is the difference between this and the lines of development pursued in the region for some 50 years, with results that are apparent? The obstacles are well known: (1) can areas of cultivation be increased to this scale without worsening the decline in landed capital? (2) can yields be improved with the means envisaged? Excessive use of fertilizers in areas of low rainfall are, as we know, counter-productive. Have we not seen in Chad a supposed improvement of cotton yields by means of soil exhaustion? Do we not see that the models proposed to the peasants have, in the absence of research and of experience bringing the producers in touch with the results of research, no proven scientific merit? In the developed world agricultural research has produced results because it was closely integrated in rural life, financed and controlled, in part at least, by producers' associations, co-operatives and the like. The haughty and paternalistic attitude of agricultural research in Africa has been one of the main causes of the unsatisfactory results. Furthermore, it is known that the models proposed are not viable: over-costly fertilizers, pesticides and implements, excessively low prices for crops. It is not enough to say there must be a subsidy for the inputs and/or an increase for crop prices. Who will pay for these subsidies? Obviously to be able to do this, as should be done, the country must have alternative resources, a surplus arising from an alternative activity other than that of the rural community.

There is no doubt of the potential for irrigated land in the region, estimated at one million hectares. The aim of 500,000 hectares by the year 2000 with an assured supply of water is required for the region's self-sufficiency in food, on the further condition that a yield of eight tonnes to the hectare of paddy can be attained. In current circumstances the only improvement foreseen entails the construction of expensive dams whose financing is far from being guaranteed. In addition, even if these methods can be effected, there must be population transfer that the land use entails, appropriate social and economic formulae, heavy equipment, maintenance for the irrigation schemes and supply, at modest cost, of the inputs required for double cropping and high yields. None of this is impossible but it does require financial resources that, like those for dry farming, can come only from a surplus generated in some other sector of activity.

In the matter of stock-raising the CILSS strategic option is based on an extensive style not integrated with agriculture, but governed by 'pastoral codes', which makes it difficult to see resolving the actual conflicts of interest.

In the matter of forestry, the high cost of reforestation should be noted: $2,000 a hectare. Under these circumstances pursuit of extensive expansion of dry farming can have only one result: further degradation of the patrimony. Peasants can abandon existing resources only when they are offered effective and cheap alternatives. Such as? Alternative sources of energy are possible: hydro-electricity and other renewable sources (solar energy, biogas, wind-power), mining for oil, gas and coal. Modalities appropriate to the needs would doubtless entail not only hydro-electric power on a large scale from the major dams but also decentralized small-scale hydro-electric output. Likewise, as well as mining the huge reserves of oil and coal, it also entails, if possible, mining of small reserves too. All of which requires resources that must come from outside the rural sector.

Instead of highlighting the coherence (or lack of it) in the overall strategy, the Sahel Club insists on 'project evaluation'. The method proposed is technical in the extreme. It is based on research: (1) into environmental indicators, where great reliance is placed on remote sensing; (2) into economic indicators, which are no more than conventional economic aggregates on growth rate; and (3) into indicators as to 'quality of life', which add precious little to the traditional 'social indicators' (school admission rates, health, access to clean water, housing and so).

Observation of the overall environment, including modern methods of long distance measurement, and the assessment of overall economic and social factors, are of some use. But they are no substitute for a study of the relations of production, the only clue to the dynamic of the system, or in other words the 'success' or 'failure' of a policy, since they reveal the deep reasons for the system of prices and payments for the factors, and hence the significance of the comparative 'profitability' of the various economic options. That is why a project of micro-economic analysis that takes as given the basis of profitability cannot evaluate the 'successes' or 'failures', but merely take note of them without explaining them.

Food self-sufficiency is a desirable objective of development strategy, in the Sahel as elsewhere in the Third World. But that does not lead to the conclusion that development should be confined exclusively to the rural domain. No rural advance is possible without industry to support it, as industry must supply the necessary inputs to raise agricultural output. These inputs cannot be met with imports from the North, because the relative prices of these inputs in comparison with the agricultural output that must be exported to pay for them is such that modernization and intensification of the Sahel's agriculture are not 'profitable'. These prices reflect the unequal relations of the international division of labour and the unequal rewards for labour this entails. The nagging issue – insoluble without an acceptance of perpetual and increasing 'current expenditure' aid which is the CILSS chorus – is a clear demonstration of this inescapable truth.

Inputs needed for agriculture modernization must, therefore, be locally produced, and be produced not only under technically adequate conditions but also under a system of economic book-keeping (prices and payments for factors) that restores the 'profitability' of intensification and modernization, whereby the latter ensures a simultaneous improvement in peasants' real income and reward for their labour. This implies a 'delinking' of this reference system from that governing the economic and social options, whether on the scale of the world system or of the sub-systems integrated in the international division of labour. This alternative system of economic book-keeping, based on an adjustment of rewards in the modern sectors (industry particularly) to those of agriculture, makes it possible to release from such industry an increasing surplus to be deployed to the concomitant financing of agricultural modernization and industrial development in support of it. This global economic system is poles apart from the system that treats agriculture as the source of financing other sectors, by exaction of a surplus from the peasants to be deployed for industry, or for administration expenses.

If parallel development of agriculture and industry is an absolute necessity, it is also clear that 'any old industrialization' will not meet the demands of the situation. Import substitution industrialization and even more so export industrialization within the international division of labour are not therefore appropriate to secure a surplus to be deployed for the modernization of agriculture. Quite the reverse, these industrial modalities presuppose unequal relations with the rural community, to their own advantage.

Once the principal of industry as a support to agricultural modernization has been grasped, the industry may vary according to particular local circumstances; one form is widely dispersed 'rural industry'. 'Ruralization' of industries linked to agricultural production and rural life (supply of fertilizers, farm equipment, hydro-electric power, cement) offers many advantages: management close to the consumers, maintenance of a strong rural population discouraged from joining the rural exodus, for example. The Sahel Club's report, with its proposed aim of maintaining high population densities in the rural areas, is theoretically following this option. But it draws no conclusions and remains superficial, since rural industry is not really possible unless it is based on a substantial modern industry (supplying equipment and certain manufacturing raw materials) and linked to the aim of improving agricultural output. The Sahel Club's choice is for maintaining a high rural population density essentially by expanding extensive production. In conclusion, it would appear that the strategy envisaged by the Sahel Club is based on a contradictory juxtaposition of lip service to intensification and proposals that indicate extensification. This contradiction is typical of the populism that envisages rural development without industrialization.

Industrialization and the agricultural revolution

If the African continent as a whole has not yet embarked upon the agricultural revolution, neither has it yet entered the industrial age. Agricultural stagnation is not the consequence of forced industrialization, as the World Bank argues against all the evidence, but the corollary of a no less marked industrial stagnation.[12]

Only six African countries (South Africa, Zimbabwe, Egypt, Algeria, Tunisia and Morocco) have an infrastructure that can be described as industrialized. In the continent as a whole industry employs fewer than 10% of the active population, and thus remains below the threshold from which it is possible to speak of a secondary production sector. Except for the six countries indicated there are insufficient manufacturing units to constitute an industrial network: the matrix of inter-industrial exchange is still almost blank.

Furthermore, industrial output is still essentially from the extractive sector. In this respect Africa has a virtual monopoly (more than 70% of world production) of gold, diamonds and cobalt, and is a major supplier of copper, bauxite, phosphates, uranium, ferrous metals and oil. Even when the world market share is limited, it is possible to speak of 'mining economies' in terms of production value in relation to population of the countries concerned and its contribution to the state's revenue. In global strategies Africa is above all 'a storehouse of natural resources' rather than either the locus or the outlet for capital deployment. Over the past 25 years, exploitation of these natural resources has been growing rapidly: oil production has shown a twenty-fold increase, that of ferrous metals five-fold, and that of bauxite by two and a half times.

Basic industries (steel, chemicals, engineering) are non-existent in most African countries and where they do exist reduced to small-scale unintegrated operations. The obstacles are well known and there is no sign of their being overcome in the foreseeable future: shortcomings in financial resources and home markets, extreme technological dependence even for processes that are quite routine elsewhere. Regional co-operation on markets or financing (that might have been expected from some oil-producing and minerals-exporting countries with financial surpluses) has to date been abortive.

The few industrial units that do exist are virtually all concentrated in the light industrial sector (mainly textiles and food processing) either to give added value to agricultural exports, or more usually for import substitution, which finds its main market among the middle or higher income groups, who rarely form more than 10% of the population. In these circumstances the 'industrial redeployment' that was keenly discussed in the 1970s has not touched the continent, and the establishment of export manufacturing industries (on the model of some newly industrializing countries of Asia and Latin America) has not begun. Among the many obstacles it should be noted that if unskilled manpower is abundant and cheap, the proletarian milieu is still embryonic, and recruitment, even at subordinate level, costly and inefficient.

Industry as a whole is almost entirely under the direct control of foreign capital. This is the case almost without exception in the continent's French-speaking countries and, despite the apparently more significant association of local interests, almost the same in the English-speaking countries. Some North African countries, and South Africa obviously, are exceptions to the rule.

Elsewhere foreign monopoly generally prolongs that of the interests of the old French and British colonial trade, while there is limited penetration by North American and Japanese multinationals.

The industrial units generally enjoy a monopoly status in the countries where they operate, and a single plant is usually sufficient to meet all the demand. Under this monopoly protection with state backing (for example, tax concessions) these units are not much concerned with international competitiveness and, whether privately or publicly owned, do not usually display an efficient modern capitalist management. If the door is opened to competing imports they almost always go bankrupt and are closed down.

Despite this starting point, that is far and away the lowest on the world scale, the rates of industrial growth – even at record level in this or that instance – have remained astonishingly low and never higher than 4% a year over the decade, or of the order of half the growth rate of the potentially active urban population. Industrialization has never triggered overall growth, but always fed on that of other sectors and been encouraged by them.

It is impossible to review all the experiences of development in Africa in their varied forms. No more is it our intention to reduce them all to a single undifferentiated model. While observing the contrasts and differences and giving them more heed than their common denominator, it is possible to recall that over this vast continent, imbued with varying social options and countless political somersaults, there have been at least four kinds of experience:

(a) Cases of 'stagnation' (in terms of growth) associated with poverty of natural resources, not necessarily absolute but in terms of the demands of the world system.
(b) Cases of 'stagnation' despite the existence of such resources whether untapped (but known), or tapped (sometimes on a large scale).
(c) Cases of relatively marked (or even strong) 'growth' associated with the tapping of these resources, whether by multinationals, or the national state.
(d) Cases of 'marked growth' despite the fact that the tapped resources (often agricultural rather than mineral) are 'medium-scale', thanks in general to a broad opening-up to the outside world, and where this marked growth is associated with a more or less unequal distribution of its benefits.

These experiences may also be classified on a political scale:
(i) assertion of the aim of national independence, sometimes (or often) with a 'socialist' objective; effective related measures, at the level of state intervention at least (nationalizations, occasional land reform, co-operative systems, formal control over external relations, and so on); linked (and not by chance) with general statements (on the world situation, for example) and obvious international alliances; or (ii) assertion of an apparently neutral aim of 'development first' with an appeal to (mainly Western) capital; refusal to 'condemn' the principles of capitalism, private initiative and the world strategy of the multinationals and the Western states, and so forth.

Within this formal classification, it is easy to draw further distinctions by following the conventional analysis of 'economic performance':

1) Activities triggering effective growth when this has occurred: (a) oil and mining in the first place; (b) export agriculture (fairly rich: coffee, cocoa; or poor: groundnuts); (c) light consumer industries reasonably managed, established by the multinationals or the state, using modern techniques, responsive to the home market (import substitution); (d) an active construction sector linked to accelerated urbanization and 'prosperity'; (e) administrative expenditure conceived in classic terms mimicking the West in form with varying degrees of supposedly 'social' purposes (principally education) and always rapidly increasing; (f) tertiary activities (trade, finance) nearly always showing more active growth than the other sectors. When overall growth has been weak, nil, or negative, the explanation is usually insufficient dynamism in (a) and (b) and/or the dubious character of (c). If, moreover, there has been strong pressure for (d) and (e) then the inescapable dual crisis of public expenditure and balance of payments aggravates the situation. The want of dynamism in (a), (b) and (c) is blamed primarily on the country's objective poverty, and secondarily on its rare and suspicious 'nationalism' in rejecting foreign capital. This is or can be aggravated by the lack of concern of the 'elite', its 'corruption', 'demagogy' and so on.

2) Agriculture always backward, undeveloped and nearly always stagnant or virtually stagnant (except perhaps in the export crops sector) and therefore incapable of releasing a surplus of marketed foodstuffs to meet the relevant urban demand. In the saddest cases, the rural community has increasing difficulty in feeding itself and famine takes hold. In the more favourable cases, the statistics record a positive performance in per capita food production (but rarely more than 2% to 3% a year over a long span of the country's overall production), an increasing marketable surplus but usually insufficient to meet the relevant urban demand, which in truth easily grows at a rate of 4% to 5% a year. It is easy to blame these disasters or shortcomings on the climate (drought) or on the administrative bureaucracy unconcerned with the rural community. It is rare for a study to be made of the policies of exaction from the rural community (the terms of trade between town and countryside . . .).

3) An industrial capacity that never triggers growth but is largely the result of adjustment to it, whose spin-off is slight: (a) upstream by the scarcity of basic industry and the low level of inter-industrial integration; (b) downstream, by the limited amount of income it distributes. Three details must be added: (i) if the industry takes the form of a defined number of production units with a virtual monopoly over a small market and these units supply consumer goods, such industry (even if efficiently managed, namely without requiring subsidy for prices competitive with those of imports) is adrift and not a driving force; (ii) if the state interferes too much in the desire to control this kind of industry, it does so badly (in the African experience) and must then subsidize the industry; (iii) some countries try to go further. They proclaim their desire to make industry the main driving force of the economy. Priority is given to the

machine tools industry in national, integrated 'industrializing industries' in order to 'catch up with' the developed world. The question then is whether this last significant detail gives the African experiences concerned a qualitative difference from the others. This fundamental issue is, in our opinion, rarely tackled.

As well as the apparent short-term economic performances, taking in the political factor, two kinds of experience in Africa can be identified. One: those that have not challenged the fundamental external driving force and have been satisfied with exploiting their international 'comparative advantage' in agriculture and mining and, hinged to these sectors, the growth of their import substitution light industries, services and administration. They are the 'national' and 'nationalist' versions – where the state is expected to control the more or less significant sectors of growth through its public ownership; and the 'social' or 'socialist' versions. But since the fruits of growth are appropriated by between 1% and 15% of the population, these modalities do not contradict the extraverted characer of development. This development, described as 'neo-colonial', warrants the name in so far as it continues colonial exploitation and is satisfied to associate with it a local elite. There is no doubt that this kind of development has been possible in some instances. But it has been objectively impossible in some neighbouring countries, where the latter were for example the suppliers of cheap manpower to the former (for example, Burkina Faso in relation to Côte d'Ivoire), or deprived of some driving export role less by nature than by the pattern of world demand.

Two: those that have sought to challenge the external driving force. As the fruit of a political and social history of the national liberation movement and the association of the mass of the people with this movement, these experiences have tried to be national. But if we look further than the intentions, it seems that these experiences (a score or so during the two decades of independence) have been unable to begin implementing an integrated national economic system with any fair degree of autonomy. The only experience that went very far in this direction (Nasser's Egypt) was overthrown by a conjuncture of its shortcomings and the West's hostility. Did the second serious experience (Algeria's), despite favourable financial factors, not come up against the same internal and external obstacles? Are not the intentions of some others (Nigeria above all) a form of words so far? To take, for example steel – one of the bases for autonomous development – it must be observed that there is no steel mill in Africa outside Eygpt and Algeria, whose autonomy not only in formal ownership but also in outlets has been established. Elsewhere steel, most frequently a continuation of colonial trade in building materials, is bound to largely luxury building needs and not to machine tools. Tunisia's attempt to copy Egypt and Algeria has been limited by the country's small market, its political options and illusions (tourism!). Nigeria's attempts warrant a closer look, for de-industrialization of the country by the penetration of multinationals (which destroy the country's small and medium size enterprises and steer national capital into trade and speculation) comes into objective conflict with the national options in official statements.

The second kind of experience and the only one of interest from the point of view of the autocentric alternative may well be described as 'national' (in reality or intention) but scarcely as 'popular'. The national industrialization envisaged would not in the first instance improve the standards of living of the poorest sections (and hence be geared to their genuine rather than money demand), but relate to the growing demand of the middle classes. The 'backwardness' of agriculture is no accident, since the demand for basic foodstuffs is of more concern to the mass of the poor than to those middle classes. So speculative agriculture (in fruit, vegetables, meat for the better-off) is given preference over the basic crops (cereals): Egypt is a fine example with the encouragement of Arab and international capital in this direction.

The consumption pattern of the middle classes, the Western model, absorbs all the so-called 'scarce' resources: (local and foreign) capital and skilled manpower. Our assessment of the use of the latter in the Arab world has brought us to the conclusion that three-quarters of this scarce resource (the stock of workers with secondary, technical or higher education, in this instance) was directly or indirectly engaged on output intended for the super-consumption of the better-off. Obviously the system of production corresponding to this option entails total technological dependence. The – apparently common sense – theory that the cake must be made bigger before it can be shared out is a nonsense. Nobody builds motorways (for the needs of motor vehicle owners) to later apportion them by the yard to the beggars. The share-out determines the character of the cake rather than its size.

If the experiences in question remain extraverted – manifestly in the first instances, and after a closer consideration of their content in the second – it is because they are not 'popular' in the sense shown here ('development for whom?').

The final characteristic, common to both sets of examples, is respect for the sacrosanct principle of 'profitability'. If this criteria is regarded as decisive (even with occasional relaxations) if it is based (as indeed it is) on the system of world prices (reflecting the international division of labour, the sharing out of the market among the monopolies, and so on), the criteria can lead only to the option of the extraverted strategy. Neither political discourse nor diplomatic alliances can affect the meaning of this option.

The history of the past three decades for Africa can be described as the history of the failure of the so-called 'modernization' strategies (cf. Chapter 2).

When the majority of the African countries attained independence, the prevailing view, even in Africa, attributed the continent's underdevelopment to a historical backwardness that must 'catch up' by the simple expedient of going flat out in a previously determined and defined direction. What the national liberation movement blamed the settlers for was for being unequal to the task. The African 'right' and 'left' were convinced that independence was the guarantee and sufficient condition for the acceleration of the rate of 'modernization'. The liberal thesis argued that the maintenance of a wide open door to integration in the international division of labour and appeal to the 'scarce resource' – foreign capital – was not incompatible with the acceleration of growth, but the reverse. The state's role was precisely that of creating the most favourable conditions to create new outlets for capital, by speeding up education and training neglected by the settlers, and by modernizing infrastructure and administration. The socialist thesis of the time, spurning foreign capital, argued that it was the state's duty to bridge the gap of the shortage of capital for the precise purpose of accelerating the process of modernization. In other words, the socialist thesis rejected neither the prospect of modernization, nor that of integration in the international division of labour.

The same fundamental views on the 'neutrality of technology' is common to these two theses, that argue that the direction of modernization was knowable and known: it is enough to look at the advanced 'Western' societies, in the West and in the East, to recognize the similarity of many of the aims – of consumption, and of methods – organization of production, administration and education. Doubtless the 'socialists' were far more sensitive to the issue of national independence and therefore on their guard as to the appeal to foreign capital. Doubtless, too, they were more sensitive to the issues of income distribution and priority to public sector services. But the 'liberals' retorted that capitalism would also solve these problems and in addition engender a gradual democratization of social and political life.

Both theses in the final analysis arose from the same Western-centred and technically economistic view, as the common denominator of a vulgarized Marxism and the finer points of conventional social science. Protests, some 15 years ago, were uncommon and poorly received – peasant utopias, culturalist nationalisms – and it is true that for want of sufficiently broad backing the protesters sank into these eccentricities. But why should Africa be singled out for such fantasies?

The actual history of these two decades has had the effect that both theses are nowadays the subject of systematic questioning to which we shall return (cf. Chapters 5 and 6).

An example of a superficial and truncated analysis of African reality: the World Bank report 'Accelerated Development in Sub-Saharan Africa'.

The 'experts' love to brag of their 'political neutrality'. They pride themselves on the hidden defect of many economists desirous of being technocrats, capable of mentally shaping a 'good development policy', 'scientific', 'devoid of any ideological prejudice'. But this kind of exercise has the supreme virtue of avoiding the real options facing currently existing societies. The truncated and superficial image of reality characteristic of the genre under discussion must of necessity lead to false conclusions.

The World Bank report entitled 'Accelerated Development in Sub-Saharan Africa' is a fine example of this substitution of 'technical prescriptions' for analysis of the causes and roots of the failure of African development.[13]

After the initial acknowledgement of the fact of the severe economic backwardness of Africa in recent decades, the World Bank might have been expected to offer an in-depth critique of the local social and economic systems and world system of division of labour responsible for the failure. Some kind of self-criticism too might have been expected of the World Bank, which for 20 years has supported most of the fundamental guidelines of the development under challenge. Not in the least; the World Bank blames the failure entirely on the African governments that had spurned agriculture and given industry too high a priority! As if a rate of growth of 3.3% on a virtually nil base in 1960, and equalling only half the urban growth rate and only just above the demographic growth rate, indicated some madcap industrialization (especially as Africa's share in world industry declined). Oddly enough and against all expectation, the World Bank attributed this 'bias against agriculture' to a prejudice on the part of foreign aid and the 'development theory'. We are on the contrary conscious of the colonial prejudice of the 'exclusively agricultural and mining role' of the African continent.

The strategy proposed by the Bank is perfectly summarized in page 4 of the report:

> The internal 'structural' problems and the external factors impeding African economic growth have been exacerbated by domestic policy inadequacies . . . trade and exchange-rate policies have overprotected industry, held back agriculture . . . public sectors frequently become overextended . . .

After which the Bank suggests a strategy of readjustment to the demands of the world system based on priority for agricultural and mining exports, by the principal method of devaluation and the restoration of a greater liberalism, combined with greater openness to private enterprise. The carrot of doubling foreign aid in real terms in the 1980s is held out to make these principles acceptable. As is known nowadays, the 'readjustment' is imposed but foreign aid declines!

If the words have any meaning this is an extraverted strategy of adjustment to the demands of transnationalization, a strategy of renouncing the construction of a diversified national and regional economy capable through its dynamism of becoming a genuine partner in the interdependent world system.

The analysis of the internal and external constraints is especially disturbing. The chapter on basic constraints notes: underdeveloped human resources, low productivity of agriculture and rapid urbanization.

The rationale for underdevelopment of human resources is trivialized to inadequate education. Infantile illusions are taken up in the chapter on human resources, treated as an area of substantial returns, without the authors of the report realizing that they are measuring these returns by the tautological indicator based on a comparison of rewards between graduates and illiterate! Education (in its present form) is not necessarily the best investment, but is definitely a means of differentiating classes and incomes . . . With no consideration of the society's problems, with no changes to suggest, the report is satisfied with proposing some minor tinkering to reduce (very slightly) the costs of education in its present form.

The low productivity of agriculture in Africa is a platitude. What the Bank report neglects to point out is that this low productivity accompanying the extensive pattern of this agriculture has been and is profitable from the point of view of the world system's division of labour. In effect it allows the West to acquire raw materials without having to invest. Transition to intensive agriculture, a necessity of today, entails a rise in the world prices of these raw materials if they are to be exported: land, along with oil or water, is no longer 'limitless' but becoming a scarce resource.

The growth of urbanization is likewise a platitude. What the Bank does not point out is that the rural exodus is the result of the impoverishment of the countryside and that it cannot be held back unless there is a transition to intensive agriculture requiring, in turn, industrial backing and fair prices (not only the internal prices but the world prices too if the output of this agriculture is to be exported). What the Bank further fails to point out is that an inadequate industrial growth (of 3.3% a year) can obviously not absorb the urban growth. The Bank's talk of deterioration in the services essential to urban life and the proposals for tinkering to reduce costs here are in these circumstances nothing but empty talk of pie in the sky.

The external factors are also treated superficially without analysis as to their causes. Noting the worsening in the balance of payments of the oil-importing countries in the region is no analysis of the problem but only a proclamation. The Bank's analysis stops short at the observation that the growth in quantity of exports has been insufficient and low: from 7.2% annual growth in the 1960s to 2% for the following decade in respect of mining output (excluding oil) and from 4.6 to 0.7% in respect of agricultural output. It offers no information as to the causes of these low figures: the world crisis in demand, the encouragement of over-production in the Third World (the Bank itself advises each country to diversify by producing what it advises for the neighbour), the aims and strategies of the multinationals in the mining sector ('shelving' of reserves) the crisis in expansion of extensive agriculture.

The critical analysis of the policies under way and consequently of the priorities proposed are governed by this disturbing vision of the global operation of the system and the 'fundamentalist' prejudices of the World Bank's Reaganite liberalism. The Bank has found only three ills afflicting Africa: (i) overvalued exchange rates; (ii) excessive taxation of farmers; and (iii) excessive growth in administrative expenditure.

It is obvious that if foreign exchange prices are maintained, devaluation allows the exporter to acquire more in local currency. But it does not permit the inference that devaluation must allow a balance without controls on the balance of payments, nor that foreign exchange prices will remain steady. Third World experience has shown repeatedly that local prices as a whole tend to adjust to those of imports, and by the same token the effects of devaluation on the structure of comparative prices and on the balance of payments are cancelled out. The absence of an autocentric economic structure with its own autonomy explains this widespread contagion reflecting the dependence of local prices on the world system of prices. How we put it is that the worldwide law of value governs the range of 'paranational' prices systems. If the per capita added value in agriculture of Third World countries is one third of the per capita added value in industry and services and if this is the case throughout the Third World, as opposed to what it is in the countries of the capitalist centre, it is for this fundamental reason. The real values of the rewards for labour determine prices and not the converse. A devaluation intended to raise real rewards (for all coffee producers for example) would not fail in its purpose: the dollar price of coffee would go down to adjust to the maintenance of the existing real (and minimal) rewards to the producers. This is the lesson of history that the World Bank grandly overlooks.

This fundamental reality obviously will not preclude the currencies of a group of countries being over-valued (or under-valued) in the world system. But there must be precision as to the character of the balances modified by juggling with exchange rates and a specific explanation of this character in case studies. It is doubtful if a general devaluation in Africa would improve the lot of the peasants and open the way for an upsurge in agricultural exports. Mali, Zaire and many others devalued without the slightest benefit accruing to the peasants.

It is correct that the hidden 'taxation' to which peasants in Africa are subjected (through the difference between the export price – after deduction of the real costs of internal marketing – and the price paid to the producer) is substantial: 40–45% according to the Bank's report. But where would the state find its resources if this margin were eliminated and if the country accorded priority in development to these export products, as the Bank suggests? Why not reduce the taxes on consumption (on coffee for example) in the developed countries for the benefit of the African peasant? It is clear that this taxation is a manifestation of the 'anti-peasant' bias of the states. But the bias is a result of the character of the relations between these states and the world system: the anti-peasant bias is not only characteristic of the local state, but also of the global system of exploitation of which that state is part.

On the subject of public expenditure, as on others, the World Bank, by neglecting to go deep into an analysis of the system is bound to throw around advice of little value, to suggest 'tinkering' methods to bring a (trifling) reduction in this expenditure. Without fail, the savings will be made on the backs of the impoverished masses, in contradiction with the talk of 'basic needs'. Furthermore does not the IMF, the Bank's close associate, always insist that devaluation should be accompanied by austerity and reductions in the standards of living of the poorest strata? 'True pricing' (with that of the world system taken as the ultimate standard) and the withdrawal of subsidies on the most essential items are always contrary to the interests of the population.

Industry, lightly discussed in chapter 7 of the report is, according to the Bank, 'over-protected'. Would not a relaxation of this 'over-protection' of an industry that remains the weakest in the world further weaken its already derisory growth rate? Wages in Africa are said to be 'high', and the lower rates of Bangladesh offered as a model. Is the World Bank seeing a Bangladeshization of the Third World? How is such language to be harmonized with the talk of satisfying 'basic needs'? Industrialization strategy is not discussed: import substitution is regarded as the desirable option par excellence (what is forgotten is that the strategy reproduces and intensifies inequalities of income distribution), but 'badly implemented' in Africa since it requires too much state protection – without which, notwithstanding the Bank's pious remarks about 'entrepreneurship', the rate of industrialization would have been even lower. The Bank also recommends increasing local processing of mineral exports, although this is known to have swallowed up substantial capital without relating the exploitation of these resources to national development. It also recommends light industrial manufacture for export: have they forgotten the frustrations of the Moroccan and Tunisian textiles industries, which after a similar 'recommendation' found doors in the West slammed against them? As for the industrialization required for agricultural development, this is apparently a strategy unknown to the Bank. In regard to exploitation of mining resources, the Bank sees no other option than that of entrusting it to the interests and strategies of the multinationals. The notion that these resources could form the basis of national and regional development never surfaces.

The 'longer-term issues' are reduced to demography and its effects. It is a commonplace that the towns, where there is a fourfold population increase every quarter century, tend – by virtue of inadequate industrialization – to turn into slum shanty-towns. It is a commonplace that in 20 years the urban population will have increased by 50%. All the more reason, with a reminder of the need to conserve soils (how? the Bank does not tell us), for hastening intensive agricultural development and the consequent demand for industrial backing and delinking.

External assistance, a topic on which the Bank concludes its report with a further flurry of pious hopes, is incapable of being the palliative to the shortcomings of the proposed plan. According to the Bank's own calculations on the most encouraging hypothesis of 'substantial aid increase', this could in the 1980s provide the continent with no better than a 2.1% per capita annual growth rate. Such aid would take the debt service burden from 10% of export earnings in 1980 to 20% in 1990. None of these assessments have stood the test of time. The 'aid' in question has not come; and the debt burden has soared far beyond the calculations of our Washington technocrats.

The World Bank's language does not conform to the basic criteria of scientific analysis. It is a language of ideology in the worst sense of the term.

Notes

1. Statistical data are taken from reports of the World Bank in Washington and the Economic Commission for Africa in Addis Ababa. See also: Amin, Samir, *Neocolonialism in West Africa*, London, Penguin, 1973; Amin, Samir and Coquery-Vidrovitch, *Histoire économique du Congo 1880–1968*, Paris, Anthropos, 1969;

Amin, Samir, *Impérialisme et sous-développement en Afrique*, (new edition) Paris, Economica, 1988; Amin, Samir, *L'échange inégal et la loi de la valeur*, (new edition) Paris, Economica, 1988.

2. Gakou, Mohamed Lamine, *The Crisis in African Agriculture*, London, Zed, 1988; Aït Amara, Hamid and Founou-Tchuigoua, (eds), *Etudes sur la crise des politiques de modernisation en Afrique*, in preparation, and Samir Amin's forewords to these books. Cf. Amin, Samir, 'Les limites de la révolution verte', *CERES*, Vol. 3, No.4, July 1970, and 'Le paradoxe africain le deficit alimentaire de l'Afrique', *CERES*, No. 25, 1973.

3. Boserup, Ester, *The Conditions of Agricultural Growth*, London, Allen & Unwin, 1965.

4. Dumont, René, *False Start in Africa*, London, Deutsch, 1966.

5. BRGM, *Les eaux souterraines de l'Afrique Sahèlienne*, Paris, 1975.

6. Founou-Tchuigoua, Bernard, *Les fondements de l'économies de traite au Sénégal*, Genoble, Silex, 1981, and preface by Samir Amin. Cf. Amin, Samir, 'Underdevelopment and dependence in Black Africa', *The Journal of Modern Africa Studies*, Vol. 10, No. 4, 172, pp. 503–24; 'The Class Struggle in Africa', *Revolution*, No. 9, 1964, pp. 23–47; introduction to Amin, Samir, (ed) *Modern Migrations in Western Africa*, Oxford, Oxford University Press for the International African Institute, 1974.

7. Amin, Samir, 'Le développement du capitalisme en Afrique noire', *L'Homme et la Société*, No. 12, 1969.

8. See thesis in preparation by Jean Pierre Leclerc and contributions on China to the MSH–State University of New York Colloquium, Paris, June 1988.

9. Data from reports of the Economic Commission for Africa, Economic Commission for Western Asia, World Bank and International Monetary Fund, and the integrated economic reports (in Arabic) of the Arab League. Cf. Amin, Samir and Yaçhir, Faysal, *La Méditerranée dans le système mondial*, Paris, La Découverte, 1988, (English edition, *The Mediterranean: Between Autonomy and Dependency*, London, Zed Books, 1989); Riad, Hassan [Amin, Samir], *L'Egypte nasserienne*, Paris, Minuit, 1964); Amin, Samir, *The Arab Nation*, London, Zed Press, 1978; *The Arab Economy Today*, London, Zed Books, 1982; Samir Amin's preface to Sertel, Yildiz, *Nord–Sud: crise et immigration; le cas turc*, Paris, Publisud, 1987; Keyder, Caglar, *State and Class in Turkey*, London, Verso, 1987.

10. Amin, Samir, *The Maghreb in the Modern World* (Trans. by Michael Perl), London, Penguin, 1970, p. 104.

11. Amin, Samir, 'Pour une stratégie alternative du développement, à propos du CILSS'. *African Development*, No. 3, 1981, and Samir Amin's introduction to Aït Amara, Hamid and Founou-Tchuigoua, Bernard (eds) *Etudes sur la crise des politiques de modernisation en Afrique*.

12. Amin, Samir, Faire, Alexandre, and Malkin, Daniel, *L'avenir industriel de l'Afrique*, Paris, Harmattan, 1981; various authors for UNU, *Crise des politiques d'industrialisation en Afrique*, (in preparation); Amin, Samir, 'L'économie politique de l'Afrique dans la crise contemporaine' in Bourges, H. and Wauthier, C., *Les 50 Afriques*, Paris, Seuil, 1979; Yachir, Faysal, *Mining in Africa Today: Strategies and Prospects*, London, Zed Books, 1988; *The World Steel Industry Today*, London, Zed Books, 1988.

13. *Accelerated Development in Sub-Saharan Africa: An Agenda for Action*, Washington D.C., World Bank, 1981. Cf. Amin, Samir, 'Critique du rapport de la Banque Mondiale pour l'Afrique', *Africa Development*, No. 1–2, 1982; 'Un

développement autocentré est-il possible en Afrique?' in Ahooja-Patel, Krishna, Drabek, Anne Gordon, and Nerfin, Marc, *World Economy in Transition:* essays presented to Surendra Patel on his 60th birthday, Oxford, Pergamon, 1986.

After this book was written, the World Bank produced a new report on adjustment in Africa. This report is a little less arrogant than the Berg report commented upon here; it pays lip service to the issue of the 'social negative aspects' of adjustment. Yet it proceeds from the same methodology and basically unscientific assumptions, which disregard the polarizing dimension of actually existing capitalism, ignoring therefore that these 'social negative aspects' are, precisely, part and parcel of the political rationale of the targets of the adjustment.

2. The Decade of Drift: 1975–1985

The 1975–85 period is one of continuing drift in the internal strategies of Third World countries and in world economic and political balance. Excitement came at the beginning with the Bandung plan, to build within the Third World a bourgeois national state with a capacity to make progress in solving the problems of underdevelopment in the framework of the interdependence imposed by the worldwide economy. History was to prove the impossibility of the plan in the light of the internal limitations of the practices of the states in question and the offensive led by the West to reject any calls for an adjustment of the international order to meet development needs at the periphery of the capitalist system. Step by step we reached the current situation that we describe as 'recompradorization' of the Third World. At the level of the international order the period is characterized by the beginning of the decline of US hegemony. But if this decline should lead almost inevitably to the reconstruction of a desirably polycentric world, what place would it hold for the Third World regions? In any event, the open crisis since the 1970s has delayed this evolution by inspiring a realignment of the West as a whole to the Atlantic pact (cf. Chapters 4 and 8).[1]

This is the canvas on which the balancing act of prevailing opinion is painted. After the phase of ingenuous illusions of Third Worldism came the phase of aggressive anti-Third Worldism. In this way analysis and critique of what is in fact an impasse for currently existing capitalism was abandoned, and the door was closed to any close examination of the proposals for delinked national and popular development, as the basis for a necessary reconstruction of a polycentric world more responsive to people's needs.

We shall try in this chapter to sketch the main stages of this drift that in Africa's case runs from the adoption of the rhetorical Lagos Plan of Action (1980), adhering to the logic of the battle for a new international economic order (NIEO) to surrender to the recolonization of the Berg plan (named after the American expert charged by the World Bank with its formulation). At the same time, we shall examine the internal reasons why the various African attempts at alternative development have not so far yielded any but the most sparse results.

The excitement of the Bandung plan (1955–73)[2]

More than 30 years ago the principal heads of state of those Asian and African countries that had regained political independence met for the first time at Bandung. The experience of the new authorities they represented was still slight: India and Indonesia had been independent for fewer than ten years, Communist China for only five, and it was only three years since the Egyptian monarchy had bowed out of history. The battle for the achievement of the historic task of independence was not over: the first Vietnamese war was only just finished and the second was already in prospect, the Korean War ended with the status quo, the Algerian war was in full flow, decolonization of sub-Saharan Africa was not even yet foreseen, and the drama of Palestine was in its first phase.

The Asian and African leaders meeting in Bandung were far from resembling one another. The political and ideological currents they represented, their vision of the future society to be built or rebuilt and its relations with the West all provoked different attitudes. But a common plan brought them together and gave their meeting meaning. On their minimum common programme was the achievement of political decolonization of Asia and Africa. Moreover they all appreciated that regaining political independence was a means and not an end, the latter being winning economic, social and cultural liberation. On this, two views divided the Bandung guests: there was a majority view of those who believed in a potential 'development' within 'interdependence' in the world economy, and a view of the communist leaders who believed that a withdrawal from the capitalist camp would lead – with, if not behind the USSR – to the building of a world socialist camp.

The leaders of the capitalist Third World who did not expect to 'leave the system' or 'delink' did not all have the same strategic and tactical view of 'development'. But in varying degrees they did think that the building of an economy and an independent developed society (albeit within global interdependence) entailed an element of 'conflict' with the dominant West (the radical wing regarded it as essential to put a stop to control over the national economy by foreign monopoly capital). In their further concern to preserve the regained independence, they refused to join the planetary war games and serve as bases for the encirclement of socialist countries that US hegemony was seeking. However, they believed too that refusing to join the Atlantic military pact did not imply a willingness to come under the umbrella of its adversary, the USSR. Hence 'neutralism' and 'non-alignment'. The then secret history of relations between China and the USSR, whose crisis was to become public knowledge two years later, was to show that this position was not really very different from the one taken by China in the 1960s. It was also the position in which Yugoslavia found itself after the break of 1948. The formation of a non-aligned front had, therefore, Tito's active sympathy from the very start.

The drawing together of the Afro-Asian states had already begun with the establishment of the Arab–Asian group in the United Nations, in order to defend the cause of independence for the struggling colonies. Bandung reinforced this drawing together and gave the struggle a fillip. Three years later, in liberated Accra, Kwame Nkrumah declared 'Africa must unite'. But once independence was gained and Nkrumahist pan-Africanism failed and there was the demonstration of the impotence of the two camps constituted around the Congo issue (the Casablanca bloc and the Monrovia bloc from 1960 to 1963) African unity was to take the minimal form of the establishment of the Organization of African Unity in 1963.

During the 1960s and the 1970s at one summit meeting after another 'non-alignment' was gradually to slide from the standpoint of a political solidarity front geared to support for liberation struggles and rejection of military alliances to a posture of 'a trade union of economic claims on the North'. The battle for a 'new international economic order' engaged upon in 1975 after the Middle East war of October 1973 and the adjustment in the price of oil was the apotheosis of this evolution only to sound its death knell.

Neither at political nor economic level was the West lightheartedly going to accept the Bandung spirit. Was it mere chance that one year later France, Britain and Israel would try to overthrow Nasser by the joint aggression of 1956? Imperialist capital's rejection of the Bandung political vision was shown by the real hatred the West manifested for the Third World radical leaders of the 1960s (Nasser, Soekarno, Nkrumah, Modibo Keita), who were nearly all overthrown in the same period, from 1965 to 1968, which included Israel's aggression of June 1967. It was, therefore, a politically hamstrung non-aligned camp that was to face the global economic crisis from 1970–71. The West's non-acceptance of the proposed NIEO showed the genuine connection between the political and economic aspects of the Afro-Asian initiative crystallized from Bandung.

What may nowadays be called 'development ideology', in a crisis that may be terminal, had its 'moment of glory' between 1955 and 1975, but never gave rise to an interpretation shared by everyone and understood in the same way.

The traditional communist camp was also not prepared to accept the aims that emerged from Bandung. In 1948 Jdanov proclaimed the division of the world into two camps – capitalist and socialist – and, in advance, condemned as illusory any attempt to stand outside them, and hence to wish to be 'non-aligned'. Within this spirit the communists could not envisage any winning of independence by a national liberation movement they had not led. India's independence was marked by the Indian Communist Party as a 'day of national mourning'; in South-East Asia the Chinese and Vietnamese models were thought desirable to be extended to Indonesia, the Philippines, Malaysia, Thailand and Burma. It was only after the first 'stabilization' of the 1950–55 period (the victory in China, armistice and partition in Korea and Vietnam, the admitted defeat of guerrillas elsewhere in South-East Asia), after the Third World 'bourgeois' new regimes had proved their viability, after the start, albeit under 'bourgeois' leadership, of their conflict with the West, and after Stalin's death (1953) and Khruschev's ideological overtures, that the notion of the possibility of a 'viable third camp' and a 'third path of development' began to be appreciated.

The non-communist Third World leaders did, however, believe in a 'third path of development' that would be neither 'capitalist', nor an imitation of the socialist models of the USSR and China. Their rejection of Marxism was tempered with considerations of varying kinds: they sometimes saw Marxism as the descendant of European culture and incompatible with their own people's value systems (and religious conviction, Islam, Hinduism or the peculiarities of negritude); sometimes they were merely fearful of losing their independence (Soviet domination of Eastern Europe, denounced by Tito, was on show to fuel their fear); sometimes they were more drawn by the Western model of efficiency and consumption, or freedom (although the latter was less highly valued), than by the Soviet and Chinese models (less efficient or too austere and so on). Out of these ambiguous attitudes were to emerge perhaps the ideologies of 'particular socialisms' (for example, African, Arab).

'Particular socialisms' or 'particular paths to a socialism of universal application'? This is the locus of debate. The question is not yet settled and may be more open today than ever. The – now open – crisis of 'existing socialisms' may in fact cast doubt on the model of a supposedly achieved socialism. But this crisis has gone through stages and indicates only the interaction of different levels of critique.

The Sino-Soviet dispute certainly had two aspects: one national and the other in regard to the social and political view of a plan for society. It cannot be doubted that China, as a potential great power, was not going to leave Moscow the sole responsibility of deciding the strategies and tactics of confrontation with the United States. It suspected the USSR of being too susceptible of sacrificing the interests of other peoples for its own, whereas Peking was convinced that the 'socialist revolution' was on the agenda in the 'storm zones', that is, the Third World. At the same time, Maoism felt bound to make a critique of the Soviet model of development and embark on an alternative path and an approach that would not reproduce the models of labour organization, consumption and the Western capitalist way of life, by replacing capital ownership with state ownership.

The subsequent arguments, polemics, realities and evolutions make it possible now to have a clearer picture of the divergences and diagnostics of the problems. But opinions and theorizations will go on producing different pictures of the Soviet and Chinese systems that call themselves socialist, of the genuine problems encountered in historical construction (development of the forces of production and new social relations), the emerging gap between the results achieved so far and the idea of socialism (especially Marx's idea), the ideological roots of these evolutions (the historical limitations of Leninism and Maoism as regards the state, the relationship with an avant-garde party, the avant-garde and the people, and so forth), and the effects of these evolutions on the world socialist movement and its integration in world politics and so on.

These realities call for a consideration of the hiatus in the leftist nationalism of Bandung, for subtle judgement and a refusal to utter 'condemnations' in the name of some absolute values supposedly achieved in nearly perfect, or truly perfect models. But they call, too, for a critical approach to the propositions of 'particular socialisms'. The latter have not proved themselves to be a step forward in the solution of problems facing the so-called socialist societies. On the contrary, they have reproduced the shortcomings of the latter, sometimes to the point of caricature: the single party (sometimes with only a paper existence), absolute power, contempt for democracy and basic human rights, without such faults bringing any compensation in terms of economic (or military) efficiency. The ease with which such efforts are overturned revealed by experience justifies some severity on this score.

There was a Bandung plan, albeit implicit and vague, that might be described as the 'bourgeois national plan for the Third World in our age. Although it has particular forms and national characteristics it could be defined as follows: (i) the desire to develop the forces of production and diversify products (namely industrialize); (ii) the desire to ensure for the national state direction and control of the process; (iii) the belief that 'technical' models provide 'neutral' data that can only be copied, albeit by mastering them; (iv) the belief that the process does not primarily require popular initiative but merely popular acquiescence in state action; (v) the belief that the process is not essentially in contradiction with participation in exchanges with the world capitalist system, even if the process does provoke occasional clashes with it.

The context of capitalist expansion in the 1955–70 period to some extent encouraged crystallization of the plan. But by what criteria is the success of the bourgeois national plan to be judged? Certainly not the apparent criterion of per capita income.

The implementation of the national bourgeois plan implies a series of controls by the hegemonic national bourgeois class, through the state, at least over the following processes: (i) control of reproduction of labour power, which entails a fairly complete and balanced development such that local agriculture can supply the essential ingredients of this quantitative reproduction and at appropriate prices to bring a return on capital; (ii) control of national resources; (iii) control of local markets and the capacity to penetrate the world market on competitive terms; (iv) control of financial machinery to ensure centralization of the surplus and a say in its productive use; (v) control of the technologies in use to the relevant level of development of the forces of production.

On this basis the Third World experiences can be classified under two headings: countries that have attempted no more than to speed up growth without worrying about the foregoing conditions (Côte d'Ivoire, Kenya, Pakistan or Saudi Arabia, among others) and the long list of countries that have attempted to fulfil those conditions (for example, Nasser's Egypt, Algeria, Tanzania, India, Brazil, South Korea). As can be seen the classification does not necessarily distinguish regimes concerned for a measure of social justice and reform, especially land reform (such as Nasser's Egypt or South Korea) from those which have had no hesitation in accepting widening social inequalities (Brazil for example). It does not necessarily distinguish attitudes in regard to transnational capital (Brazil and Kenya are both open to it but the former seeks to relate the capital to its national policy, whereas the latter is happy to adjust to capital's demands), nor even the issue of political relations of contestation or alliance with East and West. Some correlations can be found but the make-up in terms of conjunctures makes each Third World country a special case.

Putting aside the variety of the experience it can be seen that the most coherent achievements have occurred when an acute nationalist combat is combined with a powerful social movement. Nasser's Egypt was certainly one of the best examples of this.

It is no longer possible to ignore the shortcomings of these attempts that have not withstood the vagaries of fortune. The agricultural and food crisis, the foreign debt, the mounting technological dependence, the poor capacity to withstand military aggression, the arrival of the capitalist models of conspicuous waste and the effect of this on ideology and culture are all signs of the historical limitations of the attempt. Even before the current crisis brought an opportunity for a 'Western offensive' to reverse the changes, the shortcomings had already brought things to a halt. This is not to say that the experiences were bound to stop short where they did and that their 'failure' was inevitable. We should argue that to go any further, a genuine 'revolution' was crucial, one that would destroy the double illusion of national development unless it arose from genuinely popular authority, and the possibility of any such development without 'delinking' from the world system. It is not to say that some evolution in this direction was possible in this or that instance, in Egypt for example. It did not happen and now history has moved on.

It is in this sense that we say the plan warrants the description as a bourgeois national plan; and meanwhile it has been found to be impossible. In the same way history has shown that in our day the national bourgeoisie is incapable of achieving what it has done elsewhere, in Europe, North America and 19th century Japan. This thesis is no novelty and it is not the first failure of the attempt in question. Again to give just one example, Egypt's history since Mohamed Ali is one of a succession of bourgeois national attempts smashed each time by the combination of their internal fragility and imperialist aggression: in their own way Mohamed Ali, Khedive Ismail, Orabi (if his revolution has been successful), the Wafd achieved a great deal, in the context of their times, with the means that the modalities of formation of the Egyptian bourgeoisie offered within the framework of the overall capitalist system of the day; their imprint remains strong and in some respects the changes they made are irreversible. But it has to be acknowledged that their failure opened the way each time to a 'compradorization' of Egypt in the style of the time.

No more needs to be said. A study of other Third World countries and regions would in our opinion illustrate the same thesis: an unbroken succession of national bourgeois attempts, repeated abortions and surrender to the demands of the subordination that has followed each time in Latin America since the 19th century (to mention only the most recent examples of the Mexican revolution in the 1910s to 1920s and Peronist Argentina), in India (whose evolution from Nehru's 'first plan' to the return of the right to government after Congress's first failure is eloquent), and in numerous Arab and African countries.

The post-Second World War circumstances were unusually favourable. At the economic level the North's strong economic growth made 'adjustment' in the South easier. At the political level the peaceful coexistence emerging from the growth of Soviet industrial and military power (from the first Sputnik space flight to the 'strategic balance' achieved in the 1960s to 1970s) in combination with the decline of the former British and French colonialism and the upsurge of the Afro-Asian independence struggles gave the Soviet alliance real effectivenesss.

Successes are always crowned with disappointment. An illusion of 'gradual' and virtually painless evolution towards socialism was fostered by the formulation of the theory of the so-called 'non-capitalist road'. Of course this theory did not convince everybody. China denounced it forcefully in the 1960s as an opiate intended to lull the peoples to sleep and damp down the explosions in the 'storm zones'. Che Guevarism tried to counter it with immediate military revolution.

History has now moved on again. Since the early 1970s, the West's economic boom has been smothered to give way to the structural crisis under way, while competition between Europe, Japan and the United States took over from reconstruction under American protection. In the Soviet Union, Khruschev's promises – to overtake American living standards in 1989 – and the attempts at rapid democratization in the wake of the 20th Congress gave way to Brezhnev's stick-in-the-mud, timid and ineffectual reforms to overcome the management crisis of a system faced with the challenge of moving from extensive to intensive accumulation. Gorbachev's initiatives may mark a new departure, but it is early days to judge their extent and effectiveness.[3] In China, the about-turn following Mao's death showed that neither the issue of economic efficiency nor of democracy have found their 'definitive' response. Throughout the Third World the food crisis (to the extreme of chronic famine in Africa), the foreign debt crisis and the standstill of imported technology have brought a series of surrenders to the dictates of transnational capital, organized around the Paris and London Clubs, the IMF, the World Bank and the consortium of the large Western banks. In the radically inclined countries, *coups d'état* and military aggression (the 1967 war was no chance) have largely contributed to halting the experiences under way. The Bandung era is past.

The axis of the new world conjuncture is Western capitalist aggression against the Third World peoples, with the aim of subordinating their further evolution to the demands of redeployment of transnational capital.

Is this a painful but passing phenomenon that must necessarily be followed by a new blossoming of 'national bourgeois' advances? Or is it a historical turning point that will no longer allow the following of these successive national bourgeois plans characteristic of at least a century of recent history? This is where the real debate on the character of the challenges and the options for the future lies.

The battle for a new international economic order (NIEO): 1974–1980

From the late 1960s to the early 1970s (before the 'oil crisis' of 1973–74), the world system entered a long period of structural crisis from which we had not emerged some 18 years or so later. A more systematic analysis of the character of this crisis will be offered below (cf. Chapter 8).[4]

The overt crisis of the world system over more than 15 years is evidence of a new dimension to what is at stake in the international division of labour, since the crisis commits all the forces of earth to a great battle that will decide the pattern of international power for generations to come. Shall we see a perpetuation of the polarization between the United States and the USSR? Shall we see a polycentric world of five partners (United States, Europe, Japan, USSR and China)? Or shall we see a polycentric world with a more even balance between the great powers and the regions of the Third World (India, Brazil, Latin America, South-East Asia, the Arab and African world)?

The perspectives opening to Africa and the Third World must be seen in this light. More particularly the issue that arises is as follows: on what axes can the international division of labour evolve in regard to the differing strategies of the powers? What strategies can the Third World regions devise in response to the differing strategies possible?

If we must look ahead and not backwards, identify the changes under way in the international division of labour and study their significance, it is because the history of underdevelopment is one of adjustment by the periphery to mutations and evolutions at the centre. In other words 'development' of the periphery has never allowed it to 'catch up' the centre, since each stage of the centre's evolution has meant a new stage in the international division of labour, and the latter goes on being unequal and assigning the periphery subordinate roles.

We have tried elsewhere to trace this history of stages in unequal international specialization, particularly for Africa, in regard to the stages of the constitution and evolution of the world capitalist system. For the Third World as a whole we have come to an end of certain characteristics of the previous periods, but not so in the majority of African countries; these characteristics are mainly subordination of the periphery in the role of suppliers of raw materials and agricultural crops, then import substitution industrialization for the local market (a market distorted by unequal income distribution engendered by the previous stages). The next stage may be accelerated industrialization of the periphery for exports to the centre, through the dumping on the periphery of light and heavy 'classic' industries, and concentration at the centre of new industries as the basis for a renewed model of accumulation: atomic and solar energy, space, genetic engineering and synthetic food production, exploration of the seabed, information science.

This new model of distribution of tasks would remain unequal like the previous (surviving) model. The very logic of the system, the reason for dumping classic industries on the periphery is the possibility of exploiting manpower that is cheap not only in absolute terms but also relative terms, that is in comparison with the productivity of the labour it can supply.

The battles fought during the 1970s were over control of this new international division of labour in prospect. The bourgeoisies of the periphery understanding of their proposals for a new international economic order was that they would participate as partners worthy of the name, whereas the multinationals had an opposing concept of industrial relocation entirely controlled by worldwide capital.

The development of the so-called newly industrializing countries, particularly in east Asia, which did accelerate in this period, was part of this logic. Concentration of clusters of industries in certain parts of the periphery led to the question being raised of possible candidates in Africa. In this context a country can attract multinational companies' capital provided it can already offer a numerous proletariat, skilled cadres – at least of intermediate level – and some capital (to provide the necessary infrastructure and later finance the establishment of industry properly speaking) and as long as the multinational companies retain control of operations through a monopoly of technology and market influence. Few African countries fulfil these conditions, with the exception of South Africa. But the great oil producers (Algeria in particular) and the few countries less heavily populated and more advanced in urbanization and secondary and university education (Egypt primarily and then perhaps Nigeria and Morocco) did seem potential candidates.

One topic of debate of the time was the character of these potential 'sub-imperialisms'. Such 'sub-imperialism' is characterized by the concentration of exports of capital and technology from the centre, intended to enable the beneficiary to export classic industrial products to the centre and secondarily to the less favoured areas of the periphery and by this means to cover dues to the centre on capital and technology. The concentration of classic industries in these countries, combined with the high rates of exploitation of their proletariats, would enable the bourgeois 'sub-imperialists' to benefit from a sufficient share in the surplus to ensure the system's economic and political balance. If ambiguities and false issues are to be avoided in this debate, it is absolutely essential to give up the unfortunate expression 'sub-imperialism' that first came into use to describe the phenomenon of Brazil, as the expression is a poor description of the new stage in the unequal development of the periphery. The reference to imperialism suggests the export of capital, whereas in fact the 'sub-imperialisms' under discussion are importers, just as they import their technology from the centre. The significant point is agreement on content, namely the position occupied by the countries in the new international division of labour. The expression 'conveyor belt' or 'lumpen-development' would, in our opinion, be more appropriate.

The outlook implies a sharpened differentiation within the Third World. The cleavages already apparent in Africa (coastal countries and the so-called 'less developed' of the interior) are accentuated by this new factor. The great majority of African countries are still typically colonial in their economic and social structures, based on a colonial trade economy, as the 'development' policies pursued since independence have done no more than continue those implemented before the 1960s. But it was possible at the time to believe that some countries in Africa were in a position to play the role taken on by others elsewhere: Mexico and Brazil in Latin America, Iran in the Middle East, India in south Asia, Korea in east Asia.

At the time and in contrast to the prospects of the world system's reorganization, certain African countries insisted on their determination for autonomous, self-reliant, and 'socialist' development. Under the circumstances they could do no more than express a more or less serious political intention, as there had been no change in the economic and social structures; or go forward with the initiation of new social patterns characterized by internal class alliances in contradiction with the position offered the country in the international division of labour – whether that inherited from the previous stages or that in prospect.

The prospect of the new international division of labour was scarcely encouraging. For the conveyor belt countries it could mean no more than a kind of 'lumpen development', marked by rising unemployment and immiserization of the masses, for the other countries a status of 'sub-colony' and a worsening of their situation as was already to be seen in the Sahel region hit by famine, and for the cause of African unity a step backwards that might be irrecoverable.

To the degree that the 'nationalist' social patterns entered into contradiction with this outlook, it was possible to envisage an 'alternative strategy'. This proposed to compel the North to adjust to the demands of the NIEO and by this means institute a transition that could still be called socialist, with its own social aims (full employment, education, social justice). Algeria under Boumedienne's government seemed to be leading this group of countries. It must, however, be understood that so long as dependence on technology and access to external markets are not challenged, the institute of transition to socialism remains vulnerable. Here, Egypt's experience should be considered. At the level of industrialization Egypt was by far the most advanced African country. Egyptian industry, entirely nationalized, was well ahead of that in any other country on the continent. The internal social relations peculiar to Nasser's Egypt explain why these nationalizations were not accompanied by more radical challenges as to the destination and type of product, the technologies, and so on. The result was a blockage in this type of development, contradictory only in part with the international division of labour. This blockage (how was imported technology to be paid for, how could further industrialization be financed) led to the about-turn we know of, indicating the surrender of the Egyptian bourgeoisie to the dictates of world capitalism and of its American component in particular.

The actual changes that ensued, especially after 1980, dashed the hopes of the earlier years. Not only were the claims of the NIEO rejected, but also there was virtually no redeployment. The Reaganite counter-attack, aimed at restoring the threatened US hegemony, led to Western unity, albeit transitorily, and to the West's lining up as a whole against the Third World. A strategy of 'recompradorization' of the latter replaced the collective negotiations and concessions. Under the hammer blows of the 'readjustment' offensive imposed by the IMF, taking advantage of Third World debt, the nationalist regimes surrendered one by one. But the widespread recompradorization did not prevent further differentiation within the Third World. We shall come back to the significance of this in Chapter 7. In our view the so-called newly industrializing countries are the real periphery of today and tomorrow, while the others – 'delinked by default' – are passively undergoing the fate of the 'fourth world' as it is called nowadays. This sad outlook for the greater part of the African continent, and one that tempers the extent of the seeming 'economic successes' of the countries appearing to be exceptions to the rule, is not surprising. It should come as a surprise only to those who fail to understand that the process of the worldwide expansion of capitalism is not solely a process of development but likewise a process of destruction.

All these negative evolutions have wiped out past hopes in a positive drawing together of the European, Arab and African worlds within the prospect of rebuilding a polycentric, balanced world conducive to better development of the Third World. We shall return to this striking move backwards and the political regression that has occurred north and south of the Mediterranean and the Sahara (cf. Chapter 4).

Structural crisis; the stakes; the struggle for the NIEO

The claims by Third World states for a 'New International Economic Order' formed a coherent whole whose logic was perfectly comprehensible. Substantial and sustained rises in raw materials prices, strengthened by a debt reduction and more favourable conditions for the transfer of technology, were the method par excellence of improving the financial prospects of a new stage of Third World industrialization. This industrialization, based on what conventional wisdom regards as 'comparative advantages', was conceived on the dual basis of relatively cheap manpower and natural resources allowing for exports to the developed world in an expanded network of world trade. The opening up of developed countries' markets to the export of the manufactures of the Third World would, according to the conventional wisdom, serve the collective interest by making the international division of labour more responsive to the source of inputs. Furthermore, industrial exports would help bridge the Third World food gap through imports replacing aid.

The rise in oil prices at the end of 1973 strengthened the credibility of this programme by showing that it was possible to secure alternative prices for raw materials, and that these were certainly not 'unbearable' for the developed world. It showed that the financial resources generated in this way could be devoted to an acceleration of industrialization in the beneficiary countries. In this sense, October 1973 marks a turning point in the history of international relations, the moment of consciousness of the Third World countries not of their rights but of their power.

It was, therefore, a programme in total accordance with all the sacrosanct principles defended by Western liberal orthodoxy. A programme taking greater heed than ever of the objectives of world economic interdependence and seeking to place this on a footing of comparative advantages. A programme that should have been shaped and proposed by the economics professors in the most conservative institutions rather than by the governments who had constantly been lambasted by those institutions for their bent to 'nationalism', a supposedly obsolete philosophy contrary to the interests of their peoples. It is an irony of history that the initiative came from the 'nationalist' Third World and was unanimously rejected by the apostles of the principles on which it was based!

The claim of the NIEO coincided with the most serious post-war crisis. It was even argued that the oil price rise – the first (and as yet sole) indicator of the implementation of the Third World programme for the NIEO – was the 'cause' of the crisis. A veritable campaign was orchestrated on this theme in 1973 and 1974, using every kind of argument and despite all the facts: the beginning of the international monetary crisis and the appearance of US external deficits since the mid-1960s, the precedence of stagflation, the scale and persistence of inflation rates irrespective of the calculable increase attributable to oil, the (still massive) placing of oil revenues on the Western finance markets, the modest role of petro-dollars in comparison with the movable assets of the transnationals in speculative fluctuations, and so on. The campaign has of necessity long hung fire: erosion of the oil price in the 1980s and the reversal of the conjuncture ('the end of the era of OPEC') have never allowed it any further take-off.

The fact is, that the crisis has its main origin in the international division of labour in force, that challenged by the claims of the NIEO. We should remember that the former international division of labour confined the developing countries to the export of (agricultural and mineral) primary products, as their (import substitution) industrialization was strictly limited to their domestic market. This international division of labour was one of the bases on which the continuing prosperity of the previous quarter of a century was built. A prosperity confined, if truth be told, to the developed centres of the system. If the centres at the time in question enjoyed a high level of employment, continual growth in productivity and comparable growth in wages, for the underdeveloped peripheries and their growth rates the same mechanisms that give rise elsewhere to full employment and growth in real wages produced a continual rise in unemployment and underemployment, stagnation, or a fall in real wages and the rewards for rural producers; there the crisis was permanent. Only from the 1970s did the crisis begin to spread throughout the world system, that is, to pass to the developed centres as well.

If this is the case the best way to overcome the crisis would be to change the ground rules of the international division of labour and accept the claims of the Third World. It must be obvious that export industrialization in the Third World would provide work for a substantial number of the Third World's unemployed, create new outlets for the machine tools of the developed world and correct the imbalances in the profitability of various industrial sectors, since the falling rate of profit shown by the crisis arises from the inappropriateness of the current international division of activity.

Such measures to revise the international division of labour serve only to highlight the economic logic of the system. Here lies its logical strength and current weakness. Since: a) the world system cannot be reduced to a simple 'pure' economic logic, namely maximization of profit on a world scale, without regard to the division of the world into nations, the locus of operation of essential and immediate political forces; and b) the crisis cannot be surmounted except by implementation in a co-ordinated and systematic manner of the new international division of labour, nor is this the 'best' solution in the light of national factors, nor is this solution the most 'probable'.

Peaceful, co-ordinated and systematic implementation of a new international division of labour might be the dream of a technocrat with a single purpose: the maximization of profit. Oddly enough the Third World states have behaved like this collective technocrat, while the Western authorities, apostles par excellence of the philosophy of profitability, have recoiled from the logical consequences of their own philosophy and rejected the industrial relocation that was on offer.

Accordingly, the internal logic of the programme for the NIEO reflected the contradictory character of capital accumulation on a world scale. To some extent the programme was initially a scheme to deepen the international division of labour: through a levy on the rate of surplus value (super-exploitation of labour power at the periphery) it would have permitted a rising rate of profit on the world scale (and at this level looked like a programme of capitalist development), but in another way, within the framework of this common aim of capitalist development, the strategies of the monopolies and the imperialist states and those of the bourgeoisies and the peripheral states would have come into contradiction.

The imperialist monopolies took a narrow view of the 'new order'. To them it meant taking greater profit from the cheap manpower and natural resources of the Third World, by relocating segments of the production processes they themselves controlled. Under this strategy relocation was not aimed at creating integrated national industrial economies in the Third World, however outward-looking. On the contrary, the interest of the monopolies was in exporting discrete segments in such a way as to retain control over economic life as a whole on the world scale. In this framework the monopolies could make small concessions to the 'host countries', or even in extreme cases renounce formal ownership of the capital. Competition, the absence of integration of the segments, their technological dependence, such as the obligation to sell their output on the oil-rich markets controlled by the monopolies, all reduced the meaning of formal ownership of the capital; the monopolies could impose very harsh conditions on their partners. It was *laissez-faire* on the scale of a world under monopoly domination. In such circumstances, even the financing of the relocation through the Third World countries' own means could bring an additional benefit to the monopolies as vendors of turnkey factories. This profitable exaction was in effect included in the pricing structure. Meanwhile the exaction could be enlarged through visible financial transfers by way of technology sales, licenses and trade marks, and through interest on loans for plant expansion. Sometimes even the pricing structure was distorted to remove the apparent profitability from the segments transferred: loans supposed to make good 'management deficits' are nothing less than resurrected forms of capitalism's perennial tendency to plunder. Financial neo-capital, in imitation of the old mercantilist capital, appeared anew, as at the dawn of capitalism: 'primitive' accumulation is always with us.

This strategy has its own name – and not by chance – of 'redeployment'. It has the active support of the World Bank, the IMF and other institutions of the developed capitalist states, and wins acceptance as a 'new order' for the new enclaves of the 'free zone' kind. Obviously the strategy reduces to a minimum the local state's role, which becomes a mere administration policing the exploited labour force. It also aims to divide the Third World not only by widening the gap between countries of 'strong growth' and 'stagnant' countries, but also in setting the former to compete against one another.

What the Third World, or at least the driving element among the non-aligned, meant by a new international order was very different. Revision of the international division of labour along the lines described was intended to accompany and implement the establishment of a self-reliant industrial national economy.

The strengthening of the national state, and the active role of state policy were, in this strategy, to ensure that industry was not made up of discrete fragments, but of every stage of the production process. The resort to importation of the ingredients of these production lines (the purchase of turnkey factories) entailed a high level of exports, whether of 'traditional' raw materials or new industrial products. Hence the success of the strategies was largely dependent on the capacity to win concessions, which was in turn the programme for the new international economic order.

The conflict of these two 'interpretations' of the new order has appeared in all the negotiations on the industrial international division of labour and relocation. The points of discussion were the character and options of establishment, the degree of decentralized decision-making, the methods of financing the transfers, issues of personnel training and management, and access to external markets. The Third World states generally pressed for: the establishment of as complete industries as possible, with upstream and downstream links, agreed rules subjecting the management of industrial units to the state's industrial policy, an option for management of units by local staff, access to international distribution networks for manufactured goods to localized firms (as the lowering of protectionist barriers by the developed countries was not regarded as a sufficient guarantee of access to these markets), support for national technological research, regulated financing (to avoid, for example, a subsidiary of a multinational financing its investment by calling on local banking sources without bringing in new capital), regulation of transfers (a sharing of risks, ceilings on exportable profits, obligations to invest part of the profit in the national economy) and so on.

These demands were regarded as unacceptable by the multinationals whose sole interest was in partial relocation through subsidiaries under their virtual control.

Gradually, most of the Third World states have had to come to terms with the redeployment strategy. The only states in a position to negotiate are those that refuse the direct establishment of subsidiaries and seek an alternative in the purchase of turnkey factories within the framework of their overall industrialization policy.

The strategy of these states counted on the possibility of successful change of the international order through unilateral joint action, and through further action from North–South collective negotiations. The idea, it should be remembered, was to organize cartels of Third World producers who could insist on price revisions for raw materials. National control over natural resources should allow scope for manoeuvre not only on supply, but also and above all on exploitation of the resources that took into account long-term national interests and halted the rates of exploitation governed entirely by the needs of the developed world. With this new-found strength, the Third World countries hoped to enjoy a genuine negotiating power that would oblige the North to make concessions: for instance, access to its markets, a code of conduct for transfers of technology. Co-operation between Third World countries ('collective self-reliance') was part of this bid for strength (cf. Chapter 7).

This is the essential context for discussing the use of oil surpluses. On some views the NIEO was to be no more than the rise in oil prices alone and the relocation of export industry a minor operation. On this view the oil revenue surpluses should be made available to the developed financial markets to supply their own policies of intervention in relations between developed countries, and marginal support for the 'survival' of the old international division of labour in the developing countries. This rescued the attitude of 'aid' as a permanent safety-valve ensuring the perpetuation of a system that was increasingly unjust day by day. The actual use of oil surpluses has in fact served this purpose (cf. Chapter 6).

In the mid-1970s there was still the hope that the Third World would reject this narrow view. The non-aligned movement and the group of 77 were seeking a strategy for collective battle for across the board increases in raw materials prices, as the resolution on the solidarity fund and producers associations taken at Dakar in February 1977 showed. This strong and valid approach was not sustained. Under the pressure of the developed countries and the bias of UNCTAD and endless 'negotiation' and 'dialogue', the 'stabilization' fund strategy replaced that of producers associations for collective unilateral intervention where such was required.

So, in the end, the battle for the NIEO was lost. As well as the failure being noted, the causes have to be studied. Are they purely circumstantial (in the economic crisis)? Can they be attributed to 'tactical errors' by the Third World (its own divisions and weaknesses)? Or do these circumstances and weaknesses show the impossibility of autocentric development at the periphery of the modern capitalist system? We shall return to these fundamental issues (cf. Chapter 8).

This failure being so, what has actually happened? Relocation advances at tortoise-like pace, heightening differentiation with the Third World, feeding the illusion of possible compromise between the bourgeois national plan and integration in the world system for some, and marginalization for others. The seeming successes of Korea, Brazil and India have forced the collective plan of the NIEO into the background. We shall return to these successes (cf. Chapters 6 and 7) to assess their character and extent.

Africa: from the Lagos Plan (1980) to the World Bank plan and the United Nations Conference (1986)

Few now remember the Lagos Plan of Action, adopted by the OAU summit in 1980, in the tracks of the euphoria that five years earlier had marked the Third World's adoption of a charter for a 'new international economic order'.[5]

Once the euphoria of the early 1960s was over, the tares of colonial development suddenly resuscitated by the newly independent regimes were not slow to sprout. Then 15 years of systematic efforts by some to bring to Africa the concept of autocentric development were at last to find a response. The whole strength of the Lagos Plan lay in the fact that it was based on this masterfully simple idea that Africa's development could not be merely a passive result of the world system's or evolution of the European Economic Community, to which the continent's states had been bound by the association named after the agreements of Yaoundé and Lomé. The explicit option for a new, self-reliant development strategy arose from this crucial idea.

But the Lagos Plan did not draw the conclusions implied in the logic of this option. It was satisfied with the easy part of the task, namely showing how this option did make it possible to overcome the handicaps of extraversion. In this spirit the Lagos Plan set itself the target of strong growth (7% a year) based on a genuine agricultural revolution (4% annual growth) and subsequent industrialization (9.5% annual growth). At the same time, it declared the aim of economic and even cultural and social integration for the continent.

As soon as we move from intentions to a consideration of the means of implementation, however, we find the weaknesses of the plan. These were manifest in the 'technical' method employed to calculate the 'means' in question. The calculation, starting from projection of demand, then used known technologies and a tabulation of input and output to define the desirable structure of production. Hence could be deduced the amount of investment and imports needed and consequently the corresponding exports demanded. A routine methodology, whose reputation for 'neutrality' in relation to the aims is certainly vouched for by the planners. But the methodology is not neutral: it assumes the given demand and hence reproduces the distortions in the specific income distribution of peripheral capitalism, along with the negative effects of the imported model of consumption; it accepts the structure of world prices as the criterion for economic rationality, although this structure reproduces the dual polarization between the centres and the peripheries and in income distribution within the peripheral societies.

Little wonder that the use of this methodology brought results in direct contradiction with the declared principle of autocentric development. The Plan's calculations were based on imports growing faster than the GDP (8% a year for imports) and a significant contribution from foreign capital (since exports were to grow at the rate of GDP, 7% a year). The Lagos Plan, despite its declaration of principle, was a classic plan for development by way of greater integration in the world economy.

The genuine implementation of the principle of autocentric development implies very different reasoning that has the nerve to challenge the criteria of economic rationality observed by conventional economics.

Without dwelling at great length here on the details of an alternative methodology consistent with the option of autocentric development, it may be recalled that this option requires the determination of a pricing structure delinked from that governed by the worldwide law of value, such that it ensures approximately equal rewards for labour in the various sectors of production (and therefore substantially reduces the gap between town and countryside, industry and modern informal sectors, and so on). On this basis of a national and popular economic rationality it may be possible to formulate development policies whose benefits can really bring improved standards of living to the broad mass of the people (cf. Chapter 5).

Priority for agriculture must come within this framework, as was shown earlier in the critique offered of the prevailing concepts of agricultural development. Similarly industrialization within this framework must be industrialization in support of the agricultural revolution, at least as a prolonged first stage.

In these areas the Lagos Plan was content to wage a rearguard action against the colonial onslaught of the World Bank. For example, it correctly defends the principle of industrialization that had been challenged on the grounds of conflicting with agricultural development! This is a throwback to the old colonial prejudice of an Africa 'naturally agricultural', as if agricultural development was really possible without industrialization, and contrary to the whole of the world's history. In the same way the Lagos Plan correctly defends the principle of basic industry. But it stops there and fails to challenge the mundane model of industrialization followed on the continent so far. It is obvious that the industrialization required is not an industrialization on all fronts, undefined and general and mainly for import substitution and exports through the processing of mineral resources. The spurious argument about export industry or import substitution industry has obscured the real argument. The Lagos Plan could not escape from a view of industrialization subordinate to the demands of the international division of labour. By adopting the UNIDO industrialization plan (the Lima targets: a 2% share of world industrial output for Africa by the year 2000), plus the plans of the

African states, the Lagos document demonstrated both a disturbing lack of imagination and a low level of consciousness of the character of the option of self-reliance.

This is all the more serious since the Lagos Plan is still within the area of exploitation of natural resources, and the traditional colonial and neo-colonial view of Africa as a 'source of supply' for the development of others. It is not enough that the very concept of control over natural resources is overlooked (and from this point of view the Lagos document is a step backwards in comparison with the concepts of the NIEO), that the Lagos document naively declares its confidence in the multinationals developing these resources(!) and hopes that the African states will show a united front in their shared demands, but also and principally that the Lagos Plan envisages the exploitation of Africa's resources on the basis of world demand. On the energy issue, however, we note that the Lagos Plan did try to avoid the narrow and fruitless discussion of 'oil costs'.

We are brought back to the central issue of foreign trade. Development 'within the world system' (in fact based on further integration with it) does come from worldwide demand and hence always seeks to maximize exports in line with that demand. Conversely, autocentric development regards foreign trade as a remainder. It begins with a calculation of essential imports for each stage of the implementation of the autocentric strategy, and on the basis of this figure sets the level of export needed to finance imports. This approach leads to the conclusion that the maximization of exports of mineral resources is often not only useless but also dangerous because of the distortion and increased dependency it brings.

Other aspects of the Lagos Plan's development strategy are treated in the same way, in contradiction with the declared option of self-reliance. This is the case for the issue of technology, perceived simply as acquisition of technologies in use in the West. In this regard the plan is caught in the trap of the old argument on the technology said to be 'appropriate' to the factors of production, as it confuses the role of technological research with the problems of management. It does likewise with education, whose objectives are defined in purely quantitative terms without serious regard to the alienation it may bring; without any consideration of the changes necessary to keep pace with autonomous scientific and technological development; with transport and communication no more than a cumulative list of national projects. As for comments on environmental and feminist issues, they take the form of wishful thinking additions to fall in with current fashion.

The obvious result is that the Lagos Plan concludes with a giant 'finance gap'. When the UN General Assembly at its special session in 1986 came to consider the extent of foreign aid required, we were back to square one, as such aid was unimaginable in the prevailing circumstances.

In short, the Lagos Plan, despite its declaredly 'self-reliant' intentions, despite its strong criticism of the colonial and neo-colonial heritage, could not escape the conventional methodology closely associated with the conventional strategy of peripheral capitalist development. Its technical and institutional (not to mention bureaucratic) approach – whereby for each 'problem' area the plan proposes the establishment of a Pan-African organization to deal with it (!) – its naive view of African integration through 'the common market' (in contradiction with historical experience showing that the market can only aggravate inequalities between the regions it incorporates), its astonishing silence on the identification of the agents of change (states, or private enterprises, and which ones) and on the structures of economic power in Africa, are clear indicators of the unresolved conflict between praiseworthy intentions and the possible ways and means.

This might seem harsh criticism. It may be tempered by reference to numerous positive and passing aspects of the document, but unfortunately the latter do not make up for the overall line of thinking pursued.

The question of development strategy for Africa, as for the Third World, is complex and ambiguous. Should development be conceived in accordance with the demands of the international order, or conversely, is it necessarily in conflict with it? Can the international order be transformed and 'adjusted' to the priority demands for Third World development, or conversely can the latter only be the result of the reverse 'adjustment'? The merit of the NIEO proposals was that they raised these issues without prejudice. The NIEO was trying to be both 'realistic' and 'optimistic'. It accepted that the inescapable demands of autocentric development were not necessarily in total conflict with 'worldwide interdependence'. It therefore proposed a transformation in the international order conducive to a reconciliation of interests, to the advantage of all.

The facts have shown that this view was based on a naive illusion as to the laws governing existing world capitalism. The West's categorical rejection of the NIEO proposals has brought about first a resumption of the development initiative by the agencies charged with implementing traditional Western ideas, and second a range of attempted 'compromises' falling back from the NIEO plan.

The World Bank's 1980 plan for sub-Saharan Africa, drafted by the North American expert Elliot Berg is a typical example of the former. This plan, directly following the principles of Reaganite orthodoxy, seeks merely to legitimize the maximum demands of worldwide capital, as was shown above.

Whatever the deep contradictions, shortcomings and naivetés of the Lagos Plan, it was more realistic, less ideological and even more soundly scientific (notwithstanding the inadequacies of its methodology) than the virtually skimped work of the World Bank. But the powers that be in the world exchequer are such that the Lagos Plan, far from being a point of departure, was soon buried, while the World Bank's language became the leitmotiv of official policies.

Undoubtedly, the international conjuncture was altogether unpromising as the NIEO proposals were rejected even as a basis of discussion. The Europe of the EEC, with its special responsibility for Africa, inherited from colonialism, then came to the fore. The Lagos Plan had refrained from even discussing the structures of overall power accompanying the association conventions of the ACP and EEC, presumably to avoid hurting feelings beyond the Mediterranean. The inadequate aid projected within the framework of association (here, too, the Lagos Plan refrained from making any judgement on the structures of power associated with so-called 'co-operation'), the inadequate resources available to stabilize agricultural products, with Stabex unable to withstand a deep and prolonged crisis, the even more dubious character of the Sysmin mechanism, which enshrines the control of worldwide capital over the continent's principal resources, encouraged reformist circles, such as those the Brandt Commission aroused briefly, to offer modest corrective solutions. The latter have been no better received than the earlier, more radical, proposals of the NIEO.

The new language of South–South co-operation was, in the circumstances, an ambiguous advance. Undoubtedly the national and popular policies for self-reliance had every interest in mutual reinforcement through complementary South–South co-operation, if only to offset the difficulties of a too restricted market in the smaller countries, or modest amounts of such and such a resource in other cases, for example. But in the absence of a genuine autocentric option at national levels, South–South co-operation meant very little. As we shall see in Chapter 6, it was inevitably to become a complement to the North–South inequalities against which it was aimed. Despite these inevitable limitations in the current situation, genuine co-operation efforts such as Afro-Arab co-operation (cf. Chapter 6) and the establishment of the South–South Commission may be useful investments that could bear fruit later when the current wave of 'compradorization' has exhausted its disastrous impact.

The collapse of the bourgeois national plan in the Third World, combined with the eclipse of the national and popular forces exposed by this failure, created favourable conditions for an offensive by the most reactionary forces, symbolized by the IMF and World Bank.

In the light of this offensive the Western ideological currents not hostile to Third World peoples were entirely disarmed, at least for the time being. This no doubt explains why to date they have offered nothing more than proposals representing pious hopes.

The first Brandt Report shares the general philosophy – of which its very sub-title, 'A Programme for Survival', is a reminder – according to which interdependence is synonymous with the shared interests of partners. What has to be saved is therefore this threatened 'global interdependence'. The world system must be maintained, and the various national societies must find their role and fit their development to the overall development of the system. The entire report, recommendations and analyses (or more precisely lack of analyses) are based on this option. The hypothesis that the common interest prevails over the conflict of interests leads inevitably to the language of pious hopes: we quote what the world's governments would like . . .

History offers too many denials of this philosophy for its continued acceptance: (i) since history to date has been precisely that of interdependence and asymmetry of this (hence the very expression of interdependence is inaccurate and that of dependence more appropriate); (ii) the history of this unequal development is that of unequal evolution of the power of the partners and hence of a succession of phases of development in the system ('A' phases of overall growth in a system defined by rules – particularly of the division of labour – hierarchies, one or more hegemonies, and so on) and crises, enforced transition from an A1 phase to an A2 phase by B crisis (defined by challenge to the rules and hierarchies); B phases of crisis, demonstrating the conflict of interests and the change wrought by the resolution of the conflicts, are based on the acknowledgement of the new balance of power; (iii) the changes in power relations owe their origin to the cumulative effects of unequal interdependence and internal transformations in societies.

Our period is clearly one of a B phase of crisis. It serves no purpose to deny the conflicts of interest, which are primary, or to treat them as insignificant. This would prevent any understanding.

The remedy for the global crisis that the report proposes is one of world Keynesianism, in André Gunder Frank's felicitous turn of phrase. The report says: 'Advocates of various schemes of "massive transfers" of funds from North to South have argued that such action would amount to a pump-priming of the world economy. We view them as contributing to growth and employment creation in the North as in the South.' (pp. 67–8 of the report).

The NIEO proposals in this regard were better and stronger and without the dubious diversion of the 'large-scale transfers'. The NIEO proposed simply export industrialization from the South to the North, based on low wages and abundant natural resources. This massive relocation of industry would doubtless have raised the global rate of profit. In this area Keynesianism is more simple: it attributes the crisis to insufficiency of demand that may be stimulated by income redistribution. It refrains from going on to the organization of production. The NIEO was aimed directly at the latter. Relocation evidently brings both redistribution of the forces of production, and hence of income, and an increase in the rate of profit. The NIEO moreover, far from begging for additional 'transfer', whose limitations and largely harmful character have been shown in history, envisaged an increase in prices for the traditional exports from the South and the mobilization of the additional resources generated in this way (mining and oil royalties in particular) to finance the new stage of growth without any 'transfers'.

Clearly the partners of the redistribution in question are not the 'peoples', but countries. The NIEO did not make the naive mistake of confusing them. In fact export industrialization based on cheap manpower presupposes: (i) exploited agriculture that supplies the towns with a superabundance of proletarianized labour power and cheap foodstuffs; and (ii) urban unemployment, a poor working class and subordinate middle class. The plan therefore was not one of 'development to the benefit of the poor', but one of capital accumulation. Clearly, too, the partners in the conflict were the ruling classes; the battle for the redistribution in question was between capital in the North and states in the South on the ground of division of an increasing surplus.

The absence of analysis of the causes of the defeat of the states in the South leads the Brandt Report, for each issue dealt with, to propose inadequate, misleading and generally naive solutions.

a) The report's recommendation – to accord priority to agriculture – is superficial. Such a priority is unquestionable. But the models of colonial exploitation, founded on the same priority (the colonial trade economy, the concessionary companies and the reserves) are the historical source of the current wretchedness of the African countryside. The 'new' policies (bureaucratic incorporation, kulakization or agro-business – proposed by the World Bank) reducing the food priority to food production plans without questioning the overall policy of world integration – are bound to aggravate the wretchedness of the peasants.

'Food priority' should mean something very different (i) a challenge to all aspects of the global policy (income distribution, real wages and agricultural prices, taxation and finance, and so forth); (ii) establishment of industries to serve the agricultural priority and not export, or to meet the relevant demand on the basis of existing structures; (iii) autonomy for peasant communities in the conception and execution of their development plans (and this goes much wider than the land reforms proposed in the report); and finally (iv) detachment from the criteria of profitability, on the understanding that the establishment of a national and popular economy and society will be in contradiction with the demands of 'international competition'.

What has been said of agriculture is *mutatis mutandis* also true of other sectors of popular concern: small businesses and crafts serving popular consumption. The Brandt report proposes assistance to the informal sector; it overlooks that this sector, geared as it is to an economy that does not seek to satisfy popular needs, is therefore exploited. Classic language of 'social services' is no substitute for the demands for genuine autonomy for the collective bodies of the people.

Building an economy seeking to satisfy popular needs does certainly require 'internal reforms'. But history and politics show that these reforms are scarcely compatible with the demands of integration in the world system. And why does the report shy away from condemning the policies of 'destabilization' of popular regimes conducted by international powers and institutions such as the IMF?

b) In dealing with the 'less developed' countries the report acts as if it were dealing with a homogeneous group, while a historical analysis has led it to postulate various types of country 'less developed' for differing reasons and tending to their integration in the world system as 'peripheries of peripheries', with some supplying migrant labour (two examples: (1) the second degree trade economy of Burkina Faso in relation to Côte d'Ivoire; or (2) reserves, such as the bantustans or Lesotho) and others foodstuffs (an example: the Sahel countries exporting meat and recently cereals to the Benin coast).

c) The timidity in regard to dominant monopoly capital to be observed in the chapter on trade. Was it not ludicrous to propose common funds and other ways of stabilizing trade without taking account of the failure of negotiations? Why ignore the possibility, entertained in 1975, of forming cartels of Third World producers? Surely that was the only way to shift the balance of power in favour of the South?

(d) With respect to energy and mineral resources, where Northern interests are at stake, the report suggests only: (i) accelerating the search for mineral resources in the South through a special fund; (ii) that poverty in the South is produced by the high price for oil! But why accelerate the pillage of the natural resources of the South and preserve waste in the North? Why does the report remain silent on the political economy of the mineral rent and its relationship to the international division of labour?

e) On industrialization, the report seems to regard as positive the results obtained in the 'NICs' – the semi-industrialized countries of Brazil, Mexico, South Korea, etc. But it overlooks: (i) that a global strategy of localization would necessarily accentuate the unequal development of the South; (ii) that this strategy was based on repressive social policy; growth in GDP and industrial output is accompanied by a stagnation or fall in workers' pay and peasant incomes; (iii) for this very reason the populations of the NICs do not appear to welcome the proposed model; Iran's Shah fell when there was accelerated growth; the democratic revolution in South Korea, the Philippines and elsewhere directly attacks the model entailing political repression; (iv) that, contrary to the model's suppositions, the priority option for export industry does not improve the external balance; are not the NICs the most heavily indebted of all Third World countries?

f) The report limits its comments on the transnationals virtually to a case for a 'code of conduct'. But is there not a further danger for Third World countries in agreeing to bow to the demands of a new stage in the transnationals' penetration of the world economy by granting it a juridical status it does not yet enjoy?

g) Finally, the report regards international labour migrations as advantageous for both partners. What a mistake, when history has shown that the countries of emigration are for ever being impoverished (consider Ireland which had the same population as England when it was sadly conquered, and the effect of emigration), and that in the exceptional case when a country does develop, it ceases this impoverishing emigration (consider modern Italy and Spain).

Of course, the proposed compromises led nowhere. Africa went on drifting. In their weakened condition the African states surrendered. In these circumstances the UN special session on Africa (1986) produced the sad spectacle of Africa begging for 'aid' to keep the system going without any prospect of development. Naturally the aid did not come. Nor has Africa won anything in the area of debt relief, the subject of a special African summit in 1987. Africa is the most vulnerable of empty bellies throughout the contemporary Third World.

Latin America in general is characterized by the newly industrializing countries. It also seemed more resistant to the crisis and maintained respectable growth rates in the 1970s, when these were falling in the developed capitalist world and in some other Third World regions, Africa in particular. Latin America believes it can sustain this kind of development, further complementing the range of export industries by a range intended for the local, national and regional markets. It believes this is necessary to maintain access to capital markets and to massive import of technology. It is thereby accepting increased dependence, just as it tends to line up with the developed world on energy policies.

The Arab world (and Iran), although revealing a level of urbanization and industrialization comparable to that of Latin America, has suffered the consequences of its massive but unequally distributed share of oil production. Agricultural weakness (with a reduced and very uneven potential), the Palestine issue, superpower competition in the region, impasses of the political forces in the forefront over three decades, are jumbled up and lead to a fairly chaotic situation.

The NICs in east Asia are threatened by the narrowness of their internal markets and their extreme dependence on the world market, to a greater extent than in Latin America. The maintenance of their economic model may be difficult and the political chaos in South Korea is doubtless not unconnected with the difficulties of 'change-over'. The south and south-east Asian countries, like the whole of Africa, are suffering from the massive impact of the crisis. The collapse of growth and productive investment, like the worsening of public financial and external deficits, is already commonplace.

Africa's situation in general is even more grave since, as has been shown, neither agricultural revolution nor industrialization has really begun. In these circumstances Africa is on the way to being 'marginalized', to undergoing a 'passive delinking'. The modish expression 'fourth world' indicates a 'rediscovery' of the commonplace that the worldwide expansion of capitalism is not synonymous with 'development everywhere', but of development, albeit peripheral in this instance, and destruction in another. Africa, under these circumstances, is bound for such destruction. The real periphery of tomorrow will be the NICs of Asia and America (that is why describing them as 'semi-peripheral' is inaccurate, cf. Chapter 6), while the African 'fourth world' will no longer represent the 'typical periphery', but the last remnants of the periphery of yesterday en route for destruction.

Debt and the threat of a financial crash

The first Brandt Report attached great importance to immediate issues and in particular to the threat of a global financial crash, in connection with world inflation and the galloping increase in the external debt of some countries. André Gunder Frank went so far as to suspect that the real aim of the report – and of the proposed summit that eventually was held at Cancun – was to examine ways and means of avoiding a financial crash.

The solution, establishing a link between the issue of international liquidities and development aid, envisaged many years ago then dropped, was taken up by the report. This link would make it possible to avoid financial collapse for certain Third World countries whose foreign debt threatened the global balance. This, according to Gunder Frank, was the 'true ground of mutual interest, for states as a whole'. But is a link of this kind possible?

The report's general considerations on the international monetary system seemed naive. The report sought the establishment of a 'fair world monetary system . . .'. This has never been the case to date. First, there has never been a monetary system except in periods of economic hegemony of a national centre. It was the case in the 19th century, and up to 1914, when the gold (but really sterling) standard corresponded to British hegemony. It was again the case from 1944 (Bretton Woods) to 1971 (suspension of dollar convertibility) while US hegemony lasted. By contrast, during what Arrighi calls 'the 30 years war for the British succession', between the US and Germany from 1914 to 1945, there was no world monetary system but a great deal of chaos. The reason for such chaos, including the 1929 crash, was not that there was no world monetary system, but on the contrary, the fact of their being no world hegemonic power made it impossible to have a world monetary system. With the beginning of the decline of US hegemony, we have once more entered a period of this kind.

Disorder inevitably encourages inflationary pressures; this was the case during the 1914–45 period. It was the case again from the second half of the 1960s, in new guises but for the same basic reason. The crisis began in relations between the dollar and the mark, yen and other European currencies, and not by chance. The United States' incapacity to meet economic responsibilities (decreasing world market competitiveness with Japan and Germany) and political role (the Vietnamese war) led to the fall of the dollar. Artificially boosted by the Reaganite policy of high interest rates, the dollar lost ground again.

Undoubtedly inflation has its internal structural causes relating to the strategy of the monopolies to abandon price competition, and to the social order achieved through 'collective bargaining'. This is why inflation has continued to gallop since 1945. This inflation was bound sooner or later to bring a revaluation of gold, and the readjustment of exchange rates in keeping with the unequal distribution of those rates. But as long as the A phase (1945–70) was in effect, the overall structural balance (including, in general, the balance of payments; never mind the chronic invalid, Great Britain, sustained by the US boss for past services, and a few epidemic invalids in the Third World) ensured the operation of the world monetary system based on US hegemony. When the B phase began the system broke down. In a first phase (1965–80) rising inflation was at a trot, then a gallop, and its rate was increasingly unequal (from 7% to 30% a year); exchange rates fluctuated wildly; gold could no longer be pegged (from 1971) and the yellow metal rose from an official rate of US$35 to the ounce to a henceforth free market rate, around $600 to $700 to the ounce with some peaks of nearly $1,000; the crisis was then accompanied by a new phenomenon: stagflation. It serves no purpose to complain, as Robert Triffin does, of these factors: instability in exchange rates, inadequacy of reserves, the absence of machinery of adjustment: there is no monetarist cure for a disease that originates elsewhere than in the currency. Would the monetarists understand this? Since 1980 rises in domestic prices have been stifled by policies treating this control as an absolute priority, but at the cost of even more pronounced stagnation and a boost to financial speculation.

It must be supposed that there are mechanisms for adjustment. In the A phase there certainly are. This is why the IMF worked on the hypothesis that a country's deficit was due entirely to its national policy. But in the B phase the imbalance is structural and global, and the deficit of some has its counterpart in the surplus of others. It is no longer possible to blame these deficits on 'inadequate' national policies; they are the inevitable counterparts of surpluses that are no less difficult to reabsorb.

Regional or world monetary order – or monetary disorder – reflects the balance of power, or want of balance, between the developed capitalist countries, and not North–South relations; what has actually changed is relations between developed countries. Hence language such as 'specific needs of developing countries' (and the 'link') is ingenuous.

Is the threat of financial crash genuine? or only a bugbear? The failure of a great financial institution can always be avoided if the central bank prefers to come to its rescue (by nationalization) and accepts the ensuing inflation. In 1929 this option was impossible without suspending convertibility. This is not the case nowadays. Certainly the central bank of a given state may hesitate if it is acting alone, since the resulting acceleration of national inflation would weaken the standing of its currency in relation to others. But has the safeguard not already been put in place by the association in consortia of all the lender countries for any significant international loan? In this case the default of any significant borrower would threaten the entire system and the system therefore behaves with solidarity to avoid the crash.

But who are the borrowers? The countries of the East and the NICs of the Third World. In fact loans provided for these countries are never called in for repayment; the structural surplus of the lenders would forbid this. These loans, even if not always destined for determinate investments, are the modern form of foreign investment. They are intended to show their return through interest payments. They are also used as a means of constant pressure to subject local policies to the wishes of monopoly capital. By the same token an exaction is made on the real income of the Third World. This is why the threat of a crash is more remote than might be thought. Either these countries will go on mortgaging their independence (and their income) through indefinite pursuit of this kind of development, and all will be well; or, through political change, they will refuse to repay and, as in previous historical situations, will be able to do so to the degree that they are subjected to reprisals driving them into national or collective autarky. In that case the central banks associated with the lending centres will come to the rescue of their own 'victims'.

The threat of a crash comes from elsewhere: the erratic flows of liquidities held by the transnationals (rather than by the oil-producer countries) and observing only the rules of short-term speculation. In this regard the supporters of floating exchange rates have acted to the advantage of the speculators, but to the detriment of the collective interest in avoiding disaster. Hence perhaps after so much infatuation with the Milton Friedman school, for reasons of ideological alienation linked to the neo-liberal revival, the West's monetary and political authorities have begun to revert to less foolish behaviour.

The efforts of radical African nationalism: adjustment or delinking?[6]

Of all regions of the Third World Africa shows the greatest number of attempts at development other than that arising spontaneously out of the worldwide expansion of capitalism. In a score of the 50 or so African states, at some time or other, and to a more or less radical degree, the authorities have declared an intention to 'break' with the colonial and neo-colonial past and embark on a new, national and radical path, an independent socialist development, whether this socialism was specific and particular (Arab or African) or declaredly scientific, Marxist, or Marxist–Leninist. According to circumstances, this declared break with the past has been made in heat, in the aftermath of the victory of the movement seizing independence, sometimes after a long and bitter war (Algeria, Angola, Cape Verde, Guinea-Bissau, Mozambique, Zimbabwe), or in the euphoria of gaining independence (Ghana, Guinea, Mali, Tanzania), or as a sequel to significant social and political changes (the overthrow of the Egyptian and Libyan monarchies), or as a result of anti-neocolonial popular movements (Benin, Burkina Faso, Congo, Madagascar, Uganda, Rawlings' Ghana). In most, if not all cases, the army has played a significant role in the political switch in question.

But Africa also reveals among these experiences a high proportion of dubious or unimpressive results, scarcely distinguishable from those achieved by the classic neo-colonial development of others. Neither the aim of economic liberation from dependence on the world capitalist system, to complement political liberation, nor of building a new society remote from that of the capitalist Third World, seem to have made sufficient progress as to reach a point where the process cannot be reversed. Furthermore, a reversal of the trend and a sometimes vociferous return to 'development' as the Western powers want it to be has occurred in a number of countries, whether as a result of a *coup d'état* or of gradual drift. And, in today's crisis all, or virtually all, of them are severely threatened with being compelled to surrender to the dictates of the West.

A halt must be called to both sides of this equation.

World capitalist expansion has always been and continues to be divisive. From the outset it has caused and perpetuates a centre/periphery dichotomy inherent in currently existing capitalism. In this sense peripheral development has always been a story of perennial 'adjustment' to the demands and constraints of dominant capital. The centres are 'restructured', the peripheries are 'adjusted' to these new structures; never the reverse.

The violence of the effects of these successive adjustments, however, is not the same in every phase of the history of capitalism, since this worldwide expansion takes the form of a succession of long cycles (from 20 to 50 years) with alternating A phases of 'prosperity' and accelerated growth then B phases of structural crisis of the global system. During the A phases of prosperity 'adjustment' seems less difficult, or even palatable, for some countries: export demand rises at a high rate, capital is on offer and looking for a home, conflict is at a low ebb (the period is often a long one of relative peace) and so on. The adjustment amid general growth is certainly unequal. The periphery fulfils various roles in the global system and must be treated in the plural. There are 'rich' peripheries, of interest to the system at the stage in question, which supply products whose worldwide marketing is more on the increase than the products of others (as they are related to the key technological advances) and which in return provide markets of interest to capital and to the goods of the centre. The ease of their 'adjustment' encourages many illusions, such as those the World Bank and other ideological mainstays of capital have built up in regard to the NICs, although clearly the foreign debt their success engenders was not foreseen.

But there are also the 'left behind' of no interest to the characteristic structures of the system at the time. They have sometimes fulfilled a significant role at a past stage of the system's evolution, but have fallen out of favour. They become the 'fourth world', the 'less advanced', as if they were something new, when in reality they have always been a by-product of capitalist expansion. A sad but fine illustration of this former fourth world is the region of slavery in the America of the mercantilist period, north-east Brazil and the Caribbean (including Haiti). These regions were once regarded as 'prosperous', and they formed the heart of the periphery in the system of their day. Later the new structures of capitalist development marginalized the relative importance of these regions, and they are among the most appallingly wretched in the Third World of today. The history of capitalist expansion is not only that of the 'development' it has wrought, but also of the savage destruction on which it was constructed. There is within capitalism a destructive element that is too often omitted from the flattering image painted of the system.

In periods of harsh restructuring in the crisis (B phases are the moment of truth of the system's evolution) illusions fall away. The difficulties – whose menace has been denied – become the means by which dominant capital imposes its will. It is no longer a question of the fantasy of independence; the law of profit reminds the 'underdeveloped' of their fate: super-exploitation and submission. 'Recompradorization' is on the agenda, by every possible economic and financial means (nowadays the pressure exerted through the foreign debt and the food weapon), plus the political and military means (*coups d'état*, interventions such as that of the armour represented by Zionism in the Middle East).

Africa holds a specially vulnerable place in this long succession of misfortunes that capitalist expansion has meant for the peoples of the periphery. Whole regions of the continent ravaged by the slave trade for the benefit of mercantilist capitalism have yet to recover from this early destruction. Colonization has carried on this toll of destruction of the continent. We have two clear examples.

The first is settler colonialism in North Africa (principally Algeria) and in East and Southern Africa (South Africa, Kenya and Zimbabwe). The current difficulties facing Algerian agriculture – the loss of rural population accelerated by the war – have part of their origin in the distant past. In Zimbabwe the high land appropriated by the whites – leaving the Africans confined to meagre and inadequate reserves and obliging them to furnish cheap manpower – owe their apparent 'prosperity' to this exploitable manpower and to the waste they represent of the country's natural resources. The country's liberation has cast some light on the supposed 'success' of settler farming. But colonization has also bequeathed a problem that has still to be solved.

The second example is the plunder of land resources and the super-exploitation in areas of the colonial trade economy. Here, as was shown above, colonization secured a surplus at nil cost: without investment in intensified production methods (access to water, implements and mechanization, and so on), or agricultural research (except for some export crops, to the detriment of food crops). The surplus was undoubtedly modest in absolute terms, but a heavy burden on the peasantry and the country's future, through damage to the soil on which the trade was founded. Here, too, the current difficulties of African agriculture, even the famine in the Sahel, have origins in the distant past.

In truth Africa, in the heyday of the triumph of colonialism, occupied no more than a marginal role in the world system. Its essential role was as a mining reserve. Later, as independence and neo-colonialism came along, the plunder of agricultural land and mining royalties was not challenged, far from it. So neither the agricultural revolution nor industrialization have begun on a scale to respond to the demands of our day.

The discouraging prospect afforded Africa by capitalist expansion explains the frequency of the rejections and the high level of effort to 'do something else', to escape the simplistic logic of capitalism. But at the same time the objective conditions caused by this historical legacy make the task particularly difficult. This difficulty could be expressed in the formulation that the especially unfavourable external factor is combined with fairly unfavourable internal factors that have been largely shaped by that very external factor.

The response to the challenge of our age that we propose is called 'delinking'. The concept is to some extent half of an equation 'adjustment or delinking'.

We shall not expand here on the theory of delinking but, to avoid any misunderstanding, say merely that delinking is not synonymous with autarky but only subjection of external relations to the logic of internal development (whereas adjustment means binding internal development to the possibilities afforded by the world system). In more precise terms, delinking is the refusal to submit to the demands of the worldwide law of value, or the supposed 'rationality' of the system of world prices that embody the demands of reproduction of worldwide capital. It, therefore, presupposes the society's capacity to define for itself an alternative range of criteria of rationality of internal economic options, in short a 'law of value of national application'.

What social forces may be the historical subject of this option of a break? The evidently almost tautological reply is that the forces can only be such as are victims of peripheral capitalist development and not its beneficiaries. Capitalist development as it stands not only has a global polarizing effect (by creating the centre–periphery dichotomy) but also polarizing effects within the societies of the periphery (as it does not have within the central capitalist societies). In other words, income distribution is more unequal at the periphery than at the centre, being relatively stable at the centre over time, but tending to increasing inequality with the development of the periphery. The result is that the 'privileged classes' have a genuine interest in pursuing capitalist expansion as it stands, despite the subordinate position accorded them in the system and sometimes perhaps their national 'frustration'. They do have conflicts with dominant capital, and these classes will sometimes cross swords with imperialism to improve their status within the system. But only to this extent. They will judge that in the last resort there is no 'advantage' (or they would say 'possibility') in delinking. This is what they are saying day after day with their declaration of inevitable 'interdependence' ('We are all in the same boat', and so forth). The character of these privileged classes has also undergone historical evolution. Recently the dominant element of the local bloc allied to imperialism was often constituted by an oligarchy of great landowners (in Latin America, India, China, Egypt, for example) or by chiefdoms (in Africa). The national independence movement was obliged to stand against this bloc and replaced it with a new one dominated by new classes of a bourgeois character (local industrial and finance bourgeoisies, bourgeoisies of rich peasants, state bourgeoisies, and so on), and generally an industrialist force. This by no means insignificant shift of world social alliances has gone alongside a global restructuring of the system, since the worldwide social alliances, by their nature, define the appropriate structure for the stage of capitalist development attained.

The privileged classes in question form a minority in the societies of the periphery, a minority ranging from negligible (1 or 2% of the population) to more substantial (10 to 25%). As for the popular classes victimized by capitalist expansion, they have varying status and by virtue of the character of the expansion tend not to be homogenized or reduced to a single model. These include the poor peasantries (in the plural), the working classes, the urbanized jobless peasants in the shanty-towns, the former (artisan) and new (lower ranks) petty bourgeoisies. With the further point that peripheral capitalist development, with its centrifugal tendency, is an obstacle to national crystallization and tends even to disrupt the old nations where they exist, it can be seen that there are numerous additional reasons for division in the camp of the popular forces: ethnicity and dialects, religions, and – particularly marked in Africa – artificial frontiers bequeathed by colonization and balkanization.

Delinking implies a 'popular' content, that is anti-capitalist in the sense that it is in conflict with dominant capitalism but shot through by a multiplicity of divergent interests (aside from the anti-system convergence) of various fractions constituting the population in question. This is why we argue that the 'post-capitalist' period will be a very long historical phase marked by permanent conflict between three poles determining the society's internal trends, local capitalism (responding to the needs shown by the development of the forces of production), socialism (expressing the anti-capitalist aspirations of the mass of the people), and statism (produced by the autonomy of the authorities in the light of capitalist and socialist forces and expressing at the same time the aspirations of the new class in control of the state). The conflicting balance of these tendencies is itself clearly variable according to particular circumstances and the rhythm of evolution.

A social force is essential to cement the popular alliance, overcome its internal conflicts, formulate the alternative national and popular plan, lead the popular bloc in hoisting itself into power, build the new state and arbitrate the conflicts shown above as characteristic of the long national and popular transition. This is the task of the revolutionary intelligentsia, the 'organic intellectual', responding to the objective demand of our day. It is a category peculiar to the situation of the peripheries in the capitalist system, with no resemblance to the problematic of the 'petty bourgeoisie' (a confused class as always) or of the 'one party' born out of national liberation, or of the role of intellectuals as a channel of expression for various social classes.

Evidently in these historical circumstances, at least two fundamental issues are posed for the intelligentsia and people's power: democracy and the cultural content of the societal plan.

As far as the cultural aspect is concerned we should state here that the challenge is not answered by superficial Westernization of the compradorized strata following the consumerist model of the developed world (this transmission of the consumerist model is just the tip of the cultural iceberg), or its apparent opposite – but really identical twin – the culturalist nationalisms on which the so-called religious fundamentalisms feed. The dual impasse to which either of these options leads is an indication of the genuine complexity of the plan.

The only relevant consideration is what faces the option of national and popular delinking in contemporary Africa, for good or ill. The absolutely first requirement in material action is a development of the forces of production and a raising of living standards of the great mass through a dual agricultural and industrial revolution, for which colonization has done no groundwork.

Has it been realized that the European agricultural revolution occurred in a world where the concomitant population explosion was controlled through the escape-valve of massive emigration? Europe at the time populated all of the US and other parts of the world. Without this escape-valve the population to be supported by Western and central Europe would have been some three times larger (since the 400 million Europeans of today would have been supplemented by the 800 millions across the Atlantic who are of emigrant descent). The modern Third World with its population explosion does not have this option of expanding outwards. Furthermore, modern industry is incapable of absorbing the internal migration from countryside to the towns at the rate possible at the time of the European industrial revolution. It is essential, therefore, to find technological and social prescriptions for genuine progress that for a long while to come holds the majority of the population in the rural areas of origin, where this is still possible, or finds ways of useful employment for the urbanized poor masses.

Clearly the national liberation movement, rightly focusing in its early stages on the preliminary winning of simple political independence, was not fully aware of the extent and scale of the challenge. This cannot be held against it, but we must be aware that the glorious page of history it wrote is over. A re-examination of the past does not excuse the present. We must be patient. We must be aware that the first wave of national liberation is spent, and that the forces entrusted with the second wave – with its national and popular content – have not yet been assembled around an adequate alternative plan. We are passing through a trough in the wave, shown by this disarray and intellectual and political surrender.

The various studies of African radical experience show both the extent of the problems to be 'resolved' and the limitations of the conceptions held by the national–radical state.

The past 30 years have been punctuated with debates on these issues. It is worth highlighting here the debate on the so-called 'non-capitalist path', which had its moments of glory in the 1960s when Nasserism was at its height and Nkrumahist pan-Africanism had not been stifled in the gradual crystallization of new African states. It is also worth highlighting what, in the jargon of African progressive intellectuals, is called the 'Dar-es-Salaam debate', which in the ealy 1970s tried to focus on the issue of building socialism in Africa. But this is not the place to assess these arguments that have never ceased.

Along with the efforts and attempts in the national context, Africa has been the stage for a significant series of regional co-operation plans, whether the 'common market' kind (Economic Community of West Africa, of East African States, the Arab and Maghrebi common markets), or 'common concerns' kind (the Southern Africa Development Coordination Conference in the face of South Africa), or financial support (Afro-Arab co-operation). We shall return to these issues in Chapter 6.

Notes

1. See Samir Amin's contributions to Amin, Samir, Faire, Alexandre, Hussein, Mahmoud and Massiah, Gustave, *La crise de l'impérialisme*, Paris, Minuit, 1975, and Amin S., Arrighi G., Frank A. G. and Wallerstein I., *Dynamics of Global Crisis*, New York, Monthly Review Press, and London, Macmillan, 1982, Amin, Samir and Frank, André Gunder, *N'attendons pas 1984*, Paris, Maspero, 1985.

2. Amin, Samir, 'Il y a trente ans, Bandung', Cairo, UNU, 1985.

3. Amin, Samir, 'Perestroika and Glasnost', 1988, (in Arabic).

4. Amin, Samir, 'Développement et transformations structurelles', *Tiers Monde*, No. 51, 1972; 'CNUCED III, Un bilan', *Bulletin of Peace Proposals*, No. 3, 1972, Oslo; 'UNCTAD IV and the New International Economic Order', *Africa Development*, CODESRIA, Dakar, No. 1, 1976; 'A propos du NOEI, et de l'avenir des relations économiques internationales', *Africa Development*, No. 4, 1978; 'A propos du rapport de la commission Brandt', *Africa Development*, No. 3, 1980. See too references in *Delinking*, London, Zed Books, 1989.

5. OAU-ECA, The Lagos Action Plan, Addis Ababa, 1980; see too, the ECA's preparatory documents.

6. Mahjoub, Azzam, et al., *Adjustment or Delinking: The African Experience*, and Amin, Samir, *Delinking*.

3. The Crisis of State

An economic analysis of the failure of development confined to the narrow framework of economic science can offer only very limited results. Economic science relies on a threadbare concept of 'agents of economic change', limited to the abstract categories of the 'dynamic entrepreneur', the 'consumer' and when needs must, the state, but in the latter instance in a cut-down version of the 'economic functions of the state' (economic legislation and regulation). Political economy looks wider by taking into account the collective agents in the social classes and the state perceived less narrowly. But this is far from being enough. For the whole problematic of peripheral capitalism raises the theory of 'subjects of historical change' and challenges the simplifications drawn by extrapolation from European experience. It has been possible to identify a series of questions about the state, the nation and ethnicity, the character of the categories called social classes in classical Marxism, the manifestations of social movement and culture. These issues may be summarized as follows:

(1) Is the state a historical subject in itself, overriding social classes? In the currently existing centres of capitalism, the state does appear to be so. But here a concomitance can be observed between the active role played by the states in the inter-state – primarily European – world system (at the level of national economic policies as well as diplomacy) and the crystallization of that other social reality known as 'nation'. It looks very much as if this concomitance is missing in the Third World and in Africa particularly, to the advantage of so-called 'ethnic' forms otherwise defined and undoubtedly diverse. Is the result a series of particular handicaps interfering with the state's manifestation as an active historical subject? What is the role of nationalist ideologies in this context?

(2) Transnationalization sets limitations on the state. To such an extent that the state may nowadays seem powerless against the forces operating in a worldwide economic environment, in the developed centres and a fortiori in the vulnerable peripheries. What is the character of this contradiction and how are the 'adjustments' forced by transnationalization made? Are these 'adjustments' similar or different for the developed and the underdeveloped societies?

(3) The social movement in modern history has appeared in two principal shapes: organization of so-called 'class struggle' (particularly of the working

class – under trade union and partisan form – and of some peasantries), and organization of the so-called 'national struggle' (notably the national liberation movement in Africa and Asia). These two principal organizational forms of social movement seem to have run aground, whereas the wind seems to be in the sails of other social forms, whether trans-class (the feminist movement for example) or with an ethnic, religious, linguistic or provincial basis. To what extent does this evolution call in issue the concepts of classical Marxism defining social classes as subjects of history?

(4) Study of the cultural aspect of societies has scarcely been brought into any theory of global social change. The implied hypothesis here was that economic change makes itself felt and thus causes a subsequent 'cultural adaptation'. It is a hypothesis that must be questioned.

We shall go on to consider some of these issues in order to highlight the specific character of the African situation.

Our era is certainly characterized by an awakening – or reawakening – of collective social identifications other than those attributable to national and class affiliation. Regionalism, linguistic and cultural adherences, 'tribal' or 'ethnic' loyalties, devotion to a religious institution, attachment to local communities, are among the many forms of this awakening. In the West and the East or in the Third World, the catalogue of these 'new' movements, or old ones with a new lease of life, is extensive. These movements are a significant aspect of the crisis of state, and more precisely of nation-state, whether the nation in question has greater or lesser reality or is merely imaginary. This crisis of state must be viewed as a manifestation of the increasing contradiction between the transnationalization of capital (and behind this of the economic life of all countries in the capitalist world) and the persistence of the state system as the exclusive political pattern in the world. The question that arises here is: if capital is becoming more international, why do the peoples not respond with more internationalism, or by asserting their class identity? Why, instead of class consciousness coming to the fore over the diversity of 'alternative' aspects of social reality, does this consciousness lose ground to 'racial', 'ethnic' or religious identity?

It is certainly not our aim to offer a reply to the question, but more modestly to contribute to clarifying the analysis through offering an ideological critique of two of the main social 'realities' at issue: nation (or the supposed nation) and ethnicity (or the supposed ethnicity).

The state system in which we live is a system of genuine states or those allegedly being built, to such a degree that in some languages, such as English, the distinction between the two concepts is diminished by synonymous usage of the two expressions: the United Nations body is in fact an organization of states. The 'ethnicity' concept – which must in turn be open to question – is advanced by opponents of the nation-state.

The first half of the question (the nation state and the ideology of the nation in crisis) revolves around what we believe to be the main issue, the crisis of the modern state as a consequence of the increasing worldwide expansion of capital. This general crisis affecting even states outside the capitalist system (the socialist countries) hits the states of the periphery more severely than those of the centre. There are two reasons for this. The lesser reason is that the 'national question', in the sense of the nation we know as the creation of the central capitalist state, is a social reality of a particular time and space. It is the product of particular historical circumstances and this crystallization has given rise to an ideological frame, and more seriously to the export of this ideology on a world scale, including to the peripheries of the system where circumstances did not allow the nation to take shape. The greater reason is these very (economic and political) circumstances preventing the crystallization of the autocentric (and potentially national) bourgeois state at the periphery. The current phase, typified by the offensive of transnational capital to 'recompradorize' the states of the periphery and dismantle the attempts at crystallization that were underway in the previous phase, makes all too apparent the character of these unfavourable historical 'conditions'. The threat to the Third World peoples of unlimited fragmentation (on ethnic or pseudo-ethnic bases, or when the national factor is wanting or unsound) exactly in line with the aims of compradorization, can be countered only by a dual objective: organization into states as large and powerful as possible (while continuing to respect diversity) and 'delinking'.

The second half of the question (ethnicity: myth and reality) complements the analysis by considering forms of social organization in the absence of the bourgeois nation. Pre-capitalist forms that beyond their variety sometimes establish a so-called 'ethnic' crystallization but more often prevent it. Peripheral, especially colonial, forms of capitalism that are ranged about the objective of dominant capital (unity through destruction) and are the origin of the ideological illusions of ethnicity. We go on to consider the cultural aspects of the problem and their effects on the social movement.

Nation-state and the ideology of nation in crisis[1]

Our political vocabulary deploys the term 'nation' in a sense that presupposes certain articulations between this true or supposed reality and other realities – the state, the world system of states, the economy and social classes. We inherit these concepts and their articulation in a system of various social theories developed out of the historical experience of 19th century Europe, in the shape of bourgeois nationalist theories or historical Marxism.

The 19th century in Europe remains an epoch central to our modern history. During this century the essential realities that constitute the framework of the contemporary world evolved, through decisive struggles of every kind – wars, revolutions, economic, social, political and cultural upheavals. Among the realities taking shape through three centuries of gentle ripening should certainly be included the nation-state and the worldwide capitalist system, as well as the opposition of modern social classes.

Two theoretical entities have been produced in this framework, in counterpoint to one another, Marxism and the theory of class struggle on the one hand, nationalism and the theory of integration of classes into the bourgeois democratic nation-state on the other. Both take into account numerous aspects of the immediate reality, characterized at one and the same time by social struggles going as far as revolution and by struggles between nation-states going as far as war. The one and the other purport to be effective instruments to inspire strategies of action by the protagonists who are the subjects of history and see themselves as such.

The real effectiveness of political strategies nevertheless depends on a specific conjuncture defined by a correlation – that seems to us now to have been limited in time and space – between the following elements: first, correlation between the state and another social reality, the nation; second, the dominant position of the bourgeois national states thus constituted in the world capitalist system, their 'central' (as opposed to peripheral) character in our conceptual scheme; third, a certain level of worldwide expansion of the capitalist system that makes 'autocentric' economic units, interdependent but enjoying a high degree of autonomy with respect to one another, central partners.

It can be seen why this conjuncture gives the policies inspired by the theories under consideration a real effectiveness. First, there is a possible field of action for 'national' economic policy, that is applied to a given territory, delineated by frontiers and governed by a single state power. The instruments of this policy – centralized national monetary system, customs regulations, network of physical infrastructure of transport and communications, unifying education around a 'national' language, unified system of administration, and so forth – have a certain autonomy in relation to the 'constraints' of the worldwide economy. The relations of class – however conflictive – are regulated within and by the national state. There is in this sense an average price for national labour power, determined by history and internal class relations, a national system of prices that reflect the decisive social relations. In this sense too the 'law of value' has a national dimension. Nations and classes – workers, bourgeois, peasants – are the effective subjects of history. It is clearly understood that there is no Wall of China to cut these national systems off from the world system they constitute. Internal social relations depend in part on the positions held by the national states in question in the world hierarchy. All of them are 'central' capitalist economies although unequally competitive. But they can improve this by coherent national policies, if social relations permit. This effectiveness in turn facilitates social compromise and, without in any way 'abolishing class struggle', contains the conflicts within precise boundaries. In all of this complex reality, the conflicts between social classes and conflicts of competing states lead to a certain degree of balance. Even the size of these nations seems to be 'optimum': 30 million citizens for the Britain, France and Germany of the period is the right size for the industry of the time.

In this conjuncture what is the role of the 'national' reality we have yet to describe? Ideology a posteriori gives an autonomous dimension to national reality by attributing to it pre-existence to the state, which seems debatable to us. For the European bourgeoisie, from the Renaissance to the century of the Enlightenment, seems more cosmopolitan than narrowly national. Moreover, it divides its loyalties among several legitimacies, religous, or philosophical beliefs, friendships still feudal but also at the service of the absolutist monarchical state when it seemed reasonable. It is still largely mobile, at ease in the embrace of Christianity. As for the peasant population, it is more loyal to soil and province than to the future nation whose culture nor even yet really language it shares. But the state of the absolute monarchy gradually creates the nation, a task to be rounded off by bourgeois democracy. Doubtless this creation does not come from nowhere. But the ethno-linguistic collections of provinces subject to the same ruler are not 'naturally' destined to become the modern nations of Europe; it is no more than a possibility. The nation is really a product of capitalism, as moreover Marxism along with conventional sociology acknowledges for the reason that in Europe feudalism, from which capitalism emerged, took no note of the nation and knew only Christianity and the fief. It was, moreover, a product largely shaped by the sword and the fire – as much as by the market – assimilating and compelling, destroying languages and dialects, and nearly always imperfect. A product also sometimes curiously aborted – when capitalist development hangs fire – or distorted by the skew of chance conjunction between local interests, ideological (especially religious) conflicts and international balances. Only in the 19th century did the great melting pot, new industry calling for the diffusion of a national language, and the – slow – progression of Western electoral democracy really define nations. But this is in the framework of pre-existing states.

It is true that the strength of the model of the predecessors inspires those who come after. As there already exists an English, and a French nation, the German nation and the Italian nation assign themselves the task of creating themselves by creating their state. The political cunning of the promoters will be in finding social alliances and compromises that mobilize the forces in this direction.

The linguistic dimension acquires exceptional force in the European nation-states, that may even constitute the essence of the national factor as a new social factor. Certainly the material base of this reality is constituted by autocentric capitalist construction, relatively autonomous within the interdependence of the global system. But the national language to some extent constitutes its active superstructure, which operates effectively in its reproduction. Language as a means of unification is a relatively modern phenomenon. In the pre-capitalist world, local languages, of peasant and regional currency, coexist alongside an official language of religion and of the state, whose penetration is incomplete at best. Education and modern democracy turn the national language into an instrument that in the end defines the nation itself, its frontiers, its mass culture. It is attributed a mysterious power of transmitting a 'national culture'. The virtues hitherto invested in the feudal lord, the absolute monarch, the men of God, the true 'proprietors' of populations and human communities, are transferred by democracy and its ideology to the entire nation. The literature of 'national identity' that flourished in the 19th century testifies to this transfer. The slide into jingoism, and indeed racism, is inherent to it.

On a closer examination, however, it would appear that this clear correlation limited in time to the 19th century is even more limited in space. Around these few 'model' nation-states, the world of the capitalist system, structured by different pasts that lose their legitimacy and effectiveness, remains inchoate and its destiny is uncertain and confused.

For what concerns us, namely identification of the historical subjects and eventual establishment of the constituent nations of the world capitalist system, attention must be given to the state. First the state in its relations to continually expanding capitalist reproduction. And at this level, there is no state but the central, that is one that controls external relations and subjects them to the logic of autocentric accumulation. Elsewhere there are only 'countries' administered from outside as colonies and semi-colonies, or ostensibly independent but powerless not only to influence the exterior according to their own needs but even to avoid the tides and influence from the exterior. But attention must in fairness be given to the 'doubtful cases', those that until the present have not veered to one side or the other, the 'semi-peripheries'. Here the destiny of the state will determine the rest.

The European semi-peripheries – the Austro-Hungarian and Russian empires – were to veer in the direction of central evolution, but not without difficulty. The start to the constitution of a unified capitalist market, albeit initially under the influence of external penetration, represented a challenge to the old dynastic state. The challenge in the early stages would take the form of a renovation–modernization that was far from hesitant and made giant strides: education, constitutional reform (the Austro-Hungarian dual monarchy and petty parliamentarianism), social reform (abolition of serfdom in Russia) among others. But here, the nationalist ideology, largely imported along with the rest, was to prove as much a handicap as a driving force. It was to end in the break-up of the Austro-Hungarian empire, putting the small inheritor states at risk of being peripheralized until their later incorporation into the Soviet empire. And if the Russian empire survives – with and even thanks to the Bolshevik revolution – even at the cost of the loss of Poland and Finland, doubtless it is in great measure because the Russian nation is predominant there.

It is one those phenomema of discrepancy that constitute the hypothesis of this reflection. For it cannot be said that each of the bourgeoisies, assuming their existence – Czech, Slovak, Polish, Hungarian, Slovene, Croat, German – needed 'its' state and 'its' market. It cannot be said that they would have been unable to constitute segments of a single bourgeoisie on the basis of a single integrated market. It cannot be said that the mass of the peasant population would have preferred to be exploited by their own 'national' bourgeoisie. The polarization of the conflict around language is typical, largely by projection of the ideology attached to the new role of language in the developed European West. The complex interplay of real and potential social conflicts led the political forces – social democratic parties of the Second International, peasant parties, parties of the bourgeois revival – to theorize, justify and propose endless strategies that finally all fell away before the myth of the linguistically unified nation-state, as a reproduction of the 'model'.

The result is in any case rather mediocre. The inheritor states are the confirmation of incapable local bourgeois hegemonies that quickly fell into the lap of Berlin or Paris. The potential for capitalist development was thrown away and economic stagnation became a marked characteristic. With the absence of bourgeois democracy compensated for by talk of jingoistic mobilization against a neighbour, the affair was settled – oddly by the regimes put into place by the Red Army in the aftermath of the defeat of fascism – by the generalized expulsion of minorities! Since then the system inspired and dictated by the Soviet model and, with the exception of Yugoslavia, integrated into the Soviet empire, has inaugurated a new history. Not everything in this new history is negative and it cannot be said that the fate of the peoples of the region would have been better in any other way and that they would then have escaped their peripheralization. But, if it is possible to imagine, the unrealized potentialities, the maintenance and renewal of the ancient empire – and nowadays a kind of Hungary–Yugoslavia (which are not doing so badly in the present-day world) at the scale of the entire region – would perhaps have allowed more room for manoeuvre for the plans for independence and democracy.

Russia would have been inaugurated with more talent, and the invention of Bolshevism is no small thing in the history of humankind. That it has little to do with socialism, that it has given Russification a power that no Western colonization has ever had (precisely through what, despite everything, is the progressive dimension of the Soviet renewal) is not the issue.

Further to the south and east is the world that was not to escape peripheralization. First the centres carve out colonial empires there. Some regions have this status from the mercantilist period – the British and Dutch Indies, the Philippines. Other fall to the imperialist scramble for Africa at the end of the 19th century. The states that retain formal independence – China, the Ottoman Empire, Persia – are in reality 'semi-colonies'. At the level of the economic base, there is no mystery: the peripheralization is the systematic work of colonial administrations or the inevitable result of the drift by states whose sovereigns expect no more than to survive from week to week. But at the level of the superstructure, things are not so one-dimensionally uniform. Here the past is a weightier encumbrance. And it is in this regard that the most outlandish simplifications and most Eurocentric projections have flourished. As the nation in Europe is the historical product of capitalism and unknown in feudal times, in the name of Eurocentrism the possibility is denied of an analogous social factor elsewhere, for periods that can only be imagined as 'feudal' as well. Elsewhere, we have pronounced on this very point and attempted to describe the tribute-paying mode in its non-feudal Asian and African forms. A phenomenon, whose similarity with the previous national phenomenon cannot escape notice, often appears when a complete and advanced form of this tribute-paying mode is characteristic of the society. Linguistic phenomena similar to those that Europe would not develop until the capitalist epoch would also testify to this similarity, quite clearly in China and Egypt, in part at least in India and at certain epochs of Arab history.

Attention must be paid to the regions and states whose fate is not determined at the moment of European irruption into their area. Was China also on the point of inventing capitalism? Would it have strengthened the Chinese nation too, but there on the basis of a substratum already present? There are indications of this. Is it this maturity that has prevented worse: disintegration? Or is it the Confucian bonding and the sheer size of the continent that made the conqueror hesitate? But India did not dismay either Dupleix or the East India Company. It still seems that the nation-state, despite its decline, and with hindsight here, was the historical subject. It provided the framework – national is the only way to describe it – in which the historical subjects that constitute classes face one another under the successive hegemonies of the heavenly aristocracy and bureaucracy, then the bourgeoisie, and in the end under a peasant revolution led by the communist party, to regulate the conditions of internal transformation and external relations.

India, too, was pregnant with a capitalist development that Marx doubtless did not expect and whose reality has been shown by Ramkrishna Mukherjee.[2] The disappearance of the Indian state, perhaps merely the fruit of a passing conjuncture, to the benefit of colonialism, has nevertheless had longstanding, irreversible effects in the fields of national and statist construction. Indian unity is not, it must quickly be added, a product of British colonization, and its maintenance after independence is not the expression of the will of the political liberation movement without objective foundations. Hinduism certainly supplies a real common denominator; is not the proof of this that unitary efforts were to fail outside its area of dominance, in the Islamized regions? But this common denominator also operates for a family of a dozen linguistically related great nations, which includes most of the peoples of the sub-continent. Here, unification of the capitalist market is not called in question by the will of the bourgeoisies of these various nations to break up the new state to their benefit, as was the case in central and eastern Europe. Is it because the ideology of the nation-state had not penetrated into this part of the world less clouded by the West-European model than Austro-Hungary and the Balkans were?

The Ottoman state and the Egyptian state also provide food for thought. The ripening of capitalist relations is evident in the Balkans and in Rumelia, in Egypt and Syria. The state that superimposed itself over all the component populations – Arab and Turkish Muslims, Greek Christians, slaves and Armenians – was not 'naturally' an obstacle to this ripening. Its incapacity to withstand the forays of foreign capital would in the end rob it of its legitimacy. But there too, as in central Europe, the proof would be provided by the history that the inheritor states would offer scarcely more effective resistance. It was therefore possible to envisage another kind of doubtless more effective response: modernization within an Ottoman framework that had become lay and pluri-national. This is not a pipe dream. History, written after the event by the Balkans peoples, the Arabs and the Turks, suggests that the desire for 'national independence' of the populations (or bourgeoisies?) was irrepressible. That is not obvious. In the Balkans perhaps, decadent Muslim fanaticism, combined with active British, Austrian and Russian intervention strengthened the transfer of the ideology of the small nation-state to the Greek, Albanian, Serbian, Bulgarian and Romanian peoples. The real resonance of this ideology remains a matter of debate, as is shown by the lack of interest shown in it by the 'Greek bourgeoisie of the exterior'.[3]

In the Arab part of the empire, the Ottomans did not recruit solely from Muslim reaction. Intellectual bearers of the Arab national renaissance in Syria and Egypt defended Ottoman unity, not only as a tactical shield against the Europeans, but also, sometimes because, with astounding perspicacity, they believed the break-up would still further weaken the possibilities of an effective renewal. Is it known that the Arab and Muslim intellectuals defended the thesis of a laicist state (defended the Christians in the Balkans and Armenia against Turkish oppression) and a pluri-national state, and kept their distance from the Khalifate? Here, as in Inida, the European model of the nation-state had only limited appeal. Unhappily this appeal would be great in the decisive sector of the young Turks and the secret organization for 'Unity and Progress' which, taking the initiative for the creation of a then artificial 'Turkish' perspective, would begin what was to be completed by the defeat of 1918 and the Kemalist revolution. In an even more tragic version of central Europe, this option would end in making Turkey the last 'lumpen-proletarian' wagon in a Europe that would repulse it. In a necessary echo, and in the face of the deplorable behaviour of the Arabs of the Mashreq in the 1914–18 War, the Egyptian liberal bourgeoisie rallied round this thesis that was predominant in the inter-war period. This option, later abandoned for a healthy return to Arab Egypt, finds objective foundation in the 'two stage' character of the Arab nation, as I have tried to show in *The Arab Nation: Nationalism and Class Struggles*.

In the Americas likewise, on a very different historical substratum however, the state operates as an active subject, forging the nation or attempting to do so, with greater or lesser success. In the North its base is provided by the construction of an autocentric economy established from New England to be extended throughout the United States after the settlement of the question of the South. But it did not manage to establish itself in Latin America, despite the early accession to independence. The national superstructure constituted in the US has such peculiar characteristics that one hesitates to speak of nation in the singular, despite the 'purity' and unparalleled success of the capitalist development. Did the two original cultures, petty commodity of New England and slave colonial of the South, fuse? Do they continue side by side? Are they diluted in a new culture that is gradually shaped by massive immigration? Is the racially-based pyramid defining North American society to the present day more or less significant than linguistic uniformity? The insurmounted peripheralization of the economic base in Latin America substantially reduces the extent to which the state has formal existence. All the more since it is a case of a Creole state marginalizing the Indian communities. It is hardly possible to speak of a nation-state except in Mexico when, after the revolution of the 20th century, hispanification of the Indian communities reached a decisive stage. Brazil, however, constitutes one of those oddities of history, where the state – a Portuguese rather than specifically Brazilian state moreover – is able to impose itself, even without an economic base and, perhaps for a long time, even without a nation. In any case, in this field as in others in Latin America, the European model remains the sole point of reference and with it the unchallenged ideology of the nation-state.

Actual history has therefore led us through this rapid overview to challenge the ideology of the nation, whether in its bourgeois version (the nation is a pre-existing reality, the ideal state – the nation-state – is founded on it and reveals its potential) or its vulgar Marxist version (capitalism creates nations and generalizes the nation-state form to the entire world). Actual history suggests rather that the state is the active subject that sometimes creates the nation, sometimes 'regenerates' it, but often fails to do either. As actual history further suggests, the significance of the nation-state ideology is that it does not always manifest itself as a progressive active agent in capitalist development but as a deviant influencing its development in a negative direction or slowing down its rate. It is a shining success only in Western Europe, Russia, China, Japan and the US; and the nation-state/autocentric economy correlation is limited in time and space. In those cases the nation became an active historical subject, a framework for the conflicts and compromises between the subjects who, in the final analysis, constitute capitalism's social classes or emerge from it. Elsewhere, whether the economic base remains peripheral or becomes so, whether the state fragments or disappears, whether the potential national constructions emerge or fail to do so, groups and social classes, communities of various kinds and the state confront each other in a play of conflicts that does not permit control of the destiny of the people in question. The true historical subject here is the 'liberation movement' rather than the classes or nation. This liberation movement, described as 'national – such is the potency of the nation-state ideology – brings together classes, groups and communities, and assigns them their objectives: independence, 'development' and national construction. It has achieved the first, but generally failed in the essence of the others, certainly by virtue of the class character of its hegemonic component, but also because the nation-state ideology is not as effective as it is believed to be.

The nation-state ideology is, however, so powerful that when, in the aftermath of the Second World War, all the countries of the world were bidding for independence, they constituted a system of would-be nation-states. But at the very moment when the nation-state was being proclaimed everywhere, it was entering a crisis everywhere, even at its centres of origin, a crisis from which there seems no escape.

In the 1945–70 period the worldwide expansion of the capitalist system reached a stage that gave it qualitatively new characteristics. Until the end of the 19th century, the worldwide expansion had merely integrated a certain number of basic products into a market that was still an international rather than a world market. This first step allowed the operation of the laws of value of a national character, within the framework of the constraints operating through international competition, through an embryonic world capitalist law of value. At this stage, the social classes were still essentially national classes, defined by social relations confined to the limits of the state. There was, therefore, a conjunction between the struggles of these classes and the play of politics, which was regulated precisely within the framework of these states. From the end of the 19th century to the Second World War, the internationalization of monopoly capital began in parallel with the international market for basic products. But this stage is marked by the absence of world hegemony, and the monopolies, constituted on the basis of competitor central states, operated in a privileged position in the peripheral regions carved out between the colonial empires and the spheres of influence of these states. The absence of a state or its weakness in these peripheral regions had the effect that social relations confined within the frontiers of central national states could still govern the essential dynamism of capitalist expansion. The principal subjects of history remained the national social classes, even if the working classes among them would henceforth clearly align their strategies within a reformist, or imperialist, perspective. After the Second World War, began the stage of the worldwide expansion of the processes of production themselves through the break-up of systems of production into segments that the so-called 'transnational' form of enterprise would spread through the globe under its control. United States hegemony, even if it is now facing challenge, provided an adequate framework for this transnationalization.

Undoubtedly the global value and employment produced in this way was a modest proportion of the whole, but that is not the issue. It is a fact that the interests invested in these areas of economic activity are those that dominate the system, and determine its evolution by their concentration in the areas of the most advanced technological progress, and are in short the typical new forms of contemporary capitalism. Is it not the case that nearly half of world trade is now made up of internal transfers to the transnationals? And the relative mass of international capital flows of direct interest to these sectors of activity is undoubtedly at least as significant within the world capital market. For the first time, too, we see social classes taking on a world dimension; white-collar workers are employed by IBM in the US, Germany, Senegal, Morocco, Brazil and Indonesia; blue-collar workers make parts for or assemble such and such make of motor-car in a score of countries, and so on. A single world labour force has been constituted; the world dimension of the law of value wins over the local dimensions. This reality finds its obvious reflection in economistic discourse: the constraint of competitiveness on a world scale is an arresting theme of the discourse of governors of the right or the left; it is presented as an inescapable and unavoidable fact, and to ignore it is to turn one's back on 'progress', etc. But by this token, the state – national or not – forfeits its effectiveness as the locus for drawing up the strategies to control capitalist expansion or modulate it. As there is no planetary state, and while US hegemony that has partly fulfilled this role is itself in crisis, while the world institutions (IMF, and so forth) are embryonic, while the political games (elections, for example) are still confined to the state systems, the correlation between class conflicts and compromises on one side and politics on the other has vanished.

But this general crisis does not have the same impact on the various components of the world system.

a) The developed capitalist centres – the United States, Europe and Japan – do not have the essence of their advantages threatened by this evolution. The US enjoys the relative advantage of political and national homogeneity on the scale of a continent; Japan the advantage of national unity, but on the scale of a more average-sized country, and furthermore one poor in natural resources and confronted with neighbours which could threaten its security. Europe is handicapped by its historical legacy. It had been the greatest beneficiary of transnationalization in the first phase – in the 1950s and 1960s – when a decisive role was played in capitalist expansion of its fringes (Italy, Spain) and modernization of its centres (Germany especially, and France). The European construction is ambivalent. It was presented by its promoters as the means of establishing a force capable of autonomy in regard to the United States and Japan, but it has also been the framework for transatlanticism.

The effects of worldwide expansion on the developed centres must be considered in the light of the crisis of state and politics it has created. The state is no longer the effective instrument it was, even in the US and Japan, and a fortiori in a divided Europe. The renewal of ultra-liberal, anti-state ideologies is a response of surrender to this decline. But at a stroke, the scope of politics is annulled. The seeds of this erasure of the sense of political choice are not new. The dominant imperialist position had long since created conditions for the aims of the social compromise. But it was a national compromise, that is, its terms depended on internal social relations (capital working-class middle strata). Voting for left or right, in these circumstances, implementing a reformist and Keynesian policy, or choosing austerity, unemployment and an attack on social privilege, were significantly different alternative choices. They were no longer so once the society accepted the notion of the constraint of 'competition on a world scale'. The political forces that engaged in electoral battle drew together in the consciousness of the narrowing of the gap between them; their tactics tended even to reduce the gap to a minimum. To win the votes of the 'centre' one sought to speak in terms as close as possible to those of the opponent. The role of social classes as historical subjects was obscured.

The ineffectiveness of politics does, however, create an uneasy feeling. The history of the United States, again in advance of that of Europe, has shown how this vacuum may be filled by a combination of permanent elements (do not racism and religious and social side-tracks serve a useful purpose in this stability?) and conjunctural coalitions of interests (professional, local, and so on, working through lobbies). Are there not indications of similar phenomena appearing in Europe?

Worldwide expansion has also entailed, for the first time, the beginnings of a pluri-national working class within the very centres of developed capitalism. Migration is of course not a new phenomenon. But the great migrations that populated America came from capitalist centres in formation. In the countries of reception, assimilation was the rule – except of course for the slaves brought by force. France, likewise a country of immigration, readily assimilated Poles, Spaniards and Italians. The new migrations come from the periphery. They have already changed the composition of the working class in the centres and represent very large minorities in the United States (Latin Americans) and in Europe (Africans, Asians and West Indians).

The optimists nevertheless stress the appearance of 'new movements' bringing new social forces into play, perhaps even new historical subjects capable of bringing to life the prospect of a new – socialist – society on the basis of objective contemporary reality. It is far from our intention to underestimate these new trends. Beyond the conjunctures aroused by the emergence of issues evaded by the traditional organizations or by the defection from this same kind of organization (parties, trade unions), some movements indicate the emergence of a far-reaching maturity: the feminist movement, the ecological and local democracy movements, the ideological currents concerned with the reorganization of labour and the critique of commodity alienation, among others. All these movements are largely trans-class, with a strong component in the new middle classes.

Is this a case of the emergence of new historical subjects? What social changes do they offer? Do these changes come within the potential evolution of capitalism and notably the maintenance of the centres/peripheries imbalance? Can they, and under what circumstances, initiate internal socialist development and North–South relations conducive to progressive transformation of the world system? What articulation with the new functions of the state does this potential demand?

The most advanced proposals and analyses in these areas call for a political restructuring of these nascent forces around the following four axes: first, a model of 'alternative development' based on expanding the scope for non-commodity and self-management activities; second, rejection of blind surrender to the demands of international competitiveness, in short, delinking to restore the lost autonomy to the national state; third, revision, albeit by regions, of North–South relations intended to strengthen the national autonomy of the partners and widen the scope for the popular movement, the foundation of a new internationalism; and fourth, a pacifist approach to East–West relations, especially to broaden the interaction of the two Europes and provide scope to the East for democratization and progress.

All that has our entire and unhesitating support. The programme defines for the North what we mean by delinking.

But it must be noted that there is no sign of this structuring in the foreseeable future. The large organizations are deaf and the accepted mode of political regulation impenetrable. The tendency is therefore for these forces to be marginalized or to be incorporated into the system. The model of 'cantonization' of social and political life permits this absorption to the benefit of capital, and it is the latter that remains the sole dominant force trampling on regional autonomies, and absurd votes on constantly recurring minor issues, and even the progressive evolution of customs, and so forth.

Of course, the future is unpredictable, as all these prospective arguments suppose that the stability of the system is not challenged either by a worsening of East–West confrontation that might follow Europe's closer adherence to the Atlantic alliance, or by a global financial and economic slump. A crash, panic, protective chain reaction, unpredictable responses to the political plan in case of too rapid a rise in unemployment, are unknowns. But let us say that, if the relations continue in their current state of tension without a slump, an overall aggressive strategy of the North against the South, that has already begun, would be quite compatible with the apparent 'stability' of the system. This evolution would, naturally, dash the hopes placed on the new movements of the North. The future would then depend entirely on the kind of answer made by the societies of the South.

b) Capitalist expansion has directly inverse effects in the centres and in the peripheries of the system: it integrates the societies in the former, founds or eventually reinforces the nation there, but in the latter it disintegrates the society, fragments it, alienates it, and eventually destroys the nation or destroys its potential. This imbalance as to the economic basis of the system seems to us quite essential. It reflects the qualitatively different position of the local bourgeoisies in the local and world system, which is not only a matter of quantitative degree. It is a manifestation of the unequal character of capitalist development and at the origin of objective need to go beyond capitalism in the peripheries.

The question of the state and its relation to the nation and to its social components comes to the forefront of a concrete analysis of the forms of peripheralization. Generally speaking, we are brought back to the proposition supported above, that the formation of nations is limited in time and space and is in no way a 'general' product of capitalism. How many of the Third World states of today bear even a vague resemblance to nation-states? With the exception of pluri-national India, peripheral capitalism in expansion does not operate as a force dictating a bringing together, or fusion, of nearby quasi-nations, neither in Spanish-speaking America nor in the Arab world. Rather the reverse, as one sees in the latter instance, the closer world integration that oil revenues occasioned pushed back pan-Arab prospects. In Africa, the crude form of neo-colonialism has even broken up the former broader colonial groupings. And this offers no advantage of more homogeneous small units: the small African states are as heterogeneous as the big ones. The incapability of opting for unifying national languages and the concomitant and anomalous retention of linguistic duality (the foreign language – English, French or Portuguese – being designated as 'national', even when it is spoken by only a tiny minority) makes it impossible to speak of nations here.

Moreover, the new stage of worldwide expansion causes the disappearance of the last traces of social classes recognizable by their position as defined in the local social formation. The ruling classes are no more than subordinate and powerless transmission belts for worldwide capital. But the popular classes themselves lose their identity (working class, small peasantry, and so on) to blend into an ill-defined mixture. The very kind of extraverted development underway calls for this 'molecular' form in the new social structure. Can these classes and social groups, fragmented and fragmentary, make the transition from the status of class in itself to a class for itself? This seems to us very unlikely in the absence of a political struggle where the state may be at stake. The mature formation of classes occurs in this framework, when there is a correlation of state, nation, social struggles and political struggles. The non-correlation between state, nation (which is often non-existent), social classes (dispersed and fragmented in the world) cancels out the effectiveness of politics. In our opinion this loss of effectiveness explains the rise of populisms and ideological irrationalities.

These negative factors together explain the success of the recompradorization underway at the level of the Third World as a whole.

This recompradorization is nevertheless bound to clash with the rise of popular movements. It is not surprising that the populist form is confused, and founded on ambivalent ideologies. It is evidence of the broad character of an alliance of classes themselves unsure of their determination, denied their autonomy and consciousness of class for itself. But this is not to say that it is less effective as a force for disintegration of the world order, or that it could not under certain circumstances evolve into positive revolutionary constructions.

It is not our intention here to make 'forecasts' of either phenomenon or to succumb to the often futile exercise of 'scenarios'. We suggest that positive constructions entail the combination of three conditions. First, delinking as we have defined it, that is strict subjection of external relations in all fields to the logic of internal choices without regard to the criteria of world capitalist rationality. Second, political capacity to introduce profound social reforms in an egalitarian direction. The latter is also a precondition for delinking, since the hegemonic classes *in situ* have no interest in it and a possible consequence of it, since it evidently implies transfers of political hegemony. Delinking has little chance of coming about without reform, and if it occurs conjuncturally it will end up at an impasse. Third, capacity for technological absorption and ingenuity, without which the autonomy of decision that has been won cannot be put into effect. Clearly such a capacity cannot be developed through a few educational tricks; it implies an ideological opening up.

Ideological and political preparation of a response to the offensive of the North against the peoples of the South requires three axes of action.

First, strengthening the unity of the Third World, and its national and regional components. The greatness of Kwame Nkrumah and his call for pan-Africanism, which in his day made some laugh and condemned him to the ferocious hatred of others, can now more than ever before be recognized as a clear-sighted awareness of the frailty of a fragmented Africa.

Second, progress for democracy and respect for collective rights, whether of (for example, ethnic, religious) 'minorities', or of the popular classes (for example, political and trade union rights). The objective need to provide the Third World with great economic, political and military scope, as the sole means of intervening effectively in the contemporary world and winning respect as a genuine partner, entails the renunciation of the narrow ideology of nation as it has been inherited from 19th century Europe. The idea of unification by force from local Prussias and Piedmonts, ignoring regional differences and imposing, even on minorities, linguistic and administrative homogenization, does not correspond to the realities of contemporary Africa and the Third World. The rights of peoples and nations to self-determination, including their right to secession, must be tempered by outlooks sympathetic to the constitution in appropriate forms of great 'multinational' states, democratic and mindful of differences. This is the only way to check-mate the imperialist plans that always aim to divide. In Africa and the Middle East in particular, South Africa and Israel openly plan to 'bantustanize' or 'Lebanonize' to an infinite degree, counting on 'tribes' and 'religious communities' and refusing to see what, beyond their differences, unites the African peoples and the Arab peoples.

Third, strategic consciousness that the peoples of the periphery must be self-reliant. Neither a possible Soviet alliance, still less illusions about Europe, could mitigate shortcomings in the fields of delinking, internal reform and mutual support. With some justification at the tactical level, these alliances and compromises will be of no strategic value until, through the joint efforts of the peoples, the overall world system has been refashioned.

Ethnicity: myth and reality

The ethnic group, no more than 'race' or any other 'non-reality' invented for the purpose, is not the basis of social organization of the pre-capitalist worlds.

As variety was the rule here, it is essential to find some criteria of classification to assist an understanding of history. In this area the criteria of development of the forces of production and the character of the corresponding relations of production provide, in the last analysis, the only sensible solution. We suggest a distinction between two basic modes of production: the primitive–communal and tribute-paying modes. The former correspond to the long transition from virtually unknown primitive existence to the great states of the pre-capitalist classes. The tribute-paying mode defines the societies of pre-capitalist societies. On this view the slave-owning particularity is eliminated, for reasons we shall not go into here; even if we replace the 'two paths' (Western and Asiatic) – or the three, four or five inspired by more or less dogmatic interpretations of Marx's *Grundrisse* – by a distinction between a complete tribute-paying mode and its incomplete peripheral forms.

This fundamental analysis is not, however, enough, and to take account of actual history it is necessary to define the series of complex social formations that make up the pre-capitalist political societies. In this analysis the role of 'long-distance trade' is essential since, before capitalism it was practically the only way of integrating into a whole, however loosely, the disparate elementary societies. In the complete tribute-paying societies, with statist centralization of surplus is initiated political and exchange activity sufficiently intense to influence the conditions of production and eventually stimulate progress.

The rediscovery of this articulation between production and centralization (or absence thereof) of surplus – long-distance trade – is recent, at least in Marxist circles. But as happens all too often we have gone from one extreme to the other. In the past the thesis of 'primacy of production' was supported, and was a pretext for ignoring long-distance trade and its role in politics. Now, suddenly, as Marxist modes take hold, interest in analysing the productive base is lost and reserved for exchange and political and warfare organization. From Marx we move on to Pirenne, who wrote of nothing else.[4]

In the reconstruction of pre-capitalist societies, analysis of their character, their dynamic (on the basis of their contradictions), their interaction, or their complications, it is rediscovered now that the ethnic group had no essential place.

There are in fact 'peoples', the most general of terms that does not imply any a priori precise qualification. These peoples are organized in spaces that do not always coincide, for example: space for matrimonial exchanges, for long-distance trade, for eventual centralization of surplus, for political organization, for the eventually centralized states, for mythologies of kinship and origin, for religious beliefs, and space for linguistic communications (it would be possible to make an almost infinite catalogue of the areas defined).

Where is the ethnic group in this multiple reality? Everywhere and nowhere. If by ethnic group is meant a people who 'speak the same language' (even allowing for dialect variations so long as they do not prevent communication), and who obey the same political authority, there are only rarely ethnic groups in the advanced tribute-paying systems (in China and in Egypt). But why then speak of ethnic group? How does it differ from the modern nation? Furthermore – in the mediaeval West or black Africa for example – the surplus is scarcely centralized beyond the elementary constituents of the system (the feudal manor, the village). Part of the surplus is distributed through the long-distance trade. The state scarcely exists, and where it does seem to have formal existence it is without power: neither a state integrating the basic units of production of tribute-paying surplus, nor a state organized by 'warrior-merchants' as masters of long-distance trade. In these systems communal consciousness has several stages, without necessarily going through the stage of 'ethnic' identification: there is the village community and that of the villages included in the same elementary tribute-paying unit and/or close matrimonial ties, there are the broad spaces with vague religious connotation in some cases: Christianity for mediaeval Europe, for example. But there is no such thing as a

Frenchman, or even perhaps a Breton . . . Is 'provincial' (pseudo-ethnic) consciousness not a later product, of centralized monarchies (who 'create' the provinces as organizational units in order to control them), whereas the provinces are very like the advanced tribute-paying mode. Language in itself does not necessarily motivate a sense of community. In our age, when the state education system has largely brought together and imposed a 'single language', it is easy to forget that the ancient peoples were often polyglot (see Africa), that according to need they used this or that language, variant or idiom, without being perturbed by 'multiple identity' in the jargon of the modern phenomenon of linguistic chauvinism.

Pre-capitalist organization is not 'homogeneous', even in fractions of the world, a fortiori over great areas. There are nearly always areas of greater population density, development of forces of production, political, cultural and religious organization, and the 'intermediate' areas, with more or less defined dependence on the former. There are also nearly always enclaves that escape the (linguistic, religious, economic or political) homogenization imposed by the rise of great states. Where the area of long-distance trade does not correlate exactly with that of minimum common disposition of power there often emerge people–classes who bridge the gaps: the Jews in mediaeval Christianity, the Dioula in West Africa, among others.

We have elsewhere suggested an interpretation of Arab and pre-colonial African history based on the method described above.

In the Arab case, we speak of the quasi-nation superimposing itself on the regional community, founded on centralization and distribution of the surplus provided by the dominant class of warrior-merchants. It was a class at its height (moving from Tangiers to Baghdad without difficulty) strongly unified through, amongst other things, a written language and a religion. It was a quasi-nation and not a nation pure and simple since the means corresponding to the development of the forces of production scarcely touched the peasant masses, especially those cut off by natural barriers (hence the survival of linguistic and religious enclaves) and since the correlation with power, often localized (especially at times of decline in the great trade), was only relative. Unification in the ruling class was, however, strong, hence our description. But this was not an 'Arab ethnic group'; any more than the enclave peoples had an 'ethnic' by the Western mass media, was of no interest to the broad masses; the 'one' people).

The case of the old Sudanic Africa is very similar to that of North Africa. It is known (i) that the great states of Sudanic Africa (Ghana, Mali, Songhai, and so on) were founded on control of the southern edge of trans-Saharan trade, just as those of the north were founded on control of its northern edge; (ii) the ruling class of these states far from being identifiable as a 'dominant ethnic group' was formed on the basis of certain warrior clans, wide open to assimilation (there were professed Malinké or Songhai here just as there were professed Turks in the Ottoman Empire); (iii) that the scope of these dominances, with fluctuating frontiers, was highly heterogeneous, or variable, especially as regards what is now called the 'ethnic' factor. These theses with their critique of 'ethnicity' are gaining ground nowadays. The Atlantic trade ruined the states and classes to the north and south of the Sahara for similar reasons that led to the decline of the Afro-Arab long-distance trade. The Atlantic slave trade completed the destruction and wrought one of the worst abuses recorded in the history of humankind. The formation of black coastal states founded on this trade was not matched by any development of the forces of production, but rather their regression.

Our political thesis on contemporary Arab unity and African unity comes within the pursuit and revival of this history. Arab unity has firm objective roots, reinforced even today despite the impact of a decline dating back several centuries and aggravated by colonization and the emergence of the present-day post-colonial states. It is in our view impossible to defend the long-term interests of the Arab peoples, their liberation from world capitalist domination and the related internal patterns of exploitation, without defending the triple objective of delinking, socialism and the building of a unified Arab nation. African unity, or African regional unities, has perhaps more tender roots, since, among other factors, it does not enjoy the unparalleled instrument represented for the Arab nation by a shared language. It is, however, the only possible response to the challenges of our age. Neither consolidation of the states emerging from colonization, often too tiny to face the problems of our time, nor the break-up desired by the proponents of ethnicity (to be seen in Nigeria of the past and Ethiopia of the present) provide a response to these issues.

The practices of colonial domination have played a decisive part in the 'creation' of 'ethnic realities' in Africa in particular. For the colonizers to dominate vast regions, often disrupted by decline associated with slave trading, they need to 'reorganize' and above all find local intermediaries for the purpose. In the absence of state, a tribute-paying or 'feudal' class, the colonizers invented 'chiefs' and invested them with an authority that was often spurious. But of what could they be chiefs anyway? It was then that poor, amateur anthropologists, who were good military and civilian servitors of colonialism, invented the 'ethnic groups' (with the frankness of the times the expressions were 'races' or 'tribes'). Professional anthropology made a half-hearted attack on these inventions. The story of these inventions has been told very wittily about the Bambara and the Bété – and of the Ibo and many others. In the most tragic instances – for the peoples victimized – colonialism linked the invention of ethnicity to the establishment of savage systems of exploitation, nowadays adorned with the description 'traditional'. J. P. Chrétien has shown how Belgian colonialism and the Catholic church jointly invented the 'Tutsi' and the 'Hutu': curious ethnic groups indistinguishable by language, culture or history, he says. Tutsi feudal domination was thus an entirely Belgian invention, then justified by a baseless theory (the vaunted distinction between Hamites and Bantu).[5]

Ideologization of ethnicity is a clear example of racism. The ethnic group – or 'race' as it was called – was supposed to exist on its own, prior to the ethnic consciousness of those affected. It defined significant qualities that have sometimes been comically described: for example, the X or the Y are 'bright' or 'stupid', dedicated to agriculture or to abstract thought, according to the needs of the colonial power. But when all is said and done the mass circulation description of 'An Englishman's view of the French' or vice versa is not much better.

The extreme form of the ideology of ethnic racism comes in apartheid South Africa and the bantustanization of the country. The black people of South Africa have, as is well known, riposted with demonstrations of unity and struggle and it might be hoped that their courage and example would give the theoreticians of ethnicity and its unconditional acceptance more pause for thought. Zionist literature showing its 'view' of the Arabs and plans based on this view are no different.

History cannot go backwards. As a consequence, if the ethnic group exists, whether or not as a product of colonialism, it must be acknowledged and taken into account. But does it really exist and if so where? Here variety is the rule and there is no substitute as is said for 'concrete analysis of concrete situations'.

In some instances it would seem clear that ethnic reality – albeit a false reality – is a given of current politics. But on closer examination it can be seen that in most situations this reality is manipulated by clans competing for power within the ruling class. The best examples of this are Zaire, Rwanda and Burundi. In the latter two countries, the quasi-racist contrast of Tutsi and Hutu has been internalized by the ruling classes. Belgian colonialism and the Catholic church favoured in the extreme a 'feudal' domination they themselves created and christened 'Tutsi'. Later the new educated *petit-bourgeoisie*, hoping to take over from the 'feudals' in the new neo-colonial framework, claimed 'Hutu' ethnicity and, with colonialism and the church showing a change of heart, were supported by imperialism when the post-independence regime was established in Rwanda. As C. Vidal has shown, the 'the ethnic excuse' was manipulated by the *petit-bourgeois* clans competing for power. But has 'ethnicity' really been internalized by the great manipulated masses? This remains to be proven. In Katanga (now renamed Shaba) it can hardly be called ethnicity but provincialism, and pluri-ethnic at that. Here it can be seen that provincialism was only the reflection of the backwardness of the *petit-bourgeoisie* of this province under the extreme domination of large-scale mining capital, in the face of the Kinshasa *petit-bourgeoisie*, who were radical nationalist in the early 1960s. Here, too, imperialism used the contradiction to try to prolong its domination of Katanga, threatened by the rise of support for Lumumba. Once again with colonial power situated in Kinshasa, imperialism had a change of heart. It should also be observed that this provincialism, speedily dubbed as 'ethic' by the Western mass media, was of no interest to the broad masses; the first workers' organizations in the province laid no claim to ethnicity.

The hydra of ethnicity and ethnic affiliation is always ready to spring up again. In fact it reappears whenever the local ruling class is slipping and when its failure is becoming unbearable. This is clearly the case in Zaire, and perhaps not the only one in Africa. But it is not the case generally. Stable neo-colonial power is founded on a ruling class more or less united at state level: this class largely transcends ethnic grouping. A comprador class as a whole it binds its destiny to the state's and the state is its means of exerting local power. Doubtless the individual components of this class may seek to 'build a following' in their region of origin. For want of power or the desire to use the 'normal' political means (as defence of social interests and conflict over programmes are barred by the widespread system of single pseudo-parties serving comprador development), they may appeal to ethnic or pseudo-ethnic solidarities. This kind of manoeuvre is limited in effect and is only serious in case of global failure and acute conflicts for 'succession' to a broken power, when imperialism has itself decided to switch horses.

The political conclusion to be drawn from this critique of ethnicity is self-evident. It can be summarized in two phrases: respect diversity, and be united despite it.

Respecting diversity means giving up empty talk of a power pretending to be what it is not, asserting 'national interest' (frequently betrayed) by appearing to internalize the ideology of the nation-state. It means accepting that there are social realities, primarily classes (although the authorities often deny their existence in order to deprive them of autonomous expression), but also gender, religious communities, regions and sometimes even ethnic groups. A social reality exists when individuals are conscious of it and desire to express it; no right has higher value than such expression. Scientific analysis may provide an understanding of the objective conditions that create this reality, but it does not justify giving 'prior warrant' to its expression. It is not the duty of thinkers and researchers (any more than of the authorities) to decree whether a reality (ethnic or otherwise) exists or not. That right belongs only to the people and to them alone, those really concerned with the issue.

A recognition of diversity does not mean allowing fragmentation through endless secession. On the contrary it must be the jumping-off point for an appeal to unity. This is the only prospect that is bound to be favourable to the development of the popular forces. But an appeal to unity remains hollow unless it is associated with a denunciation of the global and local system that, while not always and inevitably responsible for all the 'differentiations', is ready to exploit them to break the unity of the popular forces.

The cultural dimension of development in Africa and the Third World

For the following we draw on the analysis made by our colleague Faysal Yachir. His text was published with two others, Samir Amin on Islamic ideology and Mario de Andrade and Maria do Ceu Carmoreis on black African ideologies.[6] We shall not reiterate the two texts here but return to the issues they raise.

The now widely acknowledged failure of development policies followed in Africa has provoked a renewed interest in culture. Cultural issues, until recently regarded as secondary, are seen by an increasing number of researchers as an essential aspect of social change, or as the fundamental issue in development.

This irruption of culture on to the field of economic and social reflection is primarily a reflection of the recent evolution of African societies, who in some way have spontaneously included cultural issues in the forefront of their concerns. The new acuteness of linguistic questions, the religious revival in its various forms, the demand by minorities for the right to be different, or from another angle the tensions undermining traditional values, status and roles, bear witness to the relevance of questions of individual and collective identity. But this irruption of culture on to the field of economic and social reflection also arises from increasing dissatisfaction with the limitations of analytical force in the conventional approaches, in particular of sociology and development economics.

The reason why researchers studied economics and sociology rather than culture was not that economic and social issues seemed more serious. The explanation is rather the compartmentalization of the social sciences and their largely apologetic nature have led to a separation of culture from economics, with the notion that the former should adapt almost automatically to the latter. Furthermore when culture was explicitly taken into account, it was to stress its negative character as an obstacle to development. If this dichotomous approach is nowadays challenged with renewed vigour and in more and more circles, it is because its methodological premises prevent account being taken of the increasingly obvious embroilment of culture with economics.

An awareness of the crucial importance of this embroilment of culture with economics is based on two observable intuitions warranting scientific elaboration. The first is that culture in the broad sense deeply affects if not the character of economic systems at least the logic of their operation, and this impact goes further than the influence of 'traditional values' on the diffusion of attitudes of the capitalist kind – the principal theme of functionalist sociology of modernization. The second intuition is that economics, or more precisely economic (and social) changes induce phenomena of acculturation and deculturation, namely change the culture. The relationship between culture and economics is dialectic rather than functionalist or structural.

An interest in the cultural aspect of development is not merely identifying an omission and studying cultural issues after a study of the cultural aspect of economic changes.

An attempt should be made to clear up the interaction or rather embroilment of culture with economics at three distinct levels: ideology, society and state. The social changes experienced by the African countries in the past two or three decades in part reflect the impact of policies implemented by the governments or parties, which were – and are – strongly influenced by the great ideological constructs of anti-colonial Africa. Pan-Africanism throughout the continent, sub-Saharan ideologies of negritude and 'consciencism, pan-Islamism and pan-Arabism in Egypt and the Maghreb' fill the ideological horizon for Africa in the 1950–70 period. Whatever the means of justifying government policies, under the label of 'African' and 'Arab' socialisms or whatever the aspirations to dignity and freedom of the broad strata of population, these ideologies have for an era provided the fundamental bench-mark for action by individuals and groups. Research into the cultural aspect of African development must begin with an analysis of these ideologies and their complex relation to social and economic practice. Among the matters we regard as important here is the relationship these ideologies and the perception of development issues have with the corresponding formulation of economic and social strategies.

By contrast nationalism and Marxism can be seen as minority ideologies in Africa, if not as the explicit ideologies of state authorities, at least as mobilizing myths commanding the broad adherence of peoples. In some countries, particularly those that have experienced an armed struggle for national liberation, nationalism and to a lesser extent Marxism have had a strong impact, sometimes outreaching the ideologies of pan-Africanism, negritude or pan-Arabism. Moreover, nationalism and Marxism have often been in competition, before and since political independence, a competition for power and influence, but also in recruitment and programmes. It is possible to discern within this broad framework the history of troubled relations between national movements and communist parties in Africa, but only passing interest has been shown in a comparative analysis of the themes and structure of the nationalist and communist ideologies in the context of African countries, any more than interest has been shown in the way either revealed a continuity and/or break with the more widespread African ideologies. In particular, few researchers have tried to consider the two ideologies from the point of view of their comparative bearing on dependence and under-development in Africa. Finally, for more than a decade, Marxism has become the state ideology in a fair number of African countries and this factor makes it necessary to reconsider the relation between nationalism and communism in modern African history.

The recent evolution of African societies has enriched the gamut of ideologies in three main directions. The religious revival, in its various forms, from new syncretisms to Islamic fundamentalism, is to be seen nearly everywhere in Africa, to the degree that a certain acculturation to the capitalist West proceeds and there are more obvious failures and impasses in the development strategies pursued. In the Arab countries more particularly, fundamentalism appears as a 'cultural' come-back on economics and is the reaction of an indigenous culture threatened by the accelerated Westernization of the society and its elites. This truncated but real Westernization is not supported by an explicit cultural ideology, but increasingly by the vehicle of the language of neo-liberal ideology on a world scale. The contrast beween fundamentalism and 'Westernization' is not as clear-cut as might be thought from the strict letter of fundamentalist discourse. If fundamentalism emerged as a cultural protest against economics, it has its economic foundation, whereby the circumstances of its growth are largely conditioned by the forms of social and economic change. In the same way, if 'Westernization' comes with the drift of development strategies and is conveyed by neo-liberal economic discourse, it has its cultural foundation too, since it has arisen on the basis of the dissolution, albeit incomplete, of established social relations, through the diffusion of commodity and capitalist categories in the society. Finally, possibly in conjunction with the ideological duo of fundamentalism and Westernization, new ideologies emerge on particularist bases as part of the process of constituting or consolidating nations. The national formations must be distinguished between those where nationalism has been or is an active ideology, and more recent or weaker formations where the frontiers inherited from colonialism delineate a highly heterogeneous social space in ethnic, linguistic or religious terms. In either case, specific characteristics and particularities are asserted to a varying degree. An analysis of these new ideological phenomena, of very varying degrees of completeness and spread, should be carried out, with the corresponding bid to relate them to the economic and social changes occurring in Africa in the 1970s and 1980s.

A study of the cultural aspect of development should begin from a second point of view, that of relations between culture and society. Three key issues can be identified here, the search for identity, the relation between labour and technology, and the role of intellectuals, which all come back to the interaction between cultural change and economic transformation.

The question of identity, of individuals and groups and broader collectives, is at the very heart of the cultural aspect of development. The economic changes, while bearing the stamp of the pre-capitalist cultures, alter beliefs, attitudes and behaviour that define the culture as the world of being of the peoples. In the circumstances of dependent capitalism, economic development brings a 'crisis of values' of unprecedented extent and ferocity. In the West and Japan, material development has the support of internal transformation of social and human relations, a transformation achieved over a long period so that there was no break but a complex process of selective repossession of former cultural components within the context of technological and economic development. Modern capitalism is deeply rooted in a truly Western (or Japanese) tradition that it has in turn invigorated, namely in a direction favourable to technological creativity and economic initiative. In Africa, the historical circumstances of capitalist penetration, then expansion, have from the outset had a contrary effect, as economic development confronts local cultures and the transformation of social and human relations is essentially effected from outside, often with the help of ferocious violence. Identity, in this case, rather than being gradually broken down and rebuilt to productive effect, is more or less ferociously destroyed, without putting in place compensatory processes of production of new cultural components, capable in turn of supporting accumulation and innovation. Nowadays the crisis of values in African societies has reached a staggering pitch, because of the development of capitalism and because of the inadequacy ,of this development. We find accelerated urbanization, the bringing of a significant proportion of the population into the wage sector, the spread of modern forms of production to the countryside, external competition, along with the break-up of population balance, unemployment and social differentiation tending to disrupt the traditional settings of popular culture, with the latter process assisted by the various Western cultural influences. As in the West, the individual climbs out of the disaggregation of traditional collectives, but here climbs into an atmosphere of confusion. The decomposition of social values has more the effect of changing them than of purely and simply destroying them, for the reason that mentalities are slow to change, but also that the evolution of social and economic structures fails to give rise to a coherent entity. The diffusion of new reference systems, new social criteria and new aspirations occurs at the same time as a revaluation of traditional values of new import. This spontaneous repossession of values in a rapidly changing economic context is purely a holding operation, despite its many facets ranging from the simple dullardness of the collective psychology to metaphysical reactivation before the disenchantment of seeing the real world 'in the icy waters of selfish calculation'.

The crisis of values for the majority is matched by a profound cultural alienation of the social elite, which comes back to the issue of the formation of an intelligentsia. It is of the essence of the cultural problem, since only the intelligentsia is capable of helping a society to become conscious of itself and take on board its own modernization. The direct political role of the intelligentsia in the successful modernizations of the 19th and 20th centuries is open to discussion but its role as social critic has always been crucial. In most African societies the intelligentsia has not yet been able to form itself. The growing number of graduates and intellectual workers on mainly technical duties does not suffice to form an autonomous and critical corps of intellectuals. The circumstances of training the elites in Africa do not relate only to such economic factors as the relative breadth of the production and administration systems to absorb them. They also relate to the cultural remoteness induced by alienation of the elites from their peoples. It is an alienation that comes first from privileged access to the goods and services of the modern economy, but is more affected by the extraverted character of the educational systems. Just as it has not formed an intelligentsia, the intellectual elite has been unable to construct an alternative cultural model to the more or less enticing Western model whose baton it carries. A good indicator of this incapacity is shown by the relative scantiness of autonomous social study by Africans about their condition and future, as a result of cultural, scientific and technical dependence on Western metropolises and their sloth. In one way the cultural alienation of the elites is an aspect of the crisis of values in society, just as the problems of collective identity are aggravated by the alienation of elites and lack of an intelligentsia. Analysis of 'mass culture' should be closely tied to that of 'elite culture'.

The question of technology is at the heart of the problematic of identity, since creativity in all forms and technological creativity in particular, is one of the main manifestations of the identity of peoples. Throughout history communities have stamped their own genius on their physical environment even when the level of development of the forces of production was very low. In this sense, technology is culture, even when the technological underdevelopment of ancient societies frequently corresponds to and nurtures a mythological overdevelopment. In the Western and Japanese societies of today, technological innovation carries the clear imprint of attitudes, tastes, and more broadly, values appropriate to these societies. In the kind of products, the conception of forms, the working methods, the universality of capitalist norms of consumption and production adapts to a certain diversity reflecting national cultures. In Africa, the development of colonial and post-colonial capitalism has broken the unity between culture and technology, thus inhibiting national creativity at the same time as it imposed an alienating technology. If the impact of Western technology on economic structures is often taken into consideration, its impact in the field of culture is much more rarely so. Furthermore if technology is culture, modern Western culture has become technical, in that it tends to reshape itself in the light of the appropriate conditions for technical innovation. But in Africa, the culture has largely lost its former power of control over nature without managing to achieve a new technological creativity. These complex issues, of vital importance for the future, deserve a more detailed treatment, but a beginning can be made with an analysis of particular aspects, for example the problem of language in the policy of technical apprenticeship, the representations, attitudes and behaviour of workers in industry, or the patterns of creativity in the informal sector.

A third axis of possible research is the relation between culture and the state. Two main themes are relevant at this level, the cultural policies implemented by the African states and the political conditions for cultural development.

By cultural policy here is meant properly speaking "cultural policies" that could usefully be subjected to a critical survey, but particularly education, training and scientific research policies, plus policies to encourage national languages. It is obvious that the policies of education and training determine the level and character of educational service and its social catchment. Concern should be shown for the curriculum, language of instruction, literacy campaigns, and to the role of the educational systems, as an instrument of cultural, economic and technical development rather than as a means of social promotion and reproduction.

The issue of national languages deserves particular attention, as the experience of encouraging the use of national languages to the north and south of the Sahara is sufficiently long-established as to lend itself to survey.

The second theme, the political conditions for cultural development, has in fact a bearing on democracy. Political democracy is evidently a precondition for the free expression of cultural pluralism, the most commonly found situation in Africa. In general, cultural pluralism, whether on an ethnic, linguistic or religious basis, is repressed by state authorities out of fear of imperilling the attempt to build or consolidate the nation. But such repression often leads to an exacerbation of cultural pluralism as the latter is expressed in clandestine forms even more perilous for national unity.

In a more general way, democratization of political and social life bolsters a dynamic cultural development, since it promotes discussion and encourages scientific, technical, literary and artistic innovation. In many African countries control over the press and media and censorship of literature, theatre, cinema or popular music works to sustain a cultural waste and reproduce dependence on the West. A question mark over the frustration of modern cultural expression in Africa by political authoritarianism is therefore increasingly pertinent.

The cultural dimension: the example of the crisis in the Arab world today – the end of the Nahda?[7]

Think back to the image we could have of the probable or desirable future for the Arab world some 30 years ago, or even in the 19th century. Most Arab thinkers envisaged a modernized society, very similar to Western society in state organization, production and life styles, and an active partner in the modern world. As they saw it, this modernization, far from effacing Arab culture and language or undermining religious beliefs would have the opposite effect of showing their purity by freeing them from the stigmas of the decadent centuries of Ottoman domination. Without illusions as to Europe's hostility to the plan, these Arab thinkers were gradually radicalized along with the national liberation movement, and adopted an anti-imperialist element open to a perception of a more or less socialist future. A quarter of a century ago achievement of this aim seemed to be on the threshold. Nasserism appeared to be transferring the plan from the Egyptian domain to the entire Arab nation.

A description of the more recent reality – civil war in Lebanon, the Gulf war, Israel's arrogant expansionism, the rise of Islamic fundamentalism and anachronistic inward-looking, abandonment of the aim of Arab unity not only by the authorities but also by the popular masses, the impact of oil, petrodollars and the Gulf's influence – might have seemed a scarcely possible nightmare. What is the explanation of this step backward? What we offer here brings together in part a general analysis of capitalist expansion and in part a particular analysis of the plan of the Arab Nahda. The story is not unique.

Is not the entire modern history of the Third World one of repeated – and always abortive – attempts to establish a bourgeois national state as a partner in the world capitalist system? Time after time the failure leads to a closer integration into the infernal mechanism of worldwide expansion, renewing and widening the inequality inherent to capitalist expansion and showing more clearly the objective necessity for national and popular delinking to launch the long and complex transition 'beyond capitalism'.

Surely the worldwide expansion has reached the point where it dooms the Third World bourgeoisies to abandon their own plan once and for all, and accept 'neo-comprador' subordination. Nahda was the singular ideological and cultural form of the plan for Egypt and the Arab world; its time is past. The shortcomings and limitations of the Nahda, and the particular challenges confronting the region (oil and Zionism) will be discussed within this general framework.

The first manifestations of the modern Arab national plan precede what is generally called Nahda (whose first usage is attributed to Jamal al-Din al-Afghani, in the second half of the 19th century). In Egypt at the end of the 18th century, in the era of Ali Bey al-Kabir, these first manifestations were to crystallize in the reign of Mohamed Ali. They had a pan-Arab dimension from the start, clearly expressed by Ibrahim Pasha. From the start too, they expressed a plan of building a modern national state, that is, an objectively bourgeois state. It was, therefore, a bourgeois nationalist plan in the full meaning of the phrase – without any pejorative sense.

The most widespread view of the development of capitalism relies on the thesis that the societies of Africa and Asia before the irruption of colonialism were not capable on their own of transformation into capitalist societies, as they were still at a too backward state or were 'blocked' in the impasse of the notorious 'Asiatic' mode of production. Without repeating here our overall critique of this bizarre Western–centric reduction, we merely recall that in some non-European societies as advanced as Europe on the eve of the capitalist explosion, the struggles under way were precisely over the possible passage to capitalism, but aborted by European expansion which went on to distort the further development of these societies and peripheralize them. Egypt is one such case.

Current historiography treats the Mameluke regime on the eve of the French landing as a despotic and mouldering feudal regime and the country as abandoned to decline for several centuries. Ali Bey al-Kabir's attempt, in the second half of the 18th century, to turn Egypt into a modernized Arab state autonomous in regard to the Ottomans and to Europe, a kind of dress-rehearsal for what Mohamed Ali would do – in part at least – in the first half of the 19th century, does not fit into this historiography. It is attributed entirely to the individual's 'personality', that of an 'enlightened despot', along the lines of Peter the Great, just as the later modernization of Egypt was attributed entirely to the will of Pasha Mohamed Ali. But if in the latter instance the Napoleonic model may be cited as inspiration, there is no 'external' explanation for what inspired Ali Bey.

Eighteenth-century Egypt was flourishing, a bustling prelude to the imminent birth of capitalism. The Mamelukes were no longer the basic military cells of a tribute-paying organization and had become a political aristocracy in close symbiosis with the great trade and manufacture of an Egypt close to the European mercantilist model. The main class struggles were between the embryonic grand bourgeoisie (Mameluke aristocracy and great mercantile fortunes) and the numerous plebeian mass of the middle bourgeoisie: notables, artisans and rich peasants. Expansion of the internal and external market had the effect in the Delta of reinforcing private ownership of land, accentuating the differentiation between a (kulak) peasant bourgeoisie and poor and wage-earning peasants, just as it disrupted the urban corporations and began the transition from crafts to manufacture. All these violent social changes underlay the collapse of the old ideological, moral and religious order, and the birth of a new culture. The key question that arises is what was the underpinning for the reinforced and modernized central authority required for the transition to capitalism? The Mameluke aristocracy tried to replace the support of the Egyptian plebeian bourgeoisie with an alliance with foreign mercantilist interests, with particular emphasis on the minority big traders (Christians and Jews in the Ottoman Empire, agents and protégés of the French who had taken over from the Italian cities). Within this struggle between two unequally advanced mercantilisms (of France and Egypt) there were already two lines: one to lead to a crystallization of an autonomous Egyptian capitalism and another to lead to subsequent 'peripheralization'.

France's invasion has its place in this struggle. Here again bourgeois historiography is inadequate, as it attributes Napoleonic glory entirely to the logic of military strategy (cutting the route to India) that was unreliable (as it left Britain in control of the sea). What is overlooked is France's anxiety to reconstitute an empire after the losses of 1763, because of its shortfall in cereals: France's agricultural backwardness was a handicap to overall capitalist development of the country, as the famine on the eve of the French Revolution shows. Marseilles imported from Egypt the cereals needed in the French Midi. The conflict for control of a rapidly growing trade was between French and Egyptian mercantilisms. After Egypt's failure, France continued its objective with the conquest of Algeria from 1830 on.

In Egypt Napoleonic power was initially supported by the plebeian bourgeoisie in order to destroy the Mameluke state. But when it put Egyptian trade under its tutelage by turning to Levantine Christians, it alienated and eventually lost that bourgeoisie.

Mohamed Ali did the same. He relied on the big foreign traders and Levantine Christians as he sought to modernize his administration and army with the assistance of foreign technicians, relinquishing broad reliance on the plebeian bourgeoisie. Rather the reverse, he destroyed their economic status. In the countryside he imposed a return to the tribute-paying mode of production and, through a trading monopoly, established control over production and markets. In the towns he replaced the private enterprise of the bourgeoisie with state manufacture. Why this option? Largely of course because he observed the wide gap between Egypt and Europe and that modernization of the army, the essential instrument to give Egypt autonomy, would be costly. He was therefore obliged to make a heavy exaction on the peasantry and appropriate the utmost from the profits of industry and trade, and could not therefore share with the rural and urban plebeian bourgeoisie. But he then became the prisoner of the bureaucratic aristocracy, the only class he could rely on, and in the end to succumb to their exclusive control of the countryside. In 1837 he began handing out the land to the members of the aristocracy – in the form of *tchifliks* – in a process completed by Khedive Ismail, and establishing a comprador bourgeois agrarian aristocracy in Egypt and turning Egypt into an export cotton plantation. For Mohamed Ali's option also had the effect of condemning the country to eventual external dependence. It was the combination of this factor with external aggression in 1840 that brought the attempt down and drove Egypt inexorably along the path of peripheralization.

The abortion of Mohamed Ali's plan was followed by a series of attempts to reconcile the establishment of a modernized Egyptian national state (a rejection of the aspect of Arab unity) with integration in the capitalist economy. Khedive Ismail tried this first with the deliberate option for cotton specialization. It is well known that this attempt ended up with exploitation of Egyptian indebtedness by European finance capital and then the occupation of Egypt in 1882. Then the Wafdist liberal bourgeoisie tried it in the aftermath of the 1919 revolution. It is also well-known that despite progress in social organization (political independence, attempts at imposing parliamentarianism on the King and the British, educational development, as so on) and in the economy (the industrialization bid by the Misr Bank), Egypt was unable to overcome its 'underdevelopment' to put itself forward as a genuine partner in the world capitalist system. Nasser's plan tried it again in new circumstances that made it become more radical, through bitter conflict with imperialism, more open to a socialist perspective and ready to recover the Arab dimension hitherto lost.

Before Nasserism, power in Egypt was in the hands of social classes that may only loosely be described as bourgeois, despite their integration in the world capitalist system. The same was true elsewhere in the Arab world which, in the Maghreb, was still colonial as elsewhere in Asia and Africa until well after the Second World War. But gradually in the 1950s and 1960s, power in the newly independent states passed to the local bourgeoisie through various processes (land reform, nationalizations, *coups d'état*, among others); and this bourgeoisie tended to become the local hegemonic class. The bourgeoisie in power then tried to advance its plan for building a bourgeois national state as a partner in the world capitalist system. In the Arab world, attempts at capitalist modernization, previously exceptional like those of Eygpt (the only examples are the attempt of Kheireddine Pasha in Tunisia in the 19th century and of the liberal bourgeoisie in Syria and in Iraq in the 1930s) became widespread. We have described this as the Bandung plan.

Analysis of evolution in internal politics and international politics would of itself provide an understanding of the historical process that led to the failure of the crystallization of new autocentric capitalist centres from peripheral departure points. An examination of the ideology of the attempts in question would further illuminate the external/internal forces dialectic. In this respect the Nahda as an example is highly illuminating.

We return to the 18th century and the first half of the 19th in Egypt. The cultural stage was filled by the conflict between Ahl al-Hadith and Ahl al-Kalam, which too many historians regard as nothing but an absurd religious squabble. On the contrary, it marked the beginning of a potential reform of Islam, similar in many ways to the Protestantism–Catholicism conflict. The stress placed on discussion of the Hadith (the sayings and traditions of the Prophet – or attributed to him) encouraged an inventive spirit allowing the adaptation of the religion to the needs of the time. In reopening the 'gate of effort' (*bab al-ijtihad*), there was to be found a true Calvinist interpretation of Islam (and all the Eurocentrism known as necessary to believe, along with Weber, in Protestant exclusivity). At the same time in the popular milieu of the victims of the social changes underway the critique was mixed with a promising mystical odour, in the tradition of some Sufism. The analogy is inescapable with the currents that criss-crossed British religious ideology in the mercantilist era (Anglicans, Calvinists and radicals – Levellers). By contrast, the state bureaucratic power, such as Mohamed Ali's, preferred the Kalam, that is, a closed system of formally logical scholarly philosophy. Gradually, however, this turned into pragmatism: the all-encompassing philosophy was relinquished in favour of acceptance of individual sciences. This evolution went along with peripheralization and is a good indicator of the comprador bourgeoisie's acceptance of a subordinate role. Pragmatic 'moderation' with a sprinkling of orthodox, conventional and conservative Islam was to become the creed of this acculturated bourgeoisie.

From the middle of the 19th century the process of integration of the Arab and Ottoman world in the world capitalist economy was such that the scope for autonomy enjoyed by Mohamed Ali's Egypt shrank to the point of virtually vanishing. The movement of reaction to this colonization was principally determined by rejection of colonization and thus acquisition of a prevailing anti-imperialist dimension. This was the case of the Nahda.

This movement is often reduced to its religious dimension through an emphasis on successive Muslim reformers: Jamal al-Din al-Afghani, Mohamed Abdu and Rachid Rida. This is, in fact, an intolerable simplification. Nahda is also a modernizing movement in language and culture, society and politics. In the field of language, Egypt and Syria underwent a veritable revolution creating an effective instrument for the revival of Arab unity. The critique of customs, to be found on a reading of Qassem Amin's writings on women's liberation and codifications of juridical and administrative systems was no less important. This all led quite naturally to a modernist view of politics. The national movement in Egypt, far from being exclusively 'anti-foreigner', was, from the end of the 19th century, imbued with the ideas of the Western bourgeoisie; its most radical wing encountered socialism even before 1914. It was to be the same to a varying degree with the liberation movements that would later come to the fore in other Arab areas.

Consideration of this chapter of religion reveals the historical limitations and shortcomings of the Nahda. The latter did not overcome the duality for which Mohamed Ali opted: the juxtaposition of modern ideas in the civil domain and a moderately conservative interpretation of Islam. These historical limitations explain the gradual drift from reformist readings to the current anachronistic fundamentalism. This is why it may be useful to begin with an examination of the actual language of this history, with a study of the propositions of fundamentalism.

The fundamentalist state of mind looks at history from the standpoint of another language than that of a rationalism seeking the reasons for the evolutions in the real world. A particular view of society is put forward, that is endowed with the virtues of being able to resolve once and for all the problems of society and humankind. To reject this view is to opt for Evil against Good. History is regarded as the locus of this confrontation.

In contrast with the rationalist point of view, the prolonged historical resistance by those religions that have been able to withstand social change shows their flexibility. This capacity to outlive the historical circumstances of their birth makes it impossible to speak of 'Christianity' or 'Islam', as Christians or Muslims do. As social phenomena there are Christianities, Islams, which have been a living reality to Christians and Muslims at various times and places. Divergent interpretations of observances, sects and schisms, *de facto* differences of attitude to the role accorded to the fundamental value system in social life, all bear witness to this. The fundamentalists are aware of this malleability, but reject it: the betrayal of principles worries them more than an explanation of the malleability.

The fundamentalists are not primarily interested in knowing why things have been and are what they are. What interests them more is to know how things have moved away from principles. They apply this method with much vigour if not rigour when they examine their own history, that of the Muslim world in this instance. By contrast, when they venture into the history of others, the history of Christianity and Europe for example, they are no longer impelled by a concern to distinguish the moments and attitudes that accord with their principles from those that betray them, and they seem more open to reason in understanding the evolution. But this other history is of little interest to them, since it has nothing to teach them; they are concerned only to the extent that Europe has had an impact on their own lives, by imposing its universal order through its imperialism.

An examination of the view of the past held by the fundamentalists is essential for anyone who seeks to understand how they pose the questions of today and how they articulate their responses into a plan whose feasibility can then be considered.

According to the fundamentalist reading, the history of 14 centuries of the Muslim peoples is little more than the history of their betrayal of principles. As soon as the Prophet was dead, the 'deviation' began. It was marked by the accentuation of material inequality, the appropriation of land and wealth for the benefit of a minority who monopolize and abuse power. But the 'deviation' is never explained, merely noted. The question remains unanswered: could Islam have avoided the evolution it has undergone? Could the small, relatively poor community, organized first as a sect at Mecca then as a city-state at Medina, have preserved its real mode of organization once the opulent Byzantine and Sassanian Orient was integrated into a great state?

The rest of the history of the Muslim peoples is, according to the fundamentalists, no more than a sorry tale of betrayal of principles. The condemnation is total, without nuances or exceptions. Philosophical debates are impious, condemnation covers all Arabo-Muslim philosophy and there is vilification of the interpretations by the Arab liberal bourgeoisie who wanted to revive the reputation of the 'centuries of Muslim enlightenment' (Mohamed Heykal, Taha Husayn, the Nahda of the 19th century and the Muslim reformers, the efforts at opening up by the Azhar and so on, are treated as manifestations of betrayal). A fortiori, it is easy to imagine how the fundamentalists regard the attempts at a reinterpretation of the 'heritage', that is, of this philosophy, in terms of struggles between progressive ideas and those of conservative mysticism.

On this basis, the fundamentalists believe that the choice before the Muslim societies is: an Islamic society or a non-Islamic society? But if there is no 'one' undeniable Islamic response to any of the questions life poses to our societies, there are always various, differing, responses that may well be justifiable in terms of compatibility with the dogmas of Islam. That is why the fundamentalists are destined to recruit across the widest spectrum of political attitudes: from the right to the left. That is why they are destined to tear themselves apart, as can be seen day after day, without really understanding why they are incapable of forming an unambiguous social plan. For Islam, according to them, is different and specific since it does not separate the religious (faith) from the social (organization of power, family, economic life). This unity was certainly a fact at the time of the birth of Islam. Islam was certainly an option (among other possibilities) and was chosen by the Arab society of the 7th century, facing its own problems. The unity has certainly been maintained subsequently in the Muslim world; although, if the faith has changed little, the social life associated with it has undergone giant transformations.

But is that something specific and unique? The European societies of the Middle Ages and the Ancien Regime also believed that they were 'Christian' in the sense that they could not imagine a separation between their religious faith and the forms of their social life. The faith itself was, in our opinion, little different from that of Islam, or at least the differences separating it from Christianity do not explain the differences separating the social lives of Muslim societies (through the ages) from those of Christian societies (likewise through the ages). The principles to regulate social life associated with each of these two faiths are equally flexible and have demonstrated this through their adaptation to social change.

Fundamentalism postulates the Islamic society–non-Islamic society opposition as an absolute. By this token, it prevents itself understanding what the non-Islamic societies are, as evidently they cannot be reduced to a single unity through time and space. In particular, to define 'modern society' as merely 'non-Islamic' makes it impossible to understand what it is. Fundamentalism's explanation of the modern 'non-Islamic' world is drawn from a mythical picture of 'Christendom' that bears no relation to its real history. According to this explanation, Christianity is an individualist religion that does not concern itself with the organization of society. A modern Protestant might perhaps subscribe to this interpretation of what Christianity must be, but the Catholic Church of the Middle Ages would not recognize itself there.

The fundamentalists, taking this position, are obliged to deny any social reality other than the religious. One is a Muslim or one is not. Among other things national reality disappears from the analysis. It is an old debate. Since the 19th century the peoples of the Arab and (largely) Muslim Orient have been asking themselves: what are we in the face of European imperialism? On what bases can we unite to resist it? As Ottoman subjects, Muslim believers or members of the Arab nation (or nations)? Islam, like any other social reality, may be the binding force, in certain circumstances. In Pakistan, quite evidently, it is synonymous with the nation, since the latter is nothing more than a non-Hindu but Muslim Indian nation. But in the Orient, history seems to have determined another social reality for the benefit of nationality. The (Arabic) language seems to be the unifying factor, going further than religious diversity among other factors (since there are Christian Arabs).

Space does not permit a closer examination of the evolution that led from Jamal al-Din al-Afghani and Mohamed Abud to Sayed Qotb and current fundamentalism by way of Rachid Reda and the foundation of the Muslim Brothers. Just as it does not allow a closer examination of the current debates on the question of the 'heritage' (*al tiras*), its character and internal contradictions, and the discussions and polemics on Arab–Islamic philosophy of the Middle Ages. In brief, let us say that our views on these issues may be summarized in the following three propositions.

First: Islam as a social reality (and not as a religious belief) is, like Christianity or any other ideology, flexible and susceptible of varying interpretations according to the evolution of social needs and the strategies of the social forces confronted with the issue. There have been and will continue to be conservative readings (notably put forward by authorities *in situ*) or reformist readings just as there are readings in support of social revolution and others in support of anachronistic utopias. The danger of the latter is that they do not decide between the possible (reformist or even revolutionary) justification for social changes and (conservative or even reactionary) formalism. This gives them their appeal, but also their objective weakness. In that sense we have argued that to remain bound in this problematic is to make a choice that could lead to the society's collective suicide. There are certainly objective reasons to illuminate the drift in this direction. We have proposed two complementary lines of research on this: (i) the inadequate maturity of the Egyptian (and Arab and wider) bourgeoisie in the 19th century, whose reflection can be found in the fact that the Nahda did not decide between these readings and did not root out the anachronistic nostalgia, while the authorities since Mohamed Ali opted for duality and reformist–conservative Islam; (ii) the shortcomings of peripheral capitalist development, taking into account the amorphous local class structure, the low penetration of contemporary issues among the broad strata on the population, for example. Undoubtedly, oil earnings and the migrations accompanying the recent upsurge of the Gulf have been a factor in this turn to the past. But it is mainly a result of the despair engendered by the failure of radical national efforts. If this despair is due in part to the contradictions and internal limitations of the Nasserist plan, it should not be forgotten that Western hostility and the aggressions of its age-old weapon of Zionism are the ultimate cause. There is an element of hypocrisy on the part of the West in lamenting current Islamic fundamentalism when it has fought in every way possible against the progressive alternative.

Second proposition: the Muslim societies have in the past accomplished a first great cultural revolution, thanks to which Islam has been able to adapt to the demands of the management of advanced societies in the Orient, to make them aware of their heritage and take them forward into development. It is this first revolution that the fundamentalists 'complain' of instead of celebrating. Furthermore, for complex reasons that cannot be reduced to an 'external' factor (the Turkish conquest of the Khalifate in this instance), the Arab–Ottoman world began a long decline (this is not the place to repeat the arguments presented elsewhere on this subject). To escape this, a second cultural revolution is needed to enable Islam to adapt to the needs of the present and the future, to the capitalist world and even to its socialist supersession. There is nothing in Islam to prevent this possible evolution, but the Muslim societies have so far rejected it. The Nahda itself did not pose the question in the decisive terms required.

Third proposition: the cultural renovation and reconstruction of the Arab nation have not been welded together. Here again this is not the place to reiterate the theses we have put forward elsewhere on the concept of nation and the – necessarily peculiar – history of the Arab peoples: the movement that leads in an early phase to the tribute-paying and commodity centralization of surplus for all the Arab world, then, with decline, to its enfeeblement and fragmentation; the resulting characteristics of a 'multi-stage nation'; the reinforcement of the particular interests of the local bourgeoisies crystallized by the formation of modern Arab states in the wake of worldwide capitalism; the disaster occasioned by the oil revenue and 'wealth' of the Gulf; the inappropriateness of the ideology of formal pan-Arab nationalism, and so on.

New forms of the social movement

All observers are agreed that the organizational forms through which societal movements are expressed have begun a phase of challenge whose outcome is unpredictable. This challenge is general and affects West, East and South.[8]

For a century or more it has been customary for the particular organizational forms of various currents in society to follow the logic of a certain political practice. In the developed capitalist society this organization was based on two main axes. The first, the axis of class struggle, was a justification for the industrial working-class organization (trade unions, socialist and communist workers' parties), modelled sometimes on other popular classes (the peasant or agrarian syndicate parties, small traders' parties). The second, the axis of political ideology, was a justification for the clash between the conservative right and the reformist left. Communist powers emerged from this history, whose forms they retained, even where gradually the state–party monopoly, by calling an official halt to 'class struggle' and electoral swings, stripped them of meaning. In Africa and Asia the history of the past century has been one of polarization of the social movement around the struggle for national independence. Here the typical model was of the unifying party, with the aim of grouping the social classes and various ethnic strands into a vast, disciplined movement (often ranged behind more or less charismatic leaders) and effective in action for a single goal. The powers that emerged with independence are largely immobilized in this inheritance, with the single party–state retaining its legitimacy solely from the achievement of the aim of national independence.

These practices were rationalized by what might appear to be a scientific theory of society. The ideology of the Enlightenment was the main source of its mix of values (humanist values of freedom, well-being) and 'scientific' theories of their operation (competition between individuals governing the economic mechanism). The socialist movement, including Marxism, retained the values of the inheritance of the Enlightenment and at the same time denounced the hypocrisy of the bourgeois content of the societal plan they entailed, with a call to go beyond them – by way of reform or revolution – on the basis of class struggle. The national liberation movements were inspired by one or the other approach in varying proportions according to the aims of the leading class – or stratum – in the movement.

In the end, the two practices were put on equal footing with the notion of political rationality. It was forgotten that the social movement was differently expressed in earlier periods, in Europe and elsewhere, through the channel of religion among others. It was forgotten that even in the apparently stable West, this rationality was not strong enough to resist the violent social crisis of the 1930s when large masses were rallied under the 'irrational' banners of racism and murderous folly.

Nowadays – in three parts of the world: West, East and South – the models of management of social life penned within these organizational forms seem to have exhausted their historical potential.

In the West the consensus is so broad as to reduce the historical impact of the socialist movement and the right–left polarization. The spontaneous response of the system is the 'Americanization' of political life, that is, the organization of 'lobbies' in which partial interests are crystallized (production sectors, regions, various groupings . . .) and which, without any ideological concern for an overall plan for society, compete for scraps of power. In the East the civilian society tries to break the shell of the party–state, to provide scope for the dialectic of the genuine contradictions within the society. In the Third World the legitimacy founded on a restoration of independence has worn very thin for the younger generations.

In all cases it is striking how the speeches of the authorities are linked to the past. We have built the best available society, say the candidates to elections in the West; we just need this or that adjustment (followed by the details). We have built socialism, say the authorities in the East; we just need to improve the efficiency in this area. We have built the nation and embarked on economic development, it is said in the South; we just need to keep up the effort. Here too there is no social plan to break with the logic of current reality.

Is it any wonder in these circumstances that the expression of unsatisfied social needs takes another form? The irruption of these new forms has already begun: feminist movements, ecological movements, local community action movements (for towns and neighbourhoods), ethnic or religious community movements. Their rationale in terms of broad ideologies may be still embryonic, but it is already possible to identify certain contour lines, appealing to lines that may not be entirely new but have hitherto hardly been touched upon (such as the critique of sexism or concern with ecology), or overtly the heritage of the past down-played by the 'modern' world: hence the religious renaissance, especially of the fundamentalist currents.

Are the new forms of social expression the germ of a future very different from our contemporary world? Or just the soap bubbles of a passing crisis, bound to burst when everything returns to order?

On the former hypothesis, will the future represented by the development of these new expressions (or renewed when they draw on ancient inheritances) bring progress for humankind, or will it rather be a sign of a collapse into barbarism? André Malraux, with his well-known intelligence and pessimism, said that the 21st century would be the century of religions, meaning not only the revival of tolerant faith but also of fanatically violent conflicts. In the 1930s and 1940s Nazi barbarity had already caused it to be said that ours was an age of intolerance; but the defeat of fascism had rekindled hopes: the nightmare was over, it was only an accident on the way.

Without any doubt we share Immanuel Wallerstein's view that the old organizations' (trade unions, popular and workers' parties, national liberation movements) struggle to take power from the monopoly of the bourgeois and foreign imperialist classes, achieved it to varying degrees – through reform or revolution, negotiation or war – and had in fact accomplished a great deal, if not 'everything': the welfare state, economic development and power, national dignity.

On this view these movements, which were recently 'anti-system' to the extent that they really clashed with the existing system, have nowadays been 'recuperated' and are part of the 'system', in the sense that they have turned into relatively conservative forces unwilling that anybody should want to go 'further' than they have and above all overtake them to do more.

But what is the 'system' against which, or within which, the old or new social forces operate?

Would it be wrong to describe it as capitalist in the West and in the Third World? It has certainly not yet exceeded the limits of 'existing capitalism as the world system', that is, it has not overcome the centres–peripheries polarization. It is, therefore, a system that continues to be intolerable to the great mass of people in the Third World, with or without 'development'. For them it means the squalor of the shanty-towns, the frustrations of impossible consumer hopes, cultural humiliation, the arrogance of corrupt dictators, and sometimes simply famine. But in the West, despite the social calm procured by capitalism in its advanced centres, there is a malaise indicative of the limitations of the system's capabilities. In the countries of the East, it would seem inaccurate to describe the system as capitalist, even if it is far from the image of socialism held by the Marxism from which it seeks inspiration. There the real social forces want something else, amid the confusion of conflict between the often mixed aspirations of socialists and capitalists.

'Really existing capitalism' remains the objective obstacle to the advance of the peoples. There is no alternative to popular national transformation in Third World societies. At the same time this transformation begun by the so-called 'socialist' revolutions has not completed the agenda of aims to be achieved.

In such a case it is difficult yet to say if the 'new' movements are or are not capable of going forward, with a response to the objective challenge.

Some of the movements appear to have reached an impasse. This is the case for the religious fundamentalist revivals or the 'ethnic' communal retreats. They are symptomatic of the crisis and not solutions, exclusive products of disillusionment, and they should fold-up as soon as they show their powerlessness to meet the real challenge. That is, an expression of optimism – in contrast to Malraux's pessimism – that reason will triumph.

Other movements, however, may have a place in the reconstruction of a plan for society that, 'beyond capitalism', would, after learning form the failures of the other movements, resolve the contradictions that really existing capitalism cannot overcome.

It seems to us that this is the case whenever the 'new (or old!) movements' operate not exclusively on the ground of 'winning the state', but on that of an alternative conception of social power to be won. The choice is not between 'struggling for power or struggling for an alternative' (what?), but as to the conception of power for which the struggle is waged. The organizational forms constructed out of the prevailing 'traditional' concept of power (power = state) are bound to lose much of their legitimacy as peoples take the mettle of this conservative state.

Conversely, the organizational forms emphasizing the multiple social continent of power that must be developed will reap increasing success. In this category the theme of non-party politics, expounded in India by Rajni Kothari on the basis of Gandhian culture, could be very fruitful. Likewise the anti-authoritarianism in Latin America, where Pablo Gonzales Casanova identifies the main quality of the 'new' movements: rejection of authoritarianism in state, party or leadership, and rejection of doctrinaire aspects of ideology. This is a reaction against the heavy burden of the historical formation of the continent, and is undoubtedly a reaction that encourages progress. But similarly for the same basic reason, feminism in the West, with its aim of attacking at least some of the roots of autocracy, stems from the same logic of an alternative concept of social power. To some extent the West is in the vanguard of the new advances in the liberation of society. Whether these advances mean a penetration 'beyond capitalism', or can be 'rescued' by the social system is still wide open to argument. It seems, that at least in the medium term, the advantages of a central capitalist position are such that the movements in question will not rock the foundations of capitalist management of society.

The future of the 'new movements' is uncertain, which is why it cannot be ruled out that they will collapse in the current crisis.

Extrapolating from the propositions of Frank and Fuentes and by bringing into the open what is probably implicit in their comments, it seems to us that the 'effectiveness' of the social movement cannot be judged by the same criteria at all times. In periods of 'prosperity' (the A phases of the long cycle) the movements easily adopt centralized organizational forms. The reason for this is that they operate in a system where the rules of the game are known. They can then, according to circumstance, achieve some of their aims (pay increases for example). By contrast the periods of structural crisis (the B phases of the cycle) are marked by doubts as to the rules of the game, under challenge when the 'new order' emerging from new international and internal balances has not yet crystallized. The crisis of society must surely bring a crisis of ideologies, political practices and thereby organizational forms? But is it not precisely in those periods that the new ideological forces are crystallized, to sketch the outlines of new social plans, that, to paraphrase a famous quotation, 'by seizing the masses, become material forces'?

Notes

1. Amin, Samir, 'Nation et ethnie dans la crise', *Bulletin du FTM*, No. 6, 1986, and Amin, Samir, *Class and Nation, Historically and in the Current Crisis*, New York, Monthly Review Press, and London, Heinemann, 1980; *The Arab Nation; Delinking*, London, Zed Books.

2. Mukherjee, Ramkrishna, *The Rise and Fall of the East India Company*, New York, Monthly Review Press, 1974.

3. Vergopoulos, Kostas, *La Grèce 1920–1940*, Paris, 1970.

4. Amselle, Jean-Loup and M'Bokololo, Elikia, (eds) *Au coeur de l'ethnie: ethnies, tribalisme et Etat en Afrique*. Paris, La Découverte, 1985. Cf. our observation in 'Nation et ethnie dans la crise', op. cit.

5. See articles by J. P. Dozon, J. Razin and P. Chrétien in *Au coeur de l'ethnie*, op. cit.

6. Yachir, Faysal, 'La dimension culturelle du développement'; de Andrade, Mario and Carmoreis, Maria do Ceu, 'Dimension culturelle du développement en Afrique', *Bulletin du FTM*, No. 7, 1987.

7. See Amin, Samir, 'La fin de la Nahda', *Revue d'études Palestiniennes*, No. 19, 1986; 'Y a-t-il une économie politique du fondamentalisme islamique', *Peuples Méditerranéens*, No. 21, 1982; 'Contradictions in the Capitalist Development of Egypt', *Monthly Review*, No. 4, 1984; 'Development and the Cultural Issue', *Bulletin du FTM*, No. 7, 1987; *L'Eurocentrisme*, Paris, Economica, 1988. The crisis of Arab society (in Arabic) (Azamat al-mujtama' al-arabi), Cairo, 1985; (in Arabic), Post-capitalism, 1987.

8. On the social movement cf. Amin, S., Wallerstein, I., Arrighi, G., Frank, A. F. and Fuentes, M., collective work in preparation.

4. Complexities of International Relations: Africa's Vulnerability and External Intervention

The arguments of the preceding chapters have put a finger on the spot: the African continent is par excellence one of extreme vulnerability to foreign interference. Here we shall consider the forms and effects of this vulnerability in regard to the following questions:

(i) The economic association of African states (which form the majority in the ACP) with the European Economic Community (EEC). Does the association restrict the development options in Africa? How does it relate to Europe's global strategy? It is also worth making special mention of the peculiarities of the Franc zone.

(ii) The bloody conflicts on the continent. These conflicts arise from various internal and external factors and take varying shape. How are they inter-related? How do they relate to the global strategies of the superpowers and Europe?

(iii) The South African conflict? What are the prospects for the armed struggle waged by the South African people against the apartheid regime? How does it relate to the global prospects for Africa, particularly in the Southern African region?

(iv) The economic and political strategies of the West (and of Europe in particular) towards the Arab world. Are these strategies compatible with a unitary Arab renaissance? How do they relate to the Palestinian conflict?

African economies' vulnerability vis-à-vis the challenge of capitalism's new worldwide expansion

If the quarter century (1945–70) after the Second World War was one of worldwide expansion reaching a qualitatively new stage (with the inter-nationalization of imperialism, and US hegemony that provides the framework for this almost unprecedented upsurge), for the particular region of Europe and Africa the period was one of European construction (with an impact on southern Europe) and of development of the Arab plan for unitary and popular liberation (and its confrontation with the Palestine issue) and of independence for Africa in general. European construction, initiated with the Marshall Plan and formalized with the Treaty of Rome, which came into effect in 1958, reached a new stage with its extension to Southern Europe, not without worsening the contradictions of interest between the latter and the wealthier Europe, and in a period of crisis. The post-war upsurge has, however, already had a substantial impact on the givens of the North–South issue in Europe. For the upsurge has, with its wider world impact, entailed a substantial speeding-up of the modernization of the European peripheries to such an extent that the states of Southern Europe are now so integrated into the European and world system that it is virtually impossible for the dominant political forces of these countries to envisage a response to the crisis by a withdrawal into themselves. There is a striking illustration of this change in the contrast between the attitudes of these countries in response to the crisis of the 1930s – a semi-autarkical withdrawal of populist or fascistic bent – and the current belief that acceptance of the rules of the game of worldwide competition is 'unstoppable', as is said on the right and the left.

Nevertheless, European construction remains ambiguous in meaning and prospects; and the challenges of the current crisis, far from attenuating these ambiguities, serve rather to reveal the irresolute and indecisive attitudes of the European partners.

The European construction had, from the outset, been conceived as a necessary venture to avoid the spectre of 'communism' that has today totally disappeared, if it ever really existed. In this sense, it was conceived as an integral part of the economic, political, military and ideological strategy of US domination. European economic integration, far from aiming at the creation of a new autonomous pole competing with the United States, was conceived as a sub-set of the worldwide whole. Europe was open to the Atlantic military alliance and the penetration of the US transnationals who have played a decisive role in its economic modernization. It remains so. First since it remains under the supposed protection of the United States nuclear umbrella and has not developed an autonomous defence, in the absence of which an autonomous economy is inconceivable. With a touch of bizarre economic shortsightedness, it has been suggested that savings on military expenditure will allow a better economic performance. The intention of autonomy, which De Gaulle obviously favoured, never went beyond the stage of irresolute actions. Furthermore, in response to the challenges of the crisis, Europe has rallied behind the United States in a common Western offensive intended to 'recompradorize' the Third World.

This final ambiguity leads us to the issue of imperialism in general, and of European imperialism towards the Arab and African worlds in particular. Great Britain and France had virtually shared out the Arab and African world between them; and on the morrow of the last world war they did not yet suspect that they would have to bow to the decolonization that was imposed upon them by the liberation movement and acceptable under certain conditions to American hegemony. Decolonization did not come about without conflict, and the Algerian war was colonialism's death throe.

European construction had prepared nothing in this regard, except to put the former French colonial empire in Africa at the disposal of the capital of the Community of the Six, with collective neo-colonialism replacing the former imperial colonialism and little more. Without taking up time with issues that are treated elsewhere, it is necessary to recall here:

(i) that France has *de facto* retained privileged status in its former colonies, notably by the bias of control over the Franc zone; (ii) that the conventions of the association of the African states to the EEC show a concern for reserving privileged status for Europe in regard to American and Japanese competitors, despite the general opening-up of Africa implied by worldwide expansion; (iii) that with Britain's membership of the EEC and the association of the African states, the jockeying for influence by the various powers in Africa is even more overt; (iv) that the kind of unequal relations renewed in this framework in no sense represents progress towards the liberation of Africa and development of its peoples, but on the contrary their restriction to obsolete mining and agricultural specializations that are to Europe's advantage. In that sense Europe bears a heavy responsibility for the crystallization of the power of the new local ruling classes and thereby in the continent's economic, social and political disaster.

The European view of the Arab world, especially North Africa, scarcely goes any further, except that it had to take into account the greater stability of the local ruling classes. The association agreements, drawn up with Morocco and Tunisia, made do with providing preferential and provisional access to the European market for the countries' agricultural exports (until the integration of Southern Europe into the EEC provoked a crisis for these exports), and with relocation (also provisional) of labour-intensive (mainly textile) industries directed towards European exports (until the current crisis called these concessions into question). The strategic view implicit here plunged the Arab partners deeper in the impasse of peripheral capitalism clinging to expansion of the European centre. It was the same in the end for the other Arab countries. If the oil producers among them (Algeria, Libya, Iraq and the Gulf states) believed they could mobilize their financial resources to speed up their industrialization, their ruling classes could imagine only a kind of industrialization that would offer a new outlet for the exports of developed capitalism – European, but American and Japanese too. This could only strengthen the tendency towards worldwide expansion and not offer a decisive step towards an autocentric national or regional development. Once the crisis had come, this closer entanglement proved deeply catastrophic, as is evidenced by the external debt, rudely aggravated by the conjuncture of stagnation and the impact of the American counter-attack.

In these circumstances, Saudi Arabia, Washington's traditional client, has opted, as might be expected, for unconditional support to the financial and monetary system that is the instrument of worldwide expansion and the counter-attack aimed at restoring US hegemony. If there has been any attempt at autocentric development, it has been incomplete, erratic, limited by the very character of the ruling classes of the progressive countries engaged upon it, whether they were oil producers (Algeria and Iraq) or not (Egypt and Syria). What should be noted here is that these attempts, supported by the USSR, have been fought by the West as a whole, Europe included.

To what can one ascribe this European refusal to envisage any relations with the Arabs and Africans other than neo-imperialist relations, whether they are chiefly open to US and Japanese competition (above all when the local partner insists) or relatively reserved for the Europeans?

An examination of Europe's structural and conjunctural position in international competition sheds light on this question. Europe covers the deficit on its relations with the United States and Japan by the surplus on its exchanges with the Third World and the countries of the Eastern bloc. To remain a player in the worldwide game, Europe has to maintain unequal relations within the sphere of its particular dependencies. Europe has found the main outlet for its expansion through modernization of its own peripheries (Southern Europe to be precise) and its own internal modernization. Unlike the United States and Japan who export their capital more widely (especially to Latin America and South-East Asia) in order to dominate the process of export-oriented relocation of industry in the Third World, Europe is open to massive importation of Third World manpower necessary to keep up with the rate of its internal expansion. It is also not by chance that this immigration is, in the main, precisely by those in areas of European dependence (the Arabs, the Africans, the West Indians) that are much more affected than Latin America and South-East Asia by the unequal capitalist development that Europe's strategy entails. It is now well-known just how far this immigration has created a political atmosphere inimical to improved relations with the Third World. Finally, Europe, with a paucity of natural resources in comparison with the United States, attaches much greater importance to securing its supplies. As it has renounced autonomous military powers, Europe has condemned itself to dependence upon American good will, and relies only on its rapid intervention forces (directed against the Third World of course) that are now almost entirely the essence of the European military vision.

All this inspires little confidence in the European talk of the Third World, along the lines of a Euro-Arabo-African 'trialogue'. We should not necessarily go so far as to conclude that it would be better to be dependent directly on the masters of the world – hegemonic imperialism – than on its lieutenants. That would leave out of account the military dimension of the problem, and rule out the possibility of internal change, less difficult to imagine in Europe perhaps than in the United States.

Does the crisis open new and different prospects for Euro-Arab relations? How will the conflict of economic interests henceforth between Europe and the United States be resolved, or the East–West and North–South conflicts? We shall consider these questions in Chapter 8.

Some specific aspects of Africa's economic integration in the world system, ACP-EEC association and Euro-American mercantile conflict[1]

The Berlin Act of the 1880s divided the African continent that was almost entirely subject to direct colonialism by the European powers, mainly Britain, France, Belgium and Portugal. Already by that time Britain's hegemony was declining, and until 1945 the world system was marked by constant conflict between the main imperial powers over the inheritance. It is understandable that from 1880 to 1945, the British and French metropolises should treat their colonies as preserves. The crisis of the 1930s further emphasized these 'imperial boltholes' by giving the Sterling area and Franc zone a system of strict preferences. But, at the same time, it must be admitted that Africa as a whole (apart from South Africa and North Africa) played only minor subordinate roles in imperialist exploitation of the world, in comparison with Asia and Latin America. As can be seen, the primitive forms of the exploitation of peasant labour reduced the potential size of the colonial African market. Colonization in Africa, predicated on the exploitation of mineral resources, gave no thought to industrialization and intensified agriculture.

But by the end of the Second World War the United States emerged as the new, world hegemonic power, and in this capacity insisted on relinquishment of the preserves; this was its motive for 'anti-colonialism'. Britain and France tried for a while to resist American pressure, and the adventurist Suez War of 1956 marks the end of their colonial nostalgia. The Franco-British defeat in this adventure hastened the process of decolonization of Africa, at the same time as it was an encouragement to join the path of 'European construction' inaugurated in the Treaty of Rome signed in 1957. As London was for a long time blackballed from membership of the EEC, Paris had to play the decisive political role, even if the gradual rebirth of Germany was to shift the centre of gravity of the European economy to the east of the Rhine. France brought as dowry to the EEC its African colonies, not without first ensuring the permanence of its own political and control, among other means by maintaining the rigid structures of the Franc zone. The conventions of association between the newly independent African countries and the EEC put a legal garb on European privileges in Africa, while the dual membership of former British colonies and other African countries in this association, and of Britain in the EEC, broadens the Euro-African association. But if for a decade or so there was nothing more remarkable on this theme, the general crisis the world system entered from the 1970s reopened the discussion. New prospects for reorganization were opened. The decline of US hegemony, beginning in the crisis, put on to the agenda contradictory reactions from its partners in the world system. Would Europe embark on a road ensuring it greater collective autonomy with regard to Washington? Would it therefore envisage a tightening-up of neo-imperial control over Africa? Or would it rather commit its future to a polycentric approach more favourably balanced towards the Third World, accept revision of its privileged links with Africa and agree to support a process of autocentric popular development to the south of the

Mediterranean and the Sahara? The entire ambiguity of the Euro-African association comes within this purview.

The significance of the Euro-African association goes beyond the limited framework of the association 'agreements'. The Yaoundé and Lomé conventions grant preferences on the European market for some African products (those that do not compete with European agricultural products), and – in the other direction – some trading advantages to the European partners. But in fact these 'mutual advantages' are virtually negligible. The conventions envisaged financial aid from Europe to Africa. But, so far, this has been scarcely more than to carry on the bilateral aid that the former metropolises would probably have gone on supplying the states, which it must be said are often client states. The conventions also envisaged 'establishment rights' ensuring that the African countries would be open to European capital. But so far, to our knowledge, Africa is not closed to other capital (notably the American); moreover, the European negotiator has never denied that these establishment rights were not synonymous with an open door, and the states could set – even strict – limits on their extent, and control the investments in question, provided that they put their European partners on an equal footing with third parties (American or Japanese). In other words, the African countries could determine that the 'association' should be devoid of content: a symbolic preference would be enough, without excluding control over foreign trade or over investments by local authorities, in return for which the states might benefit from financial and technical aid they could still turn down. Their sovereignty therefore remained virtually limitless. This recognized sovereignty has no greater limits than those of African inter-state relations. These are not expected to follow the same approach as in regard to the European partner: preferences actually granted to some may be less for others, an open door for some may be closed to others.

So what is at stake in association? Whether or not an associate, what difference does it make to Africa? Why does Europe cling to the symbol and the US fuss about it with such force? Are the Europeans so ingenuous as to believe that, in competition with the United States, a symbolic duty of half a per cent of value on exports is decisive, and are the Americans for their part afraid of this 'injustice'? Certainly not.

If these things occur it is because both know that what is at stake goes further than the letter of the agreement. It is a question of whether the governments in Africa will initiate a 'pro-European' policy – it has to be seen whether this conceals a singular or plural component – or hence 'anti-American' policy, or the reverse. Accepting or refusing the association agreement is, therefore, a political act, a very broad statement of intent on this issue. The trick was in seeing in the texts only secondary issues, the 'inheritance', and not foreseeing the true lines of debate, the issues that would arise along with the 'development' of Africa. Hence, positions should retain the flexibility that international uncertainty enjoins.

It has already been shown in Chapter 2 how, in the 1970s, the Third World waged a battle for a revision of the international division of labour to enable it to embark on industrialization, and how the world redeployment of capital related to this change. Over the next 15 years or so the international division of labour was changed, although more slowly than the plans for the NIEO and redeployment expected. But if these changes have occurred, it is certainly not in Africa that they have changed the terms of international specialization, but in Latin America, India and East Asia. The decline in status of Africa – trapped in its (ruinous) agricultural and mining role – is the other vector of this global evolution. Is Europe to blame? In part it is, since the EEC-ACP asociation – and other forms of its presence in Africa – gives it a particular responsibility. To say the least, the association has not been mobilized to hasten the evolution of Africa. Of course it is still true that responsibility for the disaster also and primarily falls on the local ruling classes. But were not the latter largely the traditional clients of Europe?

In these circumstances, competition between Europe and the United States disguised in the crisis operates on African territory only within the narrow limits of mercantile competition.

Special links with France: the Franc zone[2]

In addition to the special relations the African continent enjoys with the EEC, France has retained, in most of its former sub-Saharan African colonies, a position that is unmatched anywhere else in the Third World. The monetary system of these countries is, in effect, based on the principle of free and absolute movement of capital at a fixed exchange rate (subject to change by common agreement) guaranteed by the metropolis. In return for this guarantee the local central banks are permitted to support African treasuries only within very narrow limits. Furthermore, the main commercial banks operating in these countries are branches and subsidiaries of metropolitan banks, and can therefore always counter the monetary policy that the local central banks want to pursue, in the event that this policy is not attractive to them, by the simple expedient of transferring funds to or from their Paris headquarters. There is no lack of examples of this: local banks have been known to make massive transfers of their capital to France to take advantage of higher interest rates. In these circumstances the country's monetary integration in the metropolitan finance economy is total, equivalent to that of a metropolitan province; the local central banks do not deserve the description as they are no more than issuing houses circulating a French Franc printed with an unusual design; there is only one central bank for the whole of the Franc zone: the Banque de France. We have suggested calling this system the 'zone of the Franc' rather than the Franc zone. For the African countries in question, IMF membership makes no sense, and is something of a legal fiction; and the IMF interventions make no more sense, as the metropolitan system is responsible for the monetary administration of these countries.

As can be seen, the system is that of total liberalism that the 'theories' made fashionable under Reagan, proposed as a model on the world scale. To the extent that France is wide open to the worldwide financial system, this total liberalism has no boundaries. The theory of the market on which it is based is, in turn, a manifestation of the assumption that the only development 'possible' requires the widest open door. A malicious mind would note that the African countries in question belong to the group of least developed countries; consequently, reasoning on the basis of the correlation to which the advocates of these economic theories are so partial, would show the opposite of their assumption as the widest open door is associated with the least satisfactory performances.

In fact even on the view that the structures of the centres–peripheries imbalance are not based on monetary integration, which is only a consequence, and after the illusion is dropped that there can be a 'monetary solution' to this profound imbalance, it has still to be admitted that the forms of this monetary integration are an additional severe handicap to any attempt at autocentric national or regional development. All the African states that did hope to guide their development in this direction had to break out of the yoke of the Franc zone. If they have sometimes 'become bankrupt', and have even sustained the monetary illusion we are criticizing, the reasons have nothing to do with an inevitable failure of national monetary management.

The monetary management of African countries in the Franc zone is, as has been shown over and over again, 'passive', in the sense that the currency issue is adjusted to the needs of the system's reproduction without giving it any power to play any significant part in its qualitative evolution. It follows 19th century style financial orthodoxy, which has no match in other Third World countries, or in modern developed capitalism, including metropolitan France, again despite the assertions of the fashionable Reaganite–IMF theology. This systematically deflationary policy at local level does not prevent the automatic importation of possible inflation from the metropolis. We add that the organic ties between the local banks and the old colonial trading monopolies, who own the industrial plants in most of the countries in question, provide a *de facto* privilege to the economic interests of the metropolis that is no less obvious, however difficult to quantify.

The inherent faults of this system are such that it seemed to be on the verge of explosion in the 1970s. Reasonable reform proposals were put forward, to allow more substantial monetary and financial co-operation with local treasuries (for development purposes) and the expansion of productive activities, plus flexible controls over transfers. Moreover, the proposals in question were for the purpose of maintaining regional monetary unions, while taking into account the variety of situations inherited from unequal regional development; they therefore contradicted the argument currently advanced that the Franc zone was a 'factor for unity' in Africa. The general drift the African economies have suffered since the end of the 1970s put a stop to these proposals. The Franc zone in its most traditional form is again flying high, has regained some of the countries that had left and is attracting new members. This innovation is part of the widespread compradorization under way.

Evolution in Euro-Arab relations: interwoven economics and politics

The intensification of Euro-Arab relations that occurred after the Second World War must be reassessed in the context of the overall worldwide expansion.[3] It is not even necessary to draw a detailed picture of these economic relations as they are today, or as they have developed in recent history. It is enough to reiterate, as is well-known, that these relations are highly intensive in all fields. In the field of commercial exchanges, the flow from South to the North, namely Europe, assures the North the major part of its energy supplies. The flow from North to South is also significant for the Arab region: Europe is second in meeting the Arab agriculture and food shortfall and first in meeting the import requirements in producer goods for the Arab countries. This means that the relations are not only important quantitatively (revealing growth rates after the Second World War faster than the overall rate of growth in world trade), but also qualitatively crucial for both sides. The commercial exchanges are reinforced and completed by financial flows, especially since 1973 when, through the recycling of part of the surplus of some Arab countries (but less and less) some of the surplus has been invested through Euro-Arab financial institutions. These flows have considerably speeded up the transfer of technology or to be more precise the sale of turnkey factories. The earlier contribution of the Arab world to the creation of the labour force in Europe was significant; it has now become of vital importance. This migratory flow from South to North, although slowing down in the current crisis, seems destined to play an increasing role in the long term.

Post-war expansion was, however, also characterized by the deployment of a plan for national bourgeois development throughout the Third World, and especially in the Arab region. Thus from 1945 to 1970, along with the rise of the national movement, there has been apparent in the Arab world an attempt at crystallization of an Arab national bourgeoisie, or Arab national bourgeoisies, believing itself capable of forming a hegemonic political and social force at national level and becoming an equal partner in the world system.

If the Arab national plan has proved impossible to achieve, as is demonstrated by its current degeneration occasioned by the crisis, the failure is due also to internal causes (the bourgeois character of the plan) and to the fact that the West, far from supporting the development, has fought against it and continues to do so.

An analysis has already been made of the plan's internal contradictions, its historical limits and extreme vulnerability, which have in the end led to its failure (cf. Chapters 2 and 3). We insist on the point too often hidden that the 'internal causes' have not operated in isolation, or in an atmosphere conducive, or even neutral, to the plan. On the contrary, the world system – central domination, with or without hegemony (US in this case) – is far from being favourable to homogenization of the system by the gradual crystallization of new partner centres (as all versions of the 'stages' of development theory suppose), but has had rather the reverse effect of further reproduction of the centres/peripheries asymmetry.

In the Arab region, the Nahda plan began an attempt at unitary national construction, of which Nasserism was the highest point. The distant past is of great significance here despite the eight or nine centuries of degeneration that followed – a past including the character of social formations in the Arab world in its first glory (the first three or four centuries of Islam) marked by unification of the dominant class on the basis of statist/mercantile centralization of the surplus (in contrast with European feudal fragmentation), and hence the unification of culture and language. The renaissance that appeared on the horizon from the beginning of the 19th century was built progressively on Arab unitary nationalism, breaking with Ottoman influence and Pan-Islamism. But the arrival of the necessary elements for the plan's implementation, namely liquidation of the Ottoman Empire and British and French colonizations, set up obstacles. The Arab states, one by one, regained their independence but in disunion. Gradual reinforcement of these new realities, far from narrowing the differences that had been opened in the preceding centuries and worsened by colonization, served rather to entrench the differences. The Arab bourgeoisie began to be aware of its possible collective emergence only when it had given way to a series of local bourgeoisies, each integrated separately into the world system.

For all kinds of reasons, some general and fundamental (the West's hostility to the emergence of new centres in Asia and Africa), others more specific to the region (the markedly popular dimension of the national liberation struggles, conflict between states, the Palestinian question to which we shall return), the hostility of the capitalist West was unyielding and particularly violent. To recall the facts: the 1956 aggression against Egypt, the decision taken by the Americans in 1965 to go to war to bring Nasser down, and put into effect in 1967 by Israel and its sleeping partners, the prolonged Algerian war (1954–62), the invasion of Lebanon in 1982, the annexation of the Golan Heights and the West bank of the Jordan by Israel, and so on.

What is important to note here is that while this constant conflict between Arab nationalism (bourgeois though it be) and imperialism has been one of the ways in which the USSR escaped the isolation to which the Atlantic alliance sought to confine it, Europe has never dissociated itself from the United States in the conflict. The supply of Soviet weapons to Egypt in 1955 clearly marks the Soviet Union's entry on the Arab scene.

On another tack, Europe, one need hardly recall, after dragging out its efforts to hold on to colonial possessions (the Algerian war and the Anglo-French attempt against Egypt in 1956 are evidence of this) simply walked off-stage to leave the US policeman and its Israeli subordinate to act for the entire West. At least until 1973 when the 'oil crisis' sharply woke up the Europeans and reminded them of their own vulnerability and of the selfishness of the United States. But what has Europe done since? Its 'comeback' in the Orient coincided with the decline of the Arab nationalist plan; Europe was happy to show a good face – for the sake of business – to the new ruling Arab forces, especially the most reactionary and the most susceptible to accepting the compradorization underway. This cannot be said to be 'supporting an Arab attempt at autonomous development', but merely enrolling as a partner – albeit a trading competitor – in the US plan for the region.

The post-war upsurge, followed by the crisis, far from narrowing the North–South gap has widened it, setting the two shores of the Mediterranean further apart than ever, through the closer integration of Southern Europe on the one hand and the rejection and sinking of the Arab plan on the other.

How do these conflicts relate to the East–West conflict? This conflict must be situated in the context of the broad offensive of imperialism against the South in general and the Arab world in particular. Europe, through the Atantic alliance, has opted so far to act against the Arab revival. In the West, the media often portray the Middle East conflict as an East–West conflict, in which the Soviet Union is currently embroiled through Syria, and in the past through Egypt. This in no way corresponds to the truth. But the argument is used to justify the shift of NATO's military strategies towards the South and the placing of missile bases in Sicily, not aimed at the Soviet Union but at the Arab world. So under cover of a hotting up of conflict with the East, conditions are created for aggression against the South. The Mediterranean is no longer NATO's southern flank against the Soviet Union, but NATO's central flank against the South. The strategy seeks, therefore, to recompradorize the enormous space that covers, among others, all the Arab and all the African peoples.

Seen in this perspective, Euro-Arab relations are unlikely to develop in a way favourable to the liberation and progress of the Arab peoples. Euro-Arab relations are currently at a conjuncture highly unfavourable to Arab popular interests. On one side we have a Europe that after erratic changes of heart towards the Arabs between 1973 and 1980 has totally gone over to the US and Zionist plan for the region. On the other, there is the Arab world of *infitah*, a disintegrating Arab world where a half or more of the powers are already openly compradorized.

Does this mean there is no room for any other economic and political relations between Europe and the Arab world? There is, but on condition that the relations are within the prospect of reinforcing the autonomy of the states and peoples in regard to dominant US imperialism. In such a perspective of widening European and Arab states' and peoples' autonomy, one might imagine that some kind of mutual support is not impossible, despite the past and despite the difference in levels of development. This is the prospect of a non-alignment reinforced by a European non-alignment and a restored Arab non-alignment.

Conflict and national and regional security in Africa

The African continent has for some three decades been the theatre for numerous conflicts, some constant and some recurring, internal and external and often entailing foreign intervention. The development economist can purport to overlook these conflicts as they are outside his discipline. The

African intellectual cannot accept surrender to such useless exercises: what sense does 'development' make in Chad, Uganda, Ethiopia, or in the countries on the South African and Israeli front line?

To act effectively in putting a stop to these situations mortgaging any development requires an accurate scientific analysis of the causes of the insecurity in question. Are vague general theories enough in such a case? Some will see the conflict as basically a result of capitalist competition, and others as the exacerbation of fundamental and spontaneous communal loyalties that may be based on national, religious or tribal criteria; a third group will see it as the projection on to African soil of the conflict of the superpowers. Yet others will prefer to take each conflict case by case and account for them by an eclectic mix of varying causalities.

It seems to us useful to make some preliminary observations on conflict theory, before addressing the question of national and regional security in Africa.

Towards a conflict theory based on a global analysis of the system

It has been said that war is 'nothing but the continuation of politics by other means'. Studying the conflicts is therefore studying a chapter of politics. It must be admitted at the outset that our tools of analysis in this field are particularly weak. It is not our intention here to put forward a general theory of politics. We shall offer no more than a few critical comments on the theories – often more implicit than explicit – underlying the various concrete analyses made in studies of some past and present conflicts.

We shall begin with Lenin's proposition that politics is economics in tablet form. There is some truth in this proposition, but it is useful to see how far it goes, for the proposition is meaningful only for the capitalist era of history. By that we mean that capitalism is a mode of social organization characterized by the predominance of the economic dimension. It is not the same for pre-capitalist societies, characterized by the predominance of the political and ideological dimension. And how does it apply to the so-called socialist post-capitalist societies?

We have here two schools of thought, both of which may claim to be Marxist. For some, the essence of capitalism is the fundamental class contradiction between bourgeoisie and proletariat. Hence all political phenomena (including the wars of the capitalist era) must in the final analysis be explained by this fundamental conflict and the means employed to resolve it – albeit temporarily – and to relieve its acuteness. In this spirit, political attitudes adopted by this or that side must be judged from a 'proletarian class position'. Others take the view that 'really existing' capitalism (as opposed and compared with the capitalist mode of production taken in the abstract) has brought to the fore another contradiction, the driving force of history, setting the peoples of the peripheries (we say peoples advisedly, that is, a non-homogeneous collection of popular classes, and not nations, or states, or proletariats) against worldwide dominant capital. Politics and the wars are, then, largely a regulatory factor of this contradiction.

We shall move nearer to a specific analysis by defining more precisely the operation of the 'dominant capital' in question. We might make the hypothesis that the relevant question is how and to what extent is there a correlation between the emergence of a national bourgeoisie as the dominant class in a given social formation, the establishment of its state and the crystallization of capitalist interests. This has certainly been the case in the past. The formation of a nation-state in Britain, France, Germany, the United States, Japan, has corresponded to the emergence of a national (English, French, and so on) bourgeoisie and national capital. Dominant capital has plural forms, and politics (and wars) were largely governed by conflictive competition between national capitals, particularly to ensure domination over the peripheral regions subjected to the needs of the logic of the expansion of those national capitals. In this sense, as Oliver Cox, Herb Addo and generally speaking the 'world economy' school argue, imperialism (and the conflict of imperialisms)[4] is a permanent feature of capitalism, and not a fairly recent phenomenon (the 'highest stage of capitalism', as Lenin saw it).

But is this always so? The long crisis of contemporary capitalism, beginning with the American decline at the end of the 1960s, is accompanied by a worldwide expansion of capital that seems to be taking on qualitatively new characteristics. Certainly the establishment of 'transnationals' in the period before the post-war upsurge (1945–70) initiated this evolution. The economic interests of the 'transnationals' might be in conflict with those of the national capital from which they emerged, and hence their strategy could clash with that of the national state, to the extent that the latter expressed the collective interest of national capital. But two factors limited the extent of these contradictions. The first is that the transnationals were so only in their field of activity, as control over their capital remained national. It was a matter of US, British, German or Japanese transnationals. The second is that United States hegemony was asserted over them just as it was asserted over other capitalist states.

What can be seen 15 years or so on? As André Gunder Frank has shown, since the end of the 1960s recessions have come at an accelerated rate, every three or four years, and each recession has been deeper than the previous ones in real economic terms (productive employment, growth, employment), and these recessions are separated by increasingly fragile and feeble abortive recoveries, to the point that the conjuncture is one of long crisis with an unpredictable outcome. This succession of unfavourable conjunctures has brought a flurry of financial speculation manifested in Third World external indebtedness and a dual external and internal indebtedness of the United States, as the financial market-place has turned into overgrowth divorced from the material base of the economy.[5] In this flurry of financial speculation a new form of worldwide finance capital seems to have been constituted, divorced from any national base. Furthermore, certain new productive capitalist interests (in industry and non-financial services) seem to be established on the basis of a consortium of interests on a national basis of varying origin: 'European' capital, US and Japanese capital, worldwide capital. Oligopolies that had previously had a decisive national base from which they extended their 'multinational' antennae gradually became multinational oligopolies in the full meaning of the expression. Japanese capital, for instance, which had previously pursued a systematic policy of reinvestment of profits in the building-up of an industrial fortress in Japan, began to transfer the seat of its productive activities (such as the Honda motor cars) to the United States. Some forecast that this transfer could reach such proportions that the oligopoly in question could no longer be regarded as Japanese by virtue of its main headquarters and nationality of control over its capital, but rather as a new Americano-Japanese oligopoly.

We are not convinced that the extrapolation of these trends is entirely legitimate and that the future is already defined in terms of a worldwide expansion of capital going beyond capital's national bases. But the hypothesis of an evolution in this direction and to this point of no return is no longer out of the question. If this does happen the correlation of state and capital, that has been characteristic of capitalism so far, will be gone and in its place will be a new contradiction between the multiplicity of states and the worldwide expansion of capital. For it is obvious that the construction of a unified Americano-Euro-Japanese political state is not on the agenda for the foreseeable future.

This new contradiction makes it necessary to review the question of politics and conflicts that until now could be analysed in terms of conflictive competition of imperialist national capitalisms. Until now, hegemonies were exercised by national states – Britain from 1815 to 1880, the United States from 1945 to 1970 – during fairly short periods of advance for the capital of these nations at all (technological and financial) levels and for their state at the military level (British naval supremacy, US virtual nuclear monopoly until the early 1960s and a politico-military intervention capability unchallenged until the defeat in Vietnam in 1975). The rule was chiefly one of conflict of imperialisms, Britain and France throughout the 18th century, the five great powers – Britain, United States, Germany, France and Japan – from 1880 to 1945, including the 'thirty years war' (1914–45) between Germany and the United States for the succession to Britain (we owe this image to Giovanni Arrighi).[6] In the hegemonic phases, unity of the world system was to the fore – British free trade in the 19th century and American free enterprise after the Second World War – but in the phases of conflict the system had a greater tendency to break up into rival zones, crystallized in colonial empires and spheres of influence, especially between 1880 and 1914 and then during the 1930s.

The worldwide expansion of capital made it impossible to continue this schema of break-up. At the same time it also ruled out the re-establishment of the hegemony of a police state, in the absence of a new Americano-Euro-Japanese state. Some would say that this impossibility gave a second wind to United States hegemony, for want of a viable competitor. But in that case the fatal hiatus between the interests of worldwide capital and US policy (necessarily dictated by the demands of the dominant social alliance in the

United States) would lead only to a disorder ungovernable by any rationality.

Within the framework of this theoretical analytical scheme of politics and international conflicts comes the national dialectic between politics and economics. This means that the stability of the bourgeois national state depends on an internal social alliance determining the scope for possible political manoeuvre. As an illustration of this proposition, it might be said that in the 19th century the French bourgeois state depended on an alliance of capital with the middle classes of the time – the then numerous peasantry, petty craft production, and so forth – intended to isolate the working class, excluded from power and the social contract. Since the end of the 19th century the social contract has gradually integrated the working class, on the basis of Fordism and the welfare state, first in the US and then throughout the developed West. The language of 'consensus politics', outside right–left divergences, that makes the running in all contemporary Western electoral democracy, shows the reality of this new aspect of politics.

If we return to Lenin's dictum on the relations of economics and politics, we note that unless these shades of meaning are introduced as we have tried to do, we shall inevitably slip into reductionist language deftly formulated by Jaurès on the lines that capitalism harbours war as the cloud does a storm. Capitalism harbours war or peace according to circumstances. It harbours war only when the contradictions it encounters in its expansion – and whose characteristic has still to be situated within the proposed theoretical framework – cannot be overcome by other means. Such wars will be largely the expression of conflicts between bourgeois national states: the emergence of new states and their rejection by the old one, wars of the 1870 kind; inter-imperialist conflicts such as the two world wars; localized conflicts over the dividing up of the peripheries such as the Balkans wars; conflicts between expanding imperialist states and peripheralized peoples; internal conflicts of the civil war kind when the bourgeois hegemonic social alliance fails to take shape.

The character of the conflicts indicated above, among which class conflicts in the proper meaning of the expression play only a small part, is the factual basis for the non-Marxist schools of thought on conflicts. Bourgeois political thought wipes out economics as a system governed by the laws and demands of reproduction and expansion of capital and retains only discrete scraps of economic reality. It can therefore be made – realistically – to take into account access to natural resources, the opening-up of markets or the protection of profits. But it does so on an *ad hoc* basis, without accepting a general theory of capitalism. It is essentially concerned with research into possible conflict. In fact it comes within a simple sociological hypothesis that states are always potential competitors of each other and seek almost spontaneously to ensure their 'dominance'. In this respect contemporary political thought is the follower of Hobbes, Machiavelli and political thinkers of the absolutist and mercantilist state, without really going any further. From the 19th century it complements this hypothesis with that of the nationalism of peoples, presumed to desire the establishment of homogeneous national states and thereby in competition and always potentially in conflict. Later, colonial conquest and the ethnology it inspired grafted on to the other forms of pre-national community (ethnic group, tribe, religious community) the characteristics of spontaneous collective aggressiveness attributed to the nation-states.

The conflict thus becomes the effect of a nature inherent in humankind and its organization into gregarious communities going beyond any particular social organizational form. A fine example of this simple and absolute psychology comes in the inaugural Constitution of UNESCO where the Anglo-Saxon ideologues of the time declared that 'since wars begin in the minds of men, . . .'.

The scientific weakness of the thesis goes without saying. But the facts, that is, the frequency of violent conflicts between states, nations and communities, more common than the relatively peaceful class conflicts in the proper meaning of the expression, might seem to support the hypothesis. The political man of action might be satisfied with concrete analysis of conflictive contradictions at the immediate level, without questioning their roots. The 'realpolitik' inspiration of such analyses (the writings of a political figure such as Henry Kissinger for example) is a factor of politics and not of political science. Its reasoning in terms of geopolitics might be effective for action within the system but does not lead to an understanding of the system's character.

It must be regretted that many of the political thinkers of the Third World, trained in the American school, reproduce its clichés without more critical feeling. Hence the Persians are portrayed as the inevitable potential adversaries of the Arabs, Ethiopians of Somalis, Christians of Muslims, and so on, just as in the past the French, the British and the Germans were portrayed as 'hereditary enemies'. This evades the issue of the character of the social system and its characteristic contradictions, the social forces and ideologies operating in these contradictions, to focus only on an abstract and empty generality. This leaves no scope for formulating a strategy of change to bring Persians and Arabs or Ethiopians and Somalis together. The discussion is caught up in the ideological language of adversaries outside the liberation of the peoples in question, and in that of local authorities tossed about on vicissitudes of fortune they are unable to grasp.

The supposedly realistic acceptance of this purportedly fundamental fact of the aggressiveness of human nature, enjoined upon lay creatures from the European renaissance on, gradually obscured another ideological tendency, namely the humanist idealism of religions (Christianity and Islam and undoubtedly others). Among its principles this humanist idealism proclaimed the essential need to overcome this aggressiveness and build a world of peace. The socialist movement of the 19th century proposed a synthesis of this idea with its discoveries about the social mechanism. Socialism – and Marxism in particular – asserted that violence has its roots deep in the social system of exploitation of the labouring classes (and in our modern era in the exploitation of labour by capital). By this token the conflict of states, nations or other communities is merely a manifestation of this more basic and profound latent conflict. This analytical thesis had the necessary corollary in the principle of action to the effect that abolition of exploitation (that is, in our era, abolition of capital) must ensure peaceful human relations. The withering away of the state (conceived mainly as an expression of the need for class exploitation) and of nations and sub-national communities in a liberated humankind followed this view of the social reality and the direction of its possible and desirable evolution.

This kind of programmatic language is no longer tenable. For some 70 years various states claiming to be Marxist socialist have come into being. This did not stop Sino-Soviet antagonism at one stage going to the brink of war, Vietnam invading Laos and Kampuchea, or the resurgence of unfulfilled nationalisms in the Baltic, Soviet Central Asia, Tibet, Yugoslavia, or the Hungarian minority in Romania and Turkish minority in Bulgaria. Bourgeois political thought owes much of its renewed glory to this: the facts showed that nation transcended class, that nations (even without classes) expressed themselves as states (which did not wither away), and that states continued to be driven by the desire to dominate. The ideological language of the socialist powers in question, the arbitrary justifications bending according to circumstances, could only strengthen the belief that 'realpolitik' was all there was.

It is time to break out of these two-fold shackles that keep social reflections in a double impasse. This requires at the start a better understanding of the post-capitalist transition and hence the character of the contradictions operating in the societies emerging from so-called socialist revolutions. We have suggested here a framework of analysis based on the thesis of the fundamental character of inequality in capitalist expansion. We derive the corollary that the post-capitalist transition cannot be reduced to 'socialist construction'. Through its national and popular character it has the real task of resolving an inequality that is inescapable in the framework of 'currently existing' capitalism – a world system based on a polarization of centres and peripheries. We have therefore proposed analysing the post-capitalist societies as revolving around conflictive and dynamic compromises between three social tendencies: socialist, capitalist, and national–statist. We have further suggested that the so-called socialist revolutions and the national liberation movements belonged to the same great historical movement challenging the capitalist system and differing only in the degree of their achievements.

The societies and states of 'current socialism' are riddled with new and specific contradictions, differing from those typifying capitalism. To make sense of the conflicts to which these states are party, one must start with these contradictions that can be classified in two groups.

The socialist societies and states are perceived as adversaries by the capitalist West. They are such to the degree that the national and popular construction they are pursuing escapes the logic of surrender to the demands of worldwide capitalist expansion. These states, conscious of their vulnerability, do, however, seek 'peaceful coexistence', to use the phrase they have themselves coined. But the West sees this weakness as just another reason to exert on them the pressures it regards as necessary in order to destroy the prospect of successful national and popular construction. According to time and circumstance, these pressures may take the form of cold or hot war, or the arms race, while at a particular conjuncture the balance of 'détente' may diminish the intensity. Here, the ideological language and revolutionary claptrap change place: it is the Western media that play the resonant leitmotivs (the devilish 'autocracies' of the East, their total disregard of principles, and so on) whose purpose is obviously to build up a Western 'anti-socialist consensus'.

The constant hostility to the societies and states of 'really existing socialism' is similar in kind to that the West harbours in regard to national liberation, since this too is part of the same historical movements of challenge to 'really existing' capitalism. 'Anti-Third-Worldism' is the ideological expression of this hostility.

In such circumstances the states of the East, like the Third World states at moments of radicalization of their national liberation struggle, are faced with the need for active resistance to the West's plan for 'driving back'. Their alliances, supports and interventions are at least in part explicable in this context. Are there any general principles to focus the study of this web of circumstance? Bourgeois political thought looks for them at its standard workbench, with preference nowadays, of course, for the data of geopolitics and geostrategy demanded by modern military equipment. But even if this kind of analysis does give food for thought, it by-passes the principle that seems to us fundamental to an understanding of the global strategy of the countries of the East (the USSR and China in first place). The principle is that interventions by the USSR and China outside their borders (notably in alliance with the national liberation forces in bitter conflict with the West) are means of 'counter-pressure' to make the West lessen the pressure it exercises on the two socialist powers. These 'counter-pressures' can therefore be reduced once Western pressure is reduced.

The liberation movements of the capitalist Third World are ill-equipped to understand the logic of the strategy described above. They themselves fall short of the stage of strong national and popular crystallization characteristic of the so-called socialist societies. As they are engaged upon an unequal struggle against capitalist imperialism, obliged by their own weaknesses to aim low, often forced back on the retreat, they are tempted to blame their own shortcomings on the vacillations and shifts of their external ally. It is the task of the popular forces within the country in question to push their own national liberation movement to the point where they can impose a national and popular revolution. 'Anti-imperialist solidarity' is no substitute for basic shortcomings at this level.

The 'external' contradiction between the 'socialist' societies and states (and the radical national liberation states) and world capitalism is clearly not unconnected with the 'internal' contradictions – the second group – peculiar to the societies described as national and popular. The interweaving of these two groups of contradictions – internal and external – is such that it is virtually impossible to adduce general principles as to their mode of operation. A case by case study must be done. Nevertheless as a warning perhaps, it is possible to signal what may be a risky over-simplification to the effect that the socialist forces operate in an ideological mode, on the basis of the principles of anti-imperialist solidarity, while those of national capitalism and statism, pragmatic by temperament and interest, are more easily seduced by the compromise, or cynicism, of 'realpolitik'.

The problematic of African conflicts[7]

Africa and the Middle East are the theatre for numerous and virtually permanent conflicts, whose variety and apparent insolubility are enough to discourage many analysts, whether they are political figures from within the countries or abroad. Some people stop trying to understand on the view that – 'as in feudal Europe' – the African societies, victims of their own backwardness, are the ground of continual confrontations between 'tribes', peoples and communities, on which are grafted the race for power of autocratic potentates, who call into play unprincipled alliances with such powers as will play this destructive game, whether to retain an economic and 'cultural' presence, or for overall geostrategic motives. It is a simple picture; this view, however, that gains ground as the illusions of the 1960s are thrown out, remains false.

Every case has its particularities that cannot be overlooked. Concrete analyses are therefore irreplaceable. In nearly every one of these countless cases it is possible to see, interwoven in some particular way, four sources of conflict: first, the unresolved conflict between the demands of national and popular liberation and the logic of surrender to capitalist expansion imposed by imperialism; second, the internal conflicts arising from the frailty of the national society, its popular forces and ruling classes; third, the East–West conflict whose projection on to the continent has its own logical rules; fourth, trading competition between the capitalist powers with interests in the region.

This order of presentation of the sources of conflict correspnds to their order of importance. This reflects the degree of potential violence attached to the cause of conflict and in consequence the relative significance of the results of a solution of that conflict.

It is stylish nowadays to think that political independence has put a stop to the era of national liberation and that, as a consequence, the subsequent development is mainly the result of the dynamic of 'internal causes' peculiar to the Third World societies and states. The first proposition takes little account of the fact that the capitalist Third World states gained their independence under circumstances precluding their 'delinking' and have generally increased their unequal integration in the worldwide capitalist system. These circumstances contrast with those characteristic of societies that have experienced a 'socialist revolution' and definitively delinked in the narrow sense we have given the term. The result is, that the aim of national liberation, necessary to embark upon a path that can efface the legacy of unequal capitalist development, has still to be achieved. As the local bourgeoisies, who to varying degrees have controlled the former national liberation movement (leading to independence) have pursued a developmental approach that did not challenge worldwide capitalist expansion, the responsibility for national liberation reverts to the popular classes victimized in the new state of peripheral capitalist development. The corollary of the proposition we are criticizing is that the external factor, always unfavourable and increasingly so, still largely conditions the evolution of the internal factors. The conflict between imperialism and the national and popular movement will always be just as violent.

Are not the most violent conflicts in the contemporary Third World just those where direct confrontation is in the forefront: Nicaragua in Latin America, the permanent Israeli–Arab conflict, the conflict the South African people wage in their struggle against the white apartheid regime? These two main conflicts in South Africa and the Middle East will be considered below.

The Middle East and South Africa are of course not the only areas of conflict between national and popular aspirations and Western imperialism. It may be said without any exaggeration that the entire African continent is the theatre of this greater and permanent conflict. In the past three decades various experiences in some half of African states have sought a way beyond neo-colonialism (Egypt, Algeria, Sudan, Libya, Mali, Guinea, Guinea Bissau, Burkina Faso, Cape Verde, Ghana, Benin, Congo, Zaire, Ethiopia, Somalia, Tanzania, Uganda, Zambia, Zimbabwe, Angola, Mozambique, Madagascar, Mauritius, Seychelles). All these attempts have in some way or other and to varying degrees met with hostility from the West, ranging from the use of economic and financial pressures to conspiracy and even military intervention. Undoubtedly the national aspirations of the various governments in question did not display the same degree of radicalization and often lacked sufficient popular support (and sometimes these governments did not want to see the popular movement acquire the autonomy its energy deserved). These attempts were so weak that many drifted down of their own accord – at least on the surface – and fell back into the rut of neo-colonialism. Others were unable to overcome the contradictions among their own people (including the ethnic contradictions). It is also true that the economic and political apparatus left by Europe in the wake of independence was not intended to support the popular forces but to maintain the neo-colonial order they confronted. It is scarcely surprising that there were so many 'rapid interventions' by paratroopers deployed to put back into the seat of power a dictator who was at the end of his tether but entirely devoted to Western interests. There is a strong element of hypocrisy in Western discourse when it laments the condition of Africa and its peoples, without ever mentioning the unstinted support that the West – in unison – provides to the most retrograde and corrupt of local forces, albeit against more honest forces whose errors and shortcomings the West is only too ready to point out.

Africa's association with the EEC must be seen in this framework of perpetuation of neo-colonial relations. Some of our European friends revive the argument that Africa is not ripe to go further and that the popular forces are weak. Others note that even if the association works to the advantage of neo-colonial interests, there is scope for manoeuvre within the texts and the institutions but one that is sadly under-utilized by the forces of the left in

Europe (who could influence their own governments and the EEC) or by the popular and national forces in Africa. This argument is admissible, if one believes, as we do, that choosing the worst policy is rarely the best way to work for change in the strategic relations of power. But it must not cast a shadow on the prospect of a national and popular delinking, valid here as elsewhere. Africa will not develop through the agency of a 'good paternalism' as utopian as the 'good colonialism' of the past that some sections of the European left hope to see, perhaps sincerely. The African peoples cannot escape the general rule: stand up or succumb.

It is in no way our intention to draw up a table where the conflicts Africa suffers are aligned according to their anti-imperialist aspect. The list of inter-ethnic conflicts, for example, is as long as that of conflicts between African nationalism and the West: Zaire, Uganda, Ethiopia, Sudan, Rwanda and Burundi, Angola, Mozambique, Nigeria, Chad, have been or still are theatres of violent conflict, to the extent of civil war in some cases. In other countries the conflict is latent, if it has in some instances been contained so far by repression. There is a not insignificant list of conflicts by states over frontiers or overt or hidden territorial ambitions: Ethiopia, Somalia and Sudan; Algeria and Morocco (and Western Sahara); Mali and Burkina Faso are some examples.

None of these conflicts are entirely 'fabrications' of services outside Africa. The local diplomatic talk that sometimes suggests this is hardly credible, even if, as is often the case, various external forces do seize the opportunity they are given to support one group or impede another, in the light of their own strategic or tactical objectives and in a spirit of cynicism.

Does this suggest that these conflicts are 'inevitable' as the result of the potential hostility inherent in every human 'community', as superficial political thought imagines? We suggest the hypothesis that, many of these 'communal' conflicts are the result of struggles within the ruling class, or between segments of it. What these ruling classes have most obviously in common is their fragility: whether they are comprador classes, able to operate only within the narrow limits allowed by control from world capital, or often not even attaining the status of a comprador bourgeoisie (with their own economic interests subordinated by their integration in world capitalism) but rather a comprador bureaucracy (the apparatus of a comprador state); or whether they are strata and groups with nationalist aspirations who have failed to become the intelligentsia of an alliance of genuinely popular forces. In both instances the temptation is strong for the various segments of a class of this kind to hold power by mobilizing fractions of the population behind 'symbols' that leave them masters of the game. Ethnic or religious symbols are often highly suited to this kind of competition for power.

The cause of these conflicts is not some kind of ethnocentric atavism that compels the peoples not to recognize other realities than those of the communities to which they belong, nor another sort of autocratic atavism that compels the leaders to manipulate the 'ethnic devils'. It is the weakness of the peripheral society as a whole that is at issue and especially that of its ruling classes.

The national and popular outlook therefore requires a strategy that is both democratic and unitary, that is, moving towards the maintenance – or even creation – of broad space (hence great states) commensurate with the challenges demanded by national and popular delinking, and mindful at the same time of diversity within that broad space. The rights of peoples to self-determination must be implemented within this political perspective.

The global conflict of the superpowers does not entail any necessary symmetry between the aims and the actors. The United States takes the leadership of the capitalist forces with the conservative aim of preserving the neo-colonial integration of Africa in the global system. The forces of national and popular liberation cannot therefore avoid a clash. Neither the Soviet Union, nor still less China, have the ambition – and if they did, the capability – to sustain a progressive transformation of the African continent. At most if serious and enduring détente came about, the socialist superpowers would accept an 'African retreat', left to its own peoples and solitary confrontation with internal and external enemies. But in the absence of such détente, a 'presence' in Africa may be deemed useful from two points of view. First as a means of pressure to encourage the adversary to that very détente. Then, in the still possible hypothesis of extensive armed conflict, as a location for bases in the direction of the Mediterranean, North and South Atlantic and Indian Ocean. It is true that according to some specialists on military issues, this kind of geostrategic concern tends to become less relevant in an age of intercontinental missiles or Star Wars. But is the concern over in so far as the risk of conflagration is not all or nothing, but one of intermediate options where control over a regional initiative has some significance?

So long as this is so, diplomacy will keep its options: states – Soviet and Chinese like the others – tend to consider only what is there, that is the powers *in situ*. It would be ingenuous to believe – or even hope – that longer term concerns (the desire for 'socialism') mean more that ideological discourse, albeit sincere. Furthermore, the constraints of diplomacy will not in the future, any more than they did in the past, prevent certain backsliding that might be described as 'opportunist' by anyone of the view that the national and popular objective is an inescapable condition of progress. Such backsliding will occur whenever the alliance of the more or less national local power (and hence to some extent in conflict with the West) and the 'socialist' states operates in such a way as to block rather than encourage this power's evolution to the desired irreversible national and popular crystallization.

We come finally to the last section of our fourfold analysis: Euro-American competition. What we say will be brief as we do not see that this competition entails any political conflict for Africa and the Middle East. On the contrary, the resources of the United States and those of Europe complement each other. In this region, Europe is so far perfectly in step.

The conflict in South Africa[8]

For a century, imperialism maintained a system of overall domination of the Southern African region in which the white settler colony of South Africa played an essential part. The discovery of the region's mineral wealth (gold and diamonds in South Africa, copper in Katanga and Northern Rhodesia, rare minerals), at the very moment when capitalism was embarking on a new phase of monopolistic expansion, inspired a special formula of colonization, the 'reverse economy'. This was the division of a country forcing the African peasantries, who were herded into 'reserves' purposely inadequate to ensure subsistence in the previously traditional ways, to provide the necessary proletarianized migrant labour for mining. The agricultural economy of the European plantations (in South Africa and Southern Rhodesia) and later the manufacturing industry also benefited from this system.

Apartheid, from the outset, was part of this form of expansion of peripheral capitalism, in contrast with the forms implemented in other parts of the continent, notably the coastal trade economy in West Africa. Contrary to stubborn belief it was not the Boers who in an excess of racism of their own invented the system. Until then the Boers had developed only a crude concept of their society – agrarian and patriarchal – that entailed the conquest of land and not of men, with the latter to be driven out or exterminated rather than integrated in an effectively capitalist exploitation. In short they behaved as the Zionists hoped to treat the Palestinians. But the defeat inflicted on the Boers by British imperialism gave them a new place and role in the system, invented by the British governors brought up on an interpretation of race and class inspired by an Oxbridge reading of Plato. Contrary also to a widespread prejudice, nurtured by these same British who set up the system but attributed paternity to the Boers, apartheid is not a 'remnant' in conflict with the needs of capitalist expansion, but rather in perfect harmony with this expansion. Bourgeois ideology seeks to justify the 'progressive' character of capitalism by pretending that equality before the law and electoral democracy are absolute imperatives of this mode of production. The reality suggests another interpretation stressing the qualitative difference between the centres and the peripheries in this overall capitalist expansion. If, in the centres, the struggles fought by the bourgeoisie against the absolutism of former regimes, followed by the struggles waged by the working class, have in fact imposed bourgeois democracy as we know it, in the periphery the roles assigned to the conquered peoples imposed gross forms of exploitation. Slavery in the Americas, apartheid in South Africa, colonization (and the negation of basic rights it comports) are necessary forms of capitalist expansion as it truly is, in contrast to the mythical view that bourgeois ideology attaches to it. If apartheid is under challenge nowadays in South Africa, it is not because this form is an obstacle to capitalist expansion, but because the struggles of its victims in the black people of South Africa are making it unworkable.

Dominant British imperialism constructed this complex system based on fundamental alliances between the interests of dominant mining monopoly capital and white settler colonialism, direct, semi-indirect or indirect British colonial rule according to regions. Belgian rule in the Congo and subordinate Portuguese rule in Angola and Mozambique. The place of the 'natives' in these alliances was virtually nil. A few kings and chiefs were involved with day to day issues of the 'reserves' in question (notably in Swaziland and Lesotho); there was no subordinate African bourgeoisie (not even in the rural areas), or embryo of a political bourgeoisie. From the end of 19th century to 1984 this system operated without a major crisis to challenge the dominant interests of monopoly capital. In fact, as British hegemony was already waning at the end of the 19th century it brought in North American capital into the venture from the start, as is evidenced by the establishment of Anglo-American institutions. Until the crisis of South Africa reached a decisive phase – that is, until 1984 – the United States had no need of active political intervention in the region. The British baton bearer until 1948, then the South African baton bearer, was enough to maintain 'order'. The gradual decline of British hegemony gave the Boers an opportunity to avenge their previous defeat. By breaking away from the mother country in 1948, white South Africa became the senior partner in the maintenance of order for the benefit of the overall imperialist strategy in the region. The attempt by Ian Smith to do similarly in Southern Rhodesia did not have the same capacity to succeed, for reasons we explained at the time.

The crumbling of British and Belgian colonialism did not mean the destruction of the overall system of imperialist domination in the region. The national liberation movements in the Belgian Congo, in British Southern Africa (the Rhodesias, Nyasaland, the enclave protectorates in South Africa) and East Africa (Tanganyika), similar to others in the continent, were in the end persuaded or obliged to respect essential 'Western' interests. It is true that according to the class character of the alliance within these movements and the twists and turns of their political and ideological evolution, the range of post-colonial approaches and practices is broad, ranging from the avowed neo-colonialism of Malawi, Swaziland, Lesotho and Zaire, to the national efforts of Tanzania and Zambia. But the latter have remained vulnerable and frail.

The later collapse of Portuguese colonialism in 1974 and of the UDI regime in Rhodesia in 1980 have, however, taken the threat to imperialist interests to a higher level. Undoubtedly the West does not think it has definitely lost the battle in Angola or Mozambique. The internal limits to the nationalist systems newly in power have sometimes obliged them to respect the interest of monopoly capital (as with Angola's oil), and have, in any event, kept them within the system of dependent economic relations governing the capitalist world as a whole. The Soviet Union is neither able nor even willing to replace the Western partners in this respect. In Zimbabwe, the path to independence negotiated in the Lancaster House agreement has to say the least prolonged the survival of the former economic system, left virtually untouched in the rural areas (no land reform to redistribute settler land for the benefit of the peasantry) and in industrial areas (respect for the predominance of the interests of local private capital in association with worldwide capital). It is true that for political and historical reasons, and in consequence of the South African challenge (in Namibia in particular), the regimes in these three countries remain 'unreliable' in the eyes of the West. The West has regarded it as positive and useful – for it – that South Africa pursues its destabilizing military aggression against Angola and Mozambique since 1974 and against Zimbabwe since 1980. These aggressions are complemented on the economic level by the destabilizing aggression of the IMF, acting for imperialism's global account and profiting from the – sometimes serious – weaknesses and errors of local policies. The results of this strategy, aimed at establishing overtly neo-colonial regimes, are unfortunately not disappointing for imperialism. Angola was obliged to appeal to Cuban military assistance, to face up to South African ventures, Mozambique to sign the Nkomati agreement, without this bringing security to the country, Zimbabwe to observe the Lancaster House spirit, Tanzania and Zambia to pass through the Caudine forks of the IMF. The 'Soviet presence' in the region, the rear bases for liberation in Namibia and South Africa (SWAPO, ANC, PAC), are pretexts rather than genuine reasons for the West's offensive strategy. The presence is a result – and not a cause – of the West's refusal to accept other than neo-colonial regimes in Africa and to face up to decolonization in Namibia and South Africa.

But things have changed since 1984. The heightened struggle of the people of South Africa raises the question of the region's future in new terms of an alternative: overall neo-colonialism for Southern Africa, or national and popular liberation.

On this we shall make six general points that seem useful to clarify the character of the issues and possible strategies.

One: what is in direct, immediate and violent crisis in South Africa is the political regime of apartheid and the denial it implies of any regard for the basic rights of the African majority population. Although with a substantial urban proletariat, the relations of exploitation specific to capitalism are potentially at stake in the crisis, the main thrust of the blow is the claim for majority political power (majority rule versus minority rule and apartheid). This characteristic of the movement is quite natural in the current circumstances.

Two: in such circumstances, if the struggle does not develop to the level of a real challenge to the relations of production, a neo-colonial solution remains possible, even in South Africa. After all, some kind of Lancaster House would be quite acceptable to the West. Of course, some of the white settler interests in South Africa would be sacrificed; but just as it was done at the time of the defeat of the Boers at the beginning of the century! It would be useless to go much further with 'pseudo-forecasting' of possible scenarios. The latter might, to the benefit of the Africans, include more or less major land reforms and more or less broad political representation, and to the benefit of the colonizers, more or less detailed and firm 'guarantees'. What is essential for imperialism is to preserve the capitalist relations of production in industry and the mines and the international 'specialization' of the region that flows from them.

We must carefully distinguish the too ready arguments that this outcome is totally 'impossible'. It is said there is no black bourgeoisie in South Africa, as apartheid has made its existence impossible. Granted; but in many African countries this was the case and nevertheless a political bourgeoisie has quickly been able to take up the role. South Africa's nuclear power excludes any agreement, it is said, as the West would never allow the weapon to fall into the hands of a black government. Has the possibility of dismantling the weapons capability been excluded, if such were necessary? South Africa is the sole supplier of strategic minerals, unless importers turn to the Soviet Union. Granted; but is the neo-colonial solution aimed precisely at ensuring the continuance of these supplies? A final argument: white power in South Africa enjoys an autonomy sufficient to allow it to refuse 'plans' that require unpalatable sacrifices. The analogy is often made with Israel, also able to cock a snook at the West, demand unconditional support or even dispense with it. We venture to doubt the strength of this argument. South Africa would have great difficulty in withstanding sanctions, even the merely economic, and the white regime would crumble even more quickly if they were enforced. The spread of the war within the country could even of itself bring about the collapse.

Three: it is useless nowadays to see opposition between the possible strategies of the various partners in the imperialist system, including the United States, the European community and Japan. Certainly, as Lenin realized and studied in his day, imperialism was a conflict of economic imperialisms (and even military, as the two world wars showed). But these inter-imperialist relations have evolved since the Second World War. They have apparently ruled out resort to inter-imperialist war. But they have led also to a new stage of global interpenetration of interests. The European community, United States and Japan, especially in the mining sector essential for the region, deploy fully integrated company and state strategies. The argument that the EEC, out of concern for its African friendships, might diverge from its US competitor ally does not hold water, as the surrender of neo-colonial regimes and the vulnerability of those which offer a challenge is such that the European interests may sleep easily.

Four: the neo-colonial outcome is no more inevitable that its opposite, the outcome of national liberation of a popular bent and socialist vocation. It will all depend on the strategies of the struggle waged in South Africa. If the strategies have the sole aim of 'majority rule' and actively seek negotiations on this basis, the neo-colonial compromise may be achieved sooner than is expected. But if the strategies are based on a deepening of social aims (that is, a struggle for workers' control over the means of production and a peasant war for reconquest of land), the outcome would certainly be very different. The historical responsibility of the avant gardes lies here.

Five: is it a struggle eventually to build socialism (on the best hypothesis of the development of the struggle), or one that on this hypothesis would lead only to a national and popular power with merely a socialist mission? We shall return to this point in Chapter 8.

Six: so long as national and popular construction is not embarked upon in South Africa and in the region, relations between the countries of the region will remain marked by the inequality inherent to capitalist expansion, both in their relations with imperialism and their relations with each other. Hence the overall neo-colonial solution entails the segmentation of local and regional ruling classes, leading to a conflict of their interests. A pseudo South African 'expansionism', as the channel for worldwide capitalist expansion, would then be a real possibility and probability. But does the national and popular solution remove this possibility? Here again a dogmatic and vulgar concept of a conjunction of all the popular interests is not an adequate analysis. the current conflicts between the (so-called socialist) nationalist and popular regimes, between the USSR and Eastern Europe, China and the USSR, China and Vietnam, are not the result of 'ideological deviations'. Their being of a particular character (as they are not conflicts produced by the unequal development of capitalism) does not mean they do not exist. The contradiction and hence its solution in various ways (co-operation or conflict) and in particular situations, governs the post-capitalist society just as it governs the pre-capitalist and capitalist societies.

The Middle East conflict in a world perspective

The Middle East conflict, unbroken for more than 30 years, appears to set the Arab states – and behind them the Palestinian people – against the State of Israel. The Arab states appear motivated above all by the desire to acquire sufficient political and economic autonomy to become worthy partners in the world capital system from which they cannot envisage a divorce. In their pursuit of this objective, they constitute, according to Zionist fears, a 'deadly' peril to Israel.[9]

But behind these immediate protagonists stand other forces whose interests and strategies have a secondary effect on the actors in the forefront. These forces are the Arab peoples, Western imperialism and the Soviet Union. Raising the issue in these terms also raises a series of underlying issues, namely: (i) the extent to which the Arab states are really masters of the game, and the extent to which the conflict between them and their popular forces is without solution; (ii) the extent to which Zionism and the State of Israel are an autonomous force, with their own strategy and aims; (iii) the extent to which imperialism implements a common strategy towards the region and conversely the extent to which US and European interests, for example, may diverge; and finally (iv) to what extent the Soviet Union is capable of intervening in the region and the objectives it would pursue and the means it would have.

The conflict between the Arab peoples and the expanding capitalist West clearly does not date from 1947. It dates back to the very origin of the world capitalist system. The long history of this conflict is riddled with defeats of the Arab world, from the 16th century to 1950. From the Capitulations granted by the Ottoman Empire, inaugurating the era of unequal treaties, to the defeat of the Egyptian Pasha Mohamed Ali in 1840, from the conquest of Algeria from

1830, to the occupation of Egypt and Tunisia in 1982 then of Morocco in 1911, to the division of the Middle East between the British and the French in 1919, it is a long list of defeats. For the Arab peoples, partition of Palestine in 1947 and Israel's first expansion from 1948 are obviously in line with colonial European expansion, and just a more modern example.

Colonial European expansion here as elsewhere in Asia and Africa, encountered resistance that would eventually be insurmountable with the development of the national liberation movements. While in the decades after the Second World War all the Arab countries regained their political independence and effaced the marks of colonization, in these same decades, however, from 1950 to 1980, Zionist colonization came to the fore and expelled the Palestinian people from their ancestral home. This paradox of victorious colonization in the very period when colonization was being ousted from the Afro-Asiatic whole demands an explanation.

Any attempt at an answer requires an examination of the Arab national liberation movement. In Egypt and the countries of the fertile crescent (Syria, Palestine, Iraq) the – British – imperialism then dominant governed the region through the channel of local authorities drawn mainly from the large landowners, who had benefited from integration in the world economic system carried out from the 19th century. The national liberation movement had first to manifest itself as an internal anti-latifundist (anti-'feudal', anti-imperialist) movement bringing together various peasant, popular and bourgeois social forces. Through various twists and turns this movement succeeded during the 1950s in overthrowing the reactionary defenders of the status quo first in Egypt then in Syria and Iraq. Nasserism, the dominant concept in the region in the 1950s and 1960s, was the climax of this story, carrying all Arab countries in its wake. The rise of the Ba'ath in Syria and Iraq and the Algerian war (1954–62) were concomitant. The 'progressive' nationalist regimes emerging from this phase shared common essential characteristics: for example, anti-latifundist land reform, nationalizations and industrialization, the establishment of a modernist state. This current was so strong that it forced the old British and French imperialism into a general retreat – and even into acceptance of independence for the countries and regions less forward in the struggle, from Morocco to the Gulf. It was also so persuasive that the 'moderate' states emerging from the withdrawal were obliged to align themselves, nominally at least, under Nasserist leadership.

The rise of Nasserism was, however, not without violent struggles against the new dominant imperialism, of the United States, which, taking over from Britain in Palestine after 1948, chose to turn its protégé – Israel – into the spearhead of its intervention. Nasserism, in order to assert itself and a new political and economic standard, was obliged to lean on the United States' sole adversary, the USSR, as Europe had withdrawn and lined up with the United States.

This rise of Nasserism succeeded in transforming social reality throughout the Arab world. In varying degrees the new national authorities established bourgeois hegemonic alliances, crystallizing around a bourgeoisie of the industrial state, peasant (kulak) allies and *petit bourgeoisie*, sometimes with a popular element and, conversely, sometimes drawn from the former dominant classes (large landowners and traditional chieftains). Two distinct currents can be found in this broad spectrum: a radical bourgeois tendency aiming at the construction of a modernized, industrialized and autonomous national state as an 'equal' partner in the world system of states, and a moderate bourgeois tendency willing to play a subordinate role in the international division of labour that the radical wing rejected.

The entire strategy of the United States was aimed at smashing the radical tendency. It is not by chance that for this purpose the United States used the means of Israeli military intervention – the lightning war of 1967. The Egyptian and Arab defeat was part of the very historical limitations of this radical bourgeois tendency. The latter never really accepted a popular alliance endowed with an autonomy that might threaten its own class prospects. By this token it could not unhesitatingly play the card of Arab popular unity. For the rise of the anti-imperialist struggles of the Arab peoples had put the issue of Arab unity on the agenda.

The bourgeois radical wing of the Arab liberation movement could not play the card of Arab popular unity so long as within each of the existing states it refused to allow room for a popular political hegemony. The ambiguous attitudes of this radical wing in regard to the Palestinian movement itself, confined in some kind of 'protectorate', reveal the same limitations. But similar hesitations were shown in regard to relations with the Soviet Union. An alliance with the latter was sought only as a means of pressure to win acceptance by the true spokesman – the United States. The Arab bourgeoisie, even the radical wing, hoped to persuade the United States to cease relying on Zionism as the only card in the regional game and recognize the bourgeoisie as a major partner.

The United States did not see it in this way. The United States was determined to take advantage of the weaknesses of the radical Arab camp to smash it and to subject the region to its own perceptions. This process of subordination, and of recompradorization, clearly under way since 1967, has gone through three stages marking its indisputable triumph.

The first stage was the lightning war in 1967. This war marked the end of Nasserism, that is, a turning back of the Arab unitary current and a shift 'to the right' at internal level. *Infitah*, or open door policy, as a series of concessions to the local neo-comprador bourgeoisie and dominant world finance capital, began at the end of the 1960s and beginning of the 1970s in Egypt, but also in Syria, Iraq and Algeria.

Nevertheless, the radical wing of Arab nationalism tried to re-establish a less unfavourable balance. After long and costly preparations for war, with Soviet support, the successful crossing of the Suez Canal and the destruction of the Bar Lev line between 6 and 15 October 1973, were they going to allow this bourgeoisie to take its place at last an an equal and respected partner? Arab solidarity was manifest on this occasion, the coincidence with the OPEC victory in securing the increase in oil prices, the intention attributed to

Kissinger of ditching the Zionist alliance for one with the Arab bourgeoisie mobilized behind the new financial wealth of the Gulf made it credible.

But it came to nothing. On the contrary, 1973 paved the way for a new state of recompradorization. Undoubtedly the outcome of the October 1973 war was ambiguous. But above all the Arab bourgeoisie would line up with its 'moderates' win and play the American card without hesitation as was shown in Anwar Sadat's break with the USSR and the introduction of *infitah*. At the same time the new financial wealth of the Gulf, far from strengthening Arab hands, was to integrate the region further in the world capitalist system, by 'recycling' funds that further reduced the scope for Arab bourgeois autonomy. Saudi Arabia refused to provide an alternative financial solution for Egypt and rather made its financial aid conditional on Egypt's acceptance of the IMF plan, thus becoming an active agent of this recompradorization. What followed – with the Camp David agreements – was a new stage of implementation of the plan to subordinate the Arab world. Menachem Begin must have understood it in this way: by restoring the Sinai – perhaps temporarily – he secured the dismantling of the Egyptian army and left his hands free to embark upon definitive annexation of the West Bank of the Jordan, Gaza and the Golan Heights.

Israel, encouraged by its luck, went further and in July 1982 grabbed Lebanon to the gates of Beirut and secured the PLO's departure from that country. The Arab reaction to this new state of Zionist colonial expansion was, as we know, nil. The bourgeois radical wing was decisively beaten and dismantled, the Arab bourgeoisie as a whole accepted the fate dictated by imperialism as a subordinate comprador partner. Hence its only reaction was to place its hopes in the pleas it made – through the Fes plan for example – to the masters of the world system to which it belonged.

For 30 years the political life of the Arab world has been rendered more complex by the intervention of this peculiar protagonist: the Zionism of the State of Israel. Is this an autonomous force with its own objectives and means?

Zionism is a reactive response of Jewish communities to the oppression they suffered through centuries of European history, especially in modern day Eastern and Central Europe. In this sense the story is a chapter in the sad history of Europe and has nothing to do with the Orient. The interaction between European and Oriental history is born of the choice of Palestine as the 'land of return'. It was a murderous choice as it implied the expulsion or extermination of a people whose home Palestine had been for 14 if not 20 centuries! But the choice was very convenient for Europe of the 19th and 20th centuries: it would be rid of the embarrassing 'Jews' and use them to settle Arab lands. The leaders of Zionism seized their chance and included their plan within the broader one of European colonial expansion. Without Britain's mandate over Palestine the State of Israel would have been quite impossible. The occupying power not only accepted into Palestine massive immigration taking the Jewish population from 60,000 in 1920 to 600,000 in 1948, and tolerated their organization into a military power in the state, but also actively fought the

Palestinian national liberation movement and terrorized its organization, particularly between 1936 and 1939, and thereby created the conditions for the Arab defeat of 1948.

The State of Israel, determined by the UN partition of 1947, never recognized the frontiers allocated to it and never accepted the very existence of the Palestinian people, Zionism saw its future in no other terms than indefinite expansion of its colonization. It never flinched at the means to attain its objectives: from the massacre at Deir Yassin in 1948 to those at Sabra and Chatila in 1982 (massacres for which Israel is to blame, whatever is said), by way of the violent settlement on the West Bank and the Golan Heights, the story is no different from that of other colonizations. It became clear that Israel intended not only to annex the whole of Palestine, the Golan Heights and probably South Lebanon, but also that it had not given up hope of Sinai and the West Bank. The 'greater Israel' map – stretching from the Nile to the Euphrates – and the staggering declarations of its leaders about its 'sphere of intervention' – from Zaire to Pakistan! – (however exaggerated such pretensions might seem) are not the fruit of Arab imagination, but declared intentions whose seriousness is confirmed in three decades of history.

The ideology and strategy underpinning such a plan are of necessity extremely simple. It is an ideology founded on a basic racism that was never absent from the 19th century European perception of the Arabs. The Zionists not only fail to see the Arab nation, or Arab nations, but also deny the Palestinian or Lebanese people the right of nationhood. They see them as merely a motley conglomeration whose identity is no more than that of religious or para-ethnic communities (Sunni Muslims, Shi'ites, Christians, Maronites, Druzes, and so on). Old colonial rubbish of the kind with which the French were besotted in North Africa until the day when they were proved worng by the factor of a previously denied national unity. This ideology, unbelievable in our day and shared only by the South African authorities (who in the same way are blind to any African reality except that of 'tribes') and for whom Zionism holds the greater esteem and friendship, is not exclusive to a few extremists. It is shared by Likud and the Labour Party, that is, by the main body of Israeli political forces.

The strategy adopted for the achievement of this colonial plan is itself, in the nature of things, extremely simple. Zionist expansion is not possible unless Israel's strategy sticks close to the strategy of more substantial external forces. The option of making Israel an instrument of US imperialism is a fundamental option that has never for an instant been challenged since 1948 by any Israeli political force (Labour and Likud). Israel is thus in a position to 'prove' to the United States that imperialism's utmost plan – compradorization of the Arab states – is within the bounds of possibility. If the Arab states are weak to the point of being negligible it is all the better for the interests of the West. The West takes as genuine partners only such as cannot be denied. Israel and Western imperialism share the same strategic aim: to prevent the Arab world from becoming powerful economically, socially and politically. The alliance between Israel and the West is not conjunctural. Contrary to what some imagine, it is not based on manipulation by a few 'lobbyists' motivated for one reason or another by concern for the Israeli electoral client. Israel has a key place in the United States' global strategy, it is not a formal member of the Atlantic military alliance but is *de facto* its most ardent member. It also provides for the Pentagon's strategists a test bed against Soviet weapons. When, as is currently the case, détente between the two superpowers is at a low ebb, the American–Israeli military alliance takes on a new significance. Zionism counts on this confrontation as one of its major trump cards.

The United States will never, in the foreseeable future at least, abandon its unconditional support for Israel. That is why it continues to ensure Israel's absolute military superiority, as it has always done, again despite what some ingenuous or manipulated propagandists would have us believe. Israel, systematically equipped with offensive weapons, while the Arab armies have never had more than defensive capacity, has always had overwhelming air superiority (even in October 1973, which was the moment of closest military balance, Egypt could not control the air space further than 15 kilometres east of the Suez Canal). Israel's strength is that of the West as a whole. That is why talk of Israel's 'autonomy', following its own objectives and with the means to do so and compelling the West to go along with it, must be discounted, to say the least. The truth is rather the opposite: it is a bluff skilfully used by Zionist propaganda; a bluff that the Arab bourgeoisies believe – or pretend to believe – since they hope to 'persuade' Washington . . .

The ideological component of the confrontation must not be underestimated. Israel knows how to exploit anti-semitism when it exists and even how to incite and arrange the necessary provocations to this effect, so that by posing as the victim it can stir up a current of favourable opinion, especially in the usually anti-colonialist leftist circles. Israel also knows how to make the most of the very strong feeling of solidarity of 'European' peoples against the 'barbaric threat' from Asia and Africa. Colonial and imperialist ventures have always benefited from this ambivalence in the popular classes and milieu of the European left. Obviously this pro-imperialist solidarity has objective foundations and the alignment of the European working-class parties with the imperialist policies of their bourgeoisies is neither new nor peculiar to the Israeli case. It has, on the contrary, been visible in a general way since the end of the 19th century and was denounced by Lenin as a betrayal. It should be noted that Israel's Labour Party remains a member of the Socialist International without embarrassment to that body's European members. It should also be noted that while the threats to the freedom of the Polish people disturb the European conscience, the threat of extermination of the Palestinian people disturbs it much less.

Israel is well aware that the themes of 'proletarian internationalism' and 'solidarity of the peoples against imperialism' are mere rhetoric of the left, whereas the appeal to pan-European solidarity against the peoples of Asia and Africa is a reality that still means something. Hence Zionism has succeeded in drawing on Western support from the right (and even sometimes the anti-semitic extreme right!) to the great majority of the left.

The Arab ruling classes and political leaderships, unable to rely on themselves alone – or their peoples – must perforce seek the active intervention 'on their behalf' of the Soviet Union or even of the imperialist forces.

The radical wing of the Arab bourgeoisie relied for a while on Soviet support. And the results this gave – the least unpromising in modern Arab history – might encourage false hopes. The Soviet presence in the region was genuine from 1955 – date of the first arms shipments to Egypt – to the aftermath of 1973 – when Sadat made a definitive and unfettered commitment to the US camp. Despite the fears of the Arab bourgeoisie, and even of Nasser, the USSR had no desire to set up satellite regimes in the region, and gave pledges to this effect. It simply wanted to make the American camp understand that any attempt at encirclement and military pressure aimed at isolating it or even forcing it to 'roll back' was bound to fail. In this the USSR found a natural ally in the traditional Arab willingness to resist the imperialists. Undoubtedly the possibility of Soviet expansionism cannot be ruled out, although traditionally this was reserved for contiguous areas (Turkey, Iran and at a later date Afghanistan). In the future the Soviet Union may well to make Europe understand that in case of need it could block petrol supply routes. Intervention in the Horn of Africa, the presence in South Yemen and the Indian Ocean is part of this possible line of development. But it has not happened. In the Middle East the USSR has always been concerned to reconcile its support for Arab nationalism with the demands of co-existence and détente. It would have liked to solve the local conflict through peaceful negotiated means in agreement with the United States, and has made several attempts at this but in vain.

The October 1973 war made it look for a while as if Europe would intervene in a similar way, for a peaceful settlement with definitive frontiers being imposed on Israel, Israel ceasing to be a constant threat, and a Palestinian state being established. Hitherto Europe had in effect been absent from the state and had here as elsewhere entrusted responsibility for defence of the West's collective interest to the United States. But the oil shock of 1973 reminded Europe how vulnerable it was and how selfish the United States; with this crisis, the prospect of greater European autonomy became attractive. As Europe saw Camp David operating in the opposite direction of compradorizing the Arab world mainly to the benefit of the United States and encouraging Israeli expansionism, Europe between 1973 and 1980 was moving in a new direction, distancing itself from the United States and Israel. It must be noted that this new policy of European autonomy was always wavering, and has been on the retreat since 1980. Europe's alignment with the US strategy is shown by overt or concealed support to Israel in the Lebanese war, manoeuvres to hold back recognition of the PLO, and objective complicity with Israel, with Europe securing for Israel what it probably could not have secured alone – the evacuation of Beirut by PLO forces that left Palestinian civilians at the mercy of their murderers. In 1973 a great opportunity was lost of making Israel accept Arab and Palestinian co-existence. This would have meant Europe using all its influence to support the Soviet proposal for a peace conference. Europe did not do so. Did it succumb to anti-Soviet blackmail? Or was it merely the victim of its incapability of doing more than waver, as usual? The Atlantic pact's accommodation with Reaganite blackmail, making North–South relations (the problematic where the Middle East issue belongs) dependent on East–West conflict is not a positive omen for the foreseeable future.

All the Arab bourgeoisies could do then was surrender to US dictates and beg for mercy. Undoubtedly in the confusion of 1973 Nixon and Kissinger threw out a hint that they might revise their unconditional support for Israel and opt for a better regional balance, making room for the new financial bourgeoisie of the Gulf, their long-time faithful friend, which with the decline of Nasserism had become the spokesman of the Arab ruling classes as a whole. The sequel has shown that the United States reverted to its fundamental option: unconditional support for Israel's colonial plan and the no less unconditional subjection of the recompradorized Arab bourgeoisies.

Africa and the Arab world in the world system

The Arab and African region is perhaps the empty belly of the entire world. The region at the moment seems scarcely able to respond positively to the challenges of the crisis. The gross Euro-American neo-colonialism to which Africa is subjected, its break-up into national states, manipulation by the authorities *in situ* of the ethnic, religious and other heterogeneities make the continent extremely weak. In the Arab world, corruption associated with oil revenue, the illusory 'compensatory' factor of neurotic recourse to 'specific character' – including religion – have deferred the unitary and socialist plan to the Greek calends. An uneasy balance of marginalized regions, abandoned to famine and despair (the Sahel for example) and poles of limited 'prosperity', associated with oil or mining royalties and their redistribution, is not an impossible prospect.

Since the remote time of the 15th century, the Mediterranean has been the centre of the regions of the old world to the west of the Indian and Chinese continents. Since the conquest of Alexander the region has borne the common imprint of Hellenism.

These were the foundations on which the Mediaeval Christian and Islamic universes were built. During a millenium we have here a constellation of interlocking societies enjoying cultural and ideological organic links and technological and trading exchanges sufficiently voluminous to be described as a system. Some of the constituent elements of capitalism (exchange and commodity capital, free wage labour, private property of land and enterprise) appeared in the region at an early stage and at certain moments – notably the first centuries of Islam and the period of the expansion of the Italian cities (from the 12th to 15th centuries – went so far as to form segments of that system, to the degree that it is possible to see the 'Mediterranean system' as the prehistoric forebear of the modern capitalist system.

The thesis of unequal development in the birth of capitalism is based on this contrast between the advanced (Italian and Arab) Mediterranean – that has become a handicap – and the backwardness of the European feudal periphery, that was to become an advantage in the birth of capitalism.

The Renaissance marks a qualitative break with the past, since it is then that the scattered ingredients of proto-capitalism crystallize to produce a new coherent social system, that of capitalism. By the same token the relation between power and wealth is inverted: until the Renaissance wealth had always depended on power, henceforth economic wealth would determine the content of political power. Likewise the old metaphysical ideological constructs (Hellenism, Christianity and Islam) coherent with the demands of a system based on the tribute-paying mode of production, would give place to a new political construct and a new kind of universalist aspiration. At the same time, the Renaissance saw the centre of gravity of the new capitalist world shift from the shores of the Mediterranean to those of the Atlantic. The former periphery of the Mediterranean system – north-west Europe – became the centre of the new European and Atlantic capitalist world system.

The Mediterranean region was in due course peripheralized in the development of the capitalist system. Its Arab southern shore would be colonized while the belated formation of the bourgeois national state in Italy and the Balkans would leave clear traces of underdevelopment. The Mediterranean ceased to belong to its bordering countries but became a geostrategic region for others, dominated by a hegemonic power, Britain, then the United States, or disputed by their rivals, Germany then the USSR.

The change created a new situation. Europeanism called the tune, since it was associated with the formation of the new capitalist and European centre, although it was henceforth impossible to separate the two aspects of the one reality. An avatar of Christendom? The creed, of Mediterranean and Oriental – not to say Egyptian – origin, spread into the barbarian North where it flourished, while it faded out and gave place to Islam to the south of the inland sea. The new reality of Europe seeks its supposed roots and ideological justifications in the ancient Mediterranean world that nurtured it: from the Renaissance rediscovering Greece and Rome to contemporary talk in EEC Europe making Athens the cultural capital of Europe, there is no shortage of such a quest for origins. But it is interesting to note here that these supposed roots are sought exclusively in the regions of the Mediterranean area that have remained Christian. Recognition of the role of Egypt and Islam is left to rare specialists; an appeal to popular feeling here would be regarded as almost indecent.

The crystallization of the Arab nation was a product of reaction to the new challenge, nothing to do with the challenges of the previous centuries, even allowing for that of the Crusades. The Arabization and Islamization from the Atlantic to the Gulf are undoubtedly earlier, and so an Arab nation was fully in existence in the first centuries of Islam, then in its first glory. Evidence, too, of this region's lead over feudal and fragmented Europe: the centralization of surplus by the class of warrior merchants, the alliance of the cities they led and the Khalifate, to keep control of communications and the countryside, are the foundations of this nation. Yet it later decayed, with the decline of the great trade and the call for the help of the Turkish barbarians of Central Asia. The Ottoman reunification did not halt the process, but even to some extent accelerated it. Hence the renaissance of the Arab nation would come in dual reaction to the European challenge and Ottoman domination. This renaissance began early, since the threat of European advance was quickly felt in the 18th century, that is only a century or so after the gap first came into being. On the other side there was very quickly a consciousness of the danger of an Arab renaissance. The unrelenting hostility of Europe to Mohamed Ali's attempt to modernize the Nile Valley, to raise the dignity of and free the Arab Mashreq (in the first half of the 19th century) has turned into a constant feature of the West's strategy towards Egypt. The hegemonic powers of the capitalist centre – Britain in the 19th century, the United States nowadays – have always deemed it essential to their predominance to maintain Egypt in such a ruinous condition that it could not become the pivot of a revived Arab nation, that is, a genuine partner in the worldwide capitalist system. The plan of creating an artificial European state in Palestine to undermine such a possibility, was dreamed up by Palmerston in 1839, a score of years before Zionism even took shape.

Did not colonization, a recent (19th century) phenomenon, open a definitive divide and turn the Mediterranean into a frontier zone of the main confrontation of our time: between North and South? For colonization wrought inequalities of economic development considerably more reprehensible than in the past, difficult to reverse except by recourse to a diametrically opposite perspective to that of the expansion of the world capitalist system from its outset. Colonization has also revealed a moral and political contrast, and given the religious dimension (of Christianity and Islam) a weight it did not have in the past and one now capable of nurturing fanaticism.

It is clearly understood that as the hegemonic centres of the worldwide capitalist system lie outside the Mediterranean region, the Sea ceases to be the centre of its world to become a geostrategic zone for others. From the destruction of Napleon's fleet at Trafalgar, until 1945, Britain dominated the Mediterranean – which provided her shortest route to India. This was reluctantly ceded, after the Second World War, to give way to the era of the 'American Mediterranean'.

After the Second World the European Mediterranean countries, with the exception of Yugoslavia and Albania, were absorbed into Western reconstruction under the aegis of the United States, then gradually integrated into the EEC largely subject to the dominant forces of transnationalization. And if they do show economic take-off, their future development is bound up with that of their European associates and subsequently to the evolution of the developed capitalist centres as a whole. As for the Arab states, they have tried to reconstruct themselves as bourgeois national states without any success so far.

This dual evolution has dug the Mediterranean ditch so deep as to make it the frontier of North–South confrontation. In such circumstances the possibilities are wide open. Either the popular social forces will impose reconstruction within the unity of the Arab world, in the framework of a strategy that, in the nature of things, will be delinked from the logic of the overall expansion of transnational capital; on the best hypothesis this reconstruction would be part of a peaceful transition towards a polycentric world. For this Europe would have to distance itself from the Atlantic alliance and view with favour the Arab revival. Or the drifts already under way would continue and the confrontations grow more acute. The Europeans would then be in danger of pursuing a chimerical plan of an imperialist revival, with the aim of hitching the Maghreb, like Turkey, to their wagon, while Egypt and the Mashreq would be abandoned to the regional hegemony of the Zionist state.

Notes

1. Amin, Samir and Amoa, Kwame, *Echanges internationaux et sous-développement*, Paris, Anthropos, 1974; Amoa, Kwame, 'Lomé III. Critique of a Prologue', Dakar, 1986, mimeo.

2. Amin, Samir, 'Pour un aménagement du système monétaire des pays de la zone franc', *Revue Française d'Etudes Politiques Africaines*, No. 41, 1969. See, too, Tremblay, R., (ed.), *Zone franc et développement*, Montreal, Université de Montréal, 1972.

3. Amin, Samir, 'The conditions for autonomy in the Mediterranean region' in Yachir, Faysal, *The Mediterrean: Prospects for Development*, London, Zed Books, 1989. See too Amin, Samir, 'L'Avenir du Maghreb dépend-il de la CEE?', Rabat, 1981; *Les conditions d'une solidarité euro-africaine*, Paris, Berger-Levrault, 1982; 'Le Contexte Economique des Relations Euro-Arabes', *Mons Symposium*, 1984.

4. Cox, Oliver, *Capitalism as a System*, New York, Monthly Review, 1964; Addo, Herb, *Imperialism the Permanent State of Capitalism*, Tokyo, UNU, 1986.

5. Frank A. G., *Crisis in the Third World*, London, Heinemann, 1981; articles by Paul Sweezy in Monthly Review 1985–86.

6. See Giovanni Arrighi's contribution in *Dynamics of Global Crisis*; see too Kennedy, Paul, *The Rise and Fall of the Great Powers: Economic Change and Military Conflict from 1500 to 2000*, London, Unwin Hyman, 1988.

7. Hansen, Emmanuel, (ed.) *Africa: Perspectives on Peace and Development*, London, Zed Books, 1987.

8. Amin, Samir, 'Les perspectives de l'Afrique australe', *Tiers Monde*, No. 77, 1979. See Samir Amin's preface to Amin, Samir, Chitala, Derrick, and Mandaza, Ibbo, (eds) *SADCC: Problems and Prospects for Disengagement and Development in Southern Africa*, London, Zed Books, 1987.

9. Amin, Samir, 'Le Conflict du Moyen Orient dans une Perspective Mondiale' in Khader, Bichara, (ed.) *La Coopération Euro-Arabe*, Louvain, 1982; Amin, Samir, 'Eurocentrisme et politique', *IFDA*, No. 65, 1988; Chapter 1 of Amin, Samir and Yachir, Faysal, 'La Méditerranée dans le système mondial'.

5. Alternative Development for Africa and the Third World

As the Third World is a heterogeneous entity, any general statements run the risk of exaggeration. It might, however, be said that the common social inequalities are sadly striking, or scandalous, and that the practice of democracy of the most basic kind is the exception rather than the rule. In the current orthodoxy, social inequality and the absence of democracy are the way out of poverty. Capital accumulation is necessarily accompanied in its early stages by impoverishment of the peasantry and wretchedness for the worker. Later, as the rural surplus is absorbed, the labour movement will gradually impose better material conditions and political democracy. Arthur Lewis's well-known thesis of the dualities of societies in transition to development, and that of the Latin American 'desarrollismo' school of the 1950s, are in conformity with this.

The thesis assumes that the external factor (integration in the worldwide economic system) is fundamentally 'favourable' in the sense that it offers this 'development' opportunity. The latter will be grasped more or less quickly in accordance with the internal conditions characteristic of the various societies of the Third World and that these conditions are decisive.

In fact, contrary to this orthodox view, the world expansion of capitalism is accompanied by increasing inequality in social distribution at the periphery, whereas at the centre of the system it does create conditions for lesser social inequality (and a broad stability in distribution, as the foundation for a democratic consensus). As the bourgeoisie in the periphery are unable to control the process of local accumulation, which thereby remains a process of constant 'adjustment' to the constraints of worldwide accumulation, the plan of construction of a bourgeois national state is not only handicapped by a fundamentally unfavourable external factor, but also totally impossible. The peripheral state is therefore necessarily despotic by virtue of its weakness. In order to survive it is obliged to avoid conflict with the dominant imperialist forces and tries to improve its international position at the expense of more vulnerable peripheral partners.

The conclusion that must be drawn is that social and political democracy and the international solidarity of peoples demands that we abandon the myth of the 'national bourgeoisie' and replace the 'national bourgeois' plan with a 'national and popular' plan. Democracy and social progress are inseparable and this is the price we must pay.

Inequality in income distribution at the centre and periphery[1]

Empirical research on income distribution shows that unequal income distribution is more pronounced at the periphery of the capitalist world system than in its advanced centres. The main reason is that labour productivity is considerably more unequally distributed from one sector to another at the periphery. The distribution of value added per worker from one sector to another is relatively closely grouped around the mean in the OECD countries, but very unequally distributed in the countries of the Third World. This is an illustration of the fact that the law of value operates at the level of the world capitalist system and not at the level of its national components. It is striking to see that the distribution of Lorenz curves is not at all a chance one.[2] In fact the curves of all the developed capitalist countries are grouped together in a narrow band. By contrast the distributions in all the countries of the contemporary Third World are considerably more differentiated. Two approximate medians for each of the two bands correspond to the following:

25% of the population receive 10% of the income in the centre and 5% in the periphery;
50% of the population receive 25% of the income in the centre and 10% in the periphery;
75% of the population receive 50% of the income in the centre and 33% in the periphery.

The rough congruence of the Lorenz curves for the developed countries suggests that, as we know to be so, the Western societies are very close to each other today in their daily reality. The position of different countries within the band of the Lorenz curves for the countries of the centre suggests that improvements in distribution are tied to the existence of powerful Social-Democratic forces, but that this improvement is extremely limited in its real amplitude. The most advanced Social-Democratic countries, Sweden and those of northern Europe, are to be found near the minimal inequality curve; the liberal countries (United States) and the less developed ones (of southern Mediterranean Europe) are near the maximal inequality curve.

The distribution of curves of Third World countries can at first seem disconcerting. There is no visible correlation between the degree of inequality on the one hand and, on the other, such variables as GDP per capita, the degree of urbanization, and the level of industrialization. A closer examination will however make some sense out of this distribution.

As regards the distribution of income in the capitalist centres, it is sufficient to make three theoretical hypotheses to find the median of the band of Lorenz curves for the OECD countries: (1) a division of wages and profits of the order of 60–40; (2) prices paid to the labour force distributed around the average value of labour power, such that the ratio of the lower to the upper quartile of wages is 1 to 4; (3) the existence of a certain number of small and medium-size businesses and other activities (such as the liberal professions – so that wage workers constitute 80% of the total population and that the average individual income of members of these other social groups is to be found in the middle and higher sectors of the distribution.

As regards the societies of peripheral capitalism, we initially find a good approximation of the curve illustrating distribution of agricultural income (which corresponds to the median representative of the real situations in South and South-East Asia, the Arab world and Latin America) by assuming: (a) the antecedent of a rural class society that leases at the disposal of the peasantry only about half of their production; (b) the expropriation of the surplus in the form of land rent by large landowners, and later after agrarian reform by rich peasants; (c) a 'natural' inequality of productivity of land in a range of 1 to 2; (d) an increase of rural density and constitution of a surplus labour reserve of the order of one third of rural labour force.

In a second stage the urban economy comes into the picture. In the capitalist sector, which employs half at most of the active urban population, there is: (i) a higher level of surplus-value resulting in a division between wages and profits of 40–60 instead of 60–40; (ii) a hierarchy of wages that is sharper (1–6 instead of 1–4), but persons in the 'informal' sector, which employs more or less the other half of the active urban population, receive income of the order of magnitude of that of the poorest quartile of the capitalist sector.

We then combine the two curves, taking into account: (1) the proportion of urban to rural population, which varies from one country to another; and (2) the marked gap between urban and rural net product per capita, when this product is measured in prices and current income, as it is in the statistics of the real contemporary economy. This gap is always of the order of 1 to 3, that is to say, the product per capita is three times higher in the urban economy than it is in the rural economy. The result thus obtained, that is, the curve constructed on the basis of simple elements combined together, is interesting: we find the median of the actual distributions in the contemporary Third World.

The question that arises is whether this situation is 'transitory', that is, whether the distribution that corresponds to it and that describes it is evolving towards the model of developed countries. In other words, is there a historical tendency of the movement of distribution, linked to the movement in capital accumulation? On this we note three differing kinds of response as follows:

(1) There is no historical tendency for this movement. In other words, the distribution is only the empirical result of various economic and social facts whose movements, convergent or divergent, are autonomous. One can give this proposition a 'Marxist' form by formulating it as distribution depending on class struggles in all their national complexity (for example, the alliance of the bourgeoisie and peasantry, social democracy) and international complexity (imperialism and the position occupied in the international division of labour, and so on). The capitalist system would be capable of adapting itself to all these diverse situations.

(2) There is a historical tendency operating in the direction of a progressive reduction of inequality. The situation of the contemporary periphery is simply

that of a transition towards capitalist development that has not yet been completed.

(3) There is a historical tendency of immiseration and of growing inequality. It remains to be analysed why this should be so (resulting from what predominant force that cannot be counteracted by opposing forces) and at what level it is so (at the level of each capitalist state separately, at the level of the totality of developed or underdeveloped countries, or even at the level of the world economy including both the centre and the periphery).

We know quite well the concrete history of the accumulation in the developed capitalist centres. Over and above local variations, one plausible generalization may be formulated along the following lines. The peasant revolution, which in those areas marked the beginning of the era of capital, reduced inequality in the countryside wherever it was radical. This reduction came at the expense of the 'feudal sectors' but at the same time it impoverished a minority of poor peasants who were pushed into the cities. The wage worker initially received a low level of wages determined by the income of the poor peasants. This level tended to rise after a period of stagnation at this level (or even a deterioration) when the expulsion of the landless peasants slowed down. From then on (about 1860?) workers' wages and the real income of 'middle' peasants tended to rise in a parallel fashion, in conjunction with the rise of productivity. There was even a tendency towards equality between average wages and peasant income, although this tendency is not necessarily observable at each state of the accumulation process (this depending on the structures of the alliance of hegemonic classes). At the late stage of capital, there is perhaps a 'social-democratic' tendency to reduce inequality, but this latter operates in conjunction within imperialism. A favourable position in the international division of labour favours social redistribution. Still one cannot generalize, since the comparative evolutions of Sweden and the United States, for example, are quite different.

One is thus led willy-nilly to an inability to pursue this analysis on the centres in isolation; one has to place this evolution within the framework of the world system. Our thesis here is that the stability of distribution at the centre in the contemporary era does not exclude, but rather supposes, a much more unequal distribution at the periphery. The realization of value at the level of the system as a whole requires this complementary opposition of structures. One is thus led to the unavoidable question: what is the trend of the movement of distribution in the peripheries? There can be no doubt that the trend is in the direction of the increase of inequality, at least in the course of the past century (1880–1980).

In other words, the idea of progress by stages that is reproduced with only a lag in time is obviously an idea attractive for its simplicity, but nonetheless false. The idea, therefore, that the presently developed countries offer the image of what the underdeveloped countries will be tomorrow, despite the fact that four centuries of capitalist history and particularly the past century give it the lie, remains quite alive.

In the logic of this vision of 'stages', the question of inequality in distribution is considered a question of relative quantity only, without qualitative significance. But it is not a question merely of greater inequality. The latter leads to putting into operation and developing a productive system that is qualitatively different from what it is in central capitalism.

If, in fact, one allocates different resources (unskilled labour and skilled labour, capital) to the final consumers (the different strata of the population according to their income, which they receive directly and indirectly through investments and public expenditures), one discovers:

- at the centre the different resources are allocated to the consumption of each stratum in proportions that are more or less the same as the share of consumption of each of these strata;
- at the periphery, on the other hand, the scarce resources are allocated to the consumption of the richest strata in proportions that are greater than the proportion of their consumption in total consumption. This 'distortion' of distribution to the benefit of higher strata is all the stronger since distribution is unequal.

The productive apparatus of the countries of the periphery is thus not the reproduction of that of the centre at an earlier stage of its evolution. These apparatuses differ qualitatively. That is the meaning of inequality in the international division of labour. These differences explain the fact that while the Lorenz curve for the centre is stable (or perhaps moves towards less inequality), at the periphery it moves the other way towards greater inequality. The distortion in distribution is a condition of enlarged reproduction, of accumulation on a world scale.

In this sense, Marx's thesis concerning immiseration is perfectly visible on the world scale. If distribution tends to be more and more unequal at the periphery, whose population constitutes the majority of the world system, and stable at the centre, it obviously evolves towards greater inequality at the global level. Is not the fact that immiseration is manifested at the world level but not at the level of the centre yet further proof that the law of value operates at the global level and not at that of individual, isolated, capitalist formations? But immiseration operates at the periphery not only by means of the increase of the rate of surplus value but also by way of the indirect extraction of surplus labour in non-capitalist forms whether they are long-established or newly-created.

The alternative: popular national development, social and political democracy, delinking[3]

The worldwide expansion of capitalism is therefore by its nature doubly polarizing: from the origin of capitalism four centuries ago to our own day the polarization between centres and peripheries has been and is inherent in the system; within the peripheral societies social polarization is increasing. The dual contradiction, the main aspect of the contradictions of capitalism, is insurmountable within the framework of the world system. Integration in the world system – the 'external factor' – is not only an unfavourable factor in itself, but is becoming increasingly so.

The belated attempts at crystallization of the bourgeois national state have been and continue to be bound to fail and, through compradorization, doomed to perpetuate polarization in the new forms corresponding to the system's overall development.

The polarization is to blame for the socially and politically intolerable regimes at the periphery of the system. Socially intolerable as they are based on the impoverishment and exclusion of the broad masses. Politically intolerable in the past in the sense that the introduction of the system required colonial domination; and intolerable in the present and future in the sense that pursuit of local development within a prospect of further worldwide expansion requires the newly independent state to remain despotic. Hence democracy is not the 'rule', but an exception, always vulnerable and appearing intermittently in the impasse of capitalist development. Contrary to the 'optimistic' thesis of development by stages, whereby the social suffering and despotism would gradually be overcome by capitalist expansion, such expansion constantly reproduces them.

In these circumstances, capitalism has put on the agenda its supersession from the starting point of a 'revolt of the periphery'. In this sense the 'socialist revolutions' – all produced in the peripheries and semi-peripheries of the system (Russia, China, and so on) – and the national liberation movements are the main features of the most essential change in our modern world. Together, these struggles – actually or potentially – inaugurate the 'post-capitalist' age.

Instead of contrasting agriculture and industry in a metaphysical and absolute way, consideration should first be given to their place in the conceptualization and practice of the 'modernization' theory and then how they can work within a national and popular outlook. The agricultural revolution requires industrialization but not on the lines so far envisaged for Africa and the Third World.

Over the 1980s, deterioration of the economic and social system throughout the Third World (and particularly in the vast majority of African countries) leads increasingly to a challenge to the dogmas of the theory and practice of conventional development policies. The subject of an alternative option of 'autocentric' development has thus become unexpectedly popular. The use of this term by various people in various contexts (or even in extremely vague terms) makes it worth providing a preliminary definition of the concept before considering how it operates in the conditions of Africa today.

The first formulation we proposed of this concept dates back to 1957 and says literally:

Whereas in the model of autocentric accumulation external relations are subject to the logic and imperatives of internal accumulation, in the model of extraverted development, it is on the contrary external relations that determine almost entirely the rate and character of internal accumulation.

This concise formula remains our definition of the issue, but warrants some clarification. The contrast between the autocentric model and the extraverted model was not deduced from an a priori abstract theory or from an ideological whim. It was the conclusion from a comparative historical analysis. Three kinds of historical experience were considered: a) the development of the countries and regions of developed capitalism in all its historical breadth, from the mercantilist epoch to our own time; b) development of the regions of underdeveloped capitalism in the same historical breadth; c) contemporary socialist development.

The theory of accumulation on an explicitly world scale argues that the history of (capitalist) development from its origin (about the 16th century) to our own time is not one of juxtaposition of 'national' developments, with the 'latecomers' retreading the path of their predecessors, but of a world system divided into driving centres and driven and dominated peripheries shaped by the centres. The whole (the world economic system or 'world economy') is logically superior to its parts ('local economies') and not the sum of them. It can logically be deduced that development (other than peripheral dominated growth) for the 'South' would henceforth entail a 'rupture' with the logic of worldwide accumulation and could not form part of it.

In the centres, development has been autocentric from the beginning, but never autarkic; very much the reverse. The centres, by subjecting the peripheries to the demands of their accumulation, have accelerated that accumulation. The hegemonic centres (Great Britain from 1763 to 1870, the United States from 1944 to 1970) preached the ideology of economic freedom, in the forms appropriate to the system of the time: free trade for the Pax Britannica and free enterprise for the Pax Americana. The non-hegemonic centres never accepted submission to the consequences of this ideology. They preached and above all practised various forms of protectionism (in the broad sense of the term) necessary for them to avoid their peripheralization; they thus often succeeded in accelerating their autocentric development and even in challenging the hegemonies. This protectionism (with regard to the hegemonic centres) was not synonymous with autarky but on the contrary with aggressive outreach to the peripheries.

The socialist countries as 'less advanced' countries have all not only adopted the principle of autocentric development (subjecting external relations to internal accumulation) but have also virtually moved into a quasi-autarkic phase, one imposed by the world system rather than desired by themselves. If the USSR and China are nowadays more willing to entertain the international division of labour it does not mean that these countries have renounced the principle of autocentric development.

The Third World is part of the world capitalist system but with the status of periphery. It has never practised an autocentric strategy, but at best under some circumstances begun to challenge some aspects of the extraverted peripheral strategy. It has also sometimes benefited from a relaxation of central control, during wars and crises; and it is interesting to note that it is often in these periods that autocentric development does begin, only to be destroyed in the subsequent phase. In extreme cases, during the liberation wars, the bush fighters being obliged to a *de facto* autarky, have pushed the changes bringing autocentric basic development further than anywhere else in the Third World. Such slogans as 'self-reliance', 'standing on one's own feet', which clearly have a political sense, have been born out of the popular movement for national liberation, not by chance.

As a schematic of the contrast between the autocentric model and the extraverted model we proposed to identify four sectors: 1. Production of the means of production; 2. Production of mass consumer goods; 3. Luxury production and consumption; 4. Exports. We defined the autocentric model as one governed mainly by an articulation of sectors 1 and 2, and the extraverted model as determined mainly by the articulation of sectors 4 and 3. The model leads to a major conclusion. In the autocentric model the rewards for labour (wages and peasant income) must necessarily increase at the rate of progress in productivity. By comparison, in the extraverted model, the rewards for labour may be disconnected from growth in productivity.

That conclusion has its political side in the following: (i) development for a Third World country cannot be achieved by the adjustment of its economy to the demands of the international division of labour, but on the contrary by delinking this economy from that logic; (ii) this delinking is a necessary (but not sufficient) condition for an autocentric development that remains impossible if it is not popular (that is, if the benefits of increased productivity are not immediately passed on to the broad masses); (iii) in comparison, growth whose benefits are intended mainly for a minority is not only possible on the basis of extraverted development (but not possible always and everywhere) but also calls for such development, more effective for this purpose than an autocentric model.

For the Third World, therefore, autocentric development is synonymous with national and popular development. The preceding arguments have, we hope, pointed to certain ambiguities of expression. The concept of national and popular autocentric development should not be trivialized and treated either as a series of 'protectionist measures', or autarky. No more should it be confused with 'dependence'. It is true that peripheral economies are dependent, in the sense that the rates and forms of their growth are governed by those of the centres (whereas the converse is not true). But the difference between the two concepts (of periphery and dependence) is clear as soon as we consider the case of non-peripheral dependent economies: Canada for instance, where national capital holds only a subordinate position, dominated by United States capital, but where the growth in labour incomes is parallel with that of productivity. Canada is more of a province of the United States than anything else (and as it is not in fact a province, it is to some extent a dependent state). The dynamic of its accumulation (through the articulation of sectors 1 and 2) is similar to that of California or Alabama, and not of Haiti or Brazil.

The alternative option of autocentric, national and popular development is not only possible, in Africa and elsewhere, in the sense that there is no overwhelming 'technical' obstacle making it impossible (the obstacle is always social), it is even objectively necessary, in the sense that a persistent rejection of this option means remaining in a trap.

The autocentric national and popular strategy depends primarily on the principle of the most equitable income distribution possible, especially between the countryside and the town, between the modern, more highly productive sectors and the backward sectors. The extra output on labour incomes that have been equalized is a surplus that, if it is national and is retained for accumulation, will ensure marked growth, and a parallel and equal advance in popular consumption. The structure of demand thus generated allows priority to basic needs and directs the productive system towards their satisfaction.

It should be appreciated that a schema of growth of this kind cannot be the rsult of the operation of the laws of the market on the basis of the world system's pricing. A decision to regulate rewards of labour on an egalitarian basis determined by average rural productivity (equality in the cereal 'ration' for the town and the countryside, a narrow range of urban wages not modelled on that of the West), to nationalize the surplus, to ensure its centralization and redistribution in the context of the country, all these are political decisions implying taking the system of economic options away from 'project analysis' and 'profitability', the sacrosanct principles of technocratic economics.

Without attempting a misleading description of the precise details of the steps to be taken to implement a development schema of this kind, we might say:

a) It entails not only declaring priority for agriculture, but putting it into effect. This means that other activities where productivity is superior should not occasion income distribution higher than that in agriculture. Otherwise demand is such that satisfaction of the needs expressed by the more privileged will absorb most of what is available for accumulation, and agriculture will be sacrificed. Clearly, in this case the peasants, learning from their experience, will resist the 'progress' offered them, as they know that its benefits will not come back to them. At worst, priority for 'food crops', unless overall policies are revised appropriately, will mean production of cheap food (as a burden on the peasants) to sustain conditions favourable to maintaining a supply of cheap manpower (to the detriment therefore of the urban workers and sole benefit of capital, particularly through the mechanism of the international division of labour, foreign capital).

b) It entails that industrialization be conceived primarily as a support to progress in agricultural productivity: production of appropriate inputs (fertilizers, tools, for example), infrastructural work (irrigation, transport and so on), packaging and processing of products, among others. It also entails that this industry satisfy the non-food consumption needs of rural and urban workers, on as egalitarian a basis as possible and, that on the basis of this demand, an integrated chain of intermediate and machine tool industry is established to provide for efficient manufacturing production of consumer goods. It goes without saying that this national industry cannot be foregone in favour of imports. The latter have to be paid for with exports, and the comparative advantages are those resulting from the world system prices and incomes, in contradiction with the political coherence sketched above. Importation must be reduced to the minimum at each stage and not offset by a high level of exports.

c) It entails national and popular forms of social organization of production: peasant control over agricultural projects, genuine co-operatives (that are not the means of exaction on the peasants through administrative frameworks depriving the peasant of control over production), machinery for collective negotiation of agricultural prices, national control over industry, a national wages policy, redistribution of sources of finance over the country, and so forth. It is hard to see any role for the multinationals in this schema, except to supply very occasionally and under strict national control some 'recipe' for production or organization.

d) It entails a relation to technology other than simple 'transfer'. It means, in fact, providing scope for inventiveness, not for motives of cultural nationalism, but merely because the available techniques, especially the advanced one, are not neutral in regard to the kind of product, the quality of the demand to be satisfied (Western models), the prices and incomes structure that governs the viability of these techniques, and so on.

e) It entails limited external relations radically different from those flowing from the alternative industrialization strategies of import substitution or export promotion. Import substitution is based on existing demand, within an income distribution structure of very pronounced inequality; plus regard on this basis for the principles of profitability (with arguments for 'modest protection for infant industries' in a brief transitional period). It therefore encourages imports of intermediate goods (as the industrial part is not integrated) and sophisticated producer goods (as the demand to be satisfied in competition with imports imitates the Western consumer model and is capital intensive). It therefore remains extraverted. By contrast, autocentric national and popular industry is not established in the light of existing demand; it creates demand by satisfying the people's needs (incomes policy) and the intermediate and related needs. The continued importation is to bridge gaps in the range of these related needs, gradually reducing their relative importance (but not necessarily their absolute volume). It therefore subjects external relations to the logic of internal accumulation and thereby warrants its description. As for export industry, it is by definition extraverted. All the more so as in the effort to compete with the industry of the advanced countries on their own ground it must resort to massive importation of advanced technology. This explains why the NICs, which are the most advanced in this direction, are also the most heavily indebted; export industry does not relieve the external balance of payments (contrary to the argument in its favour made by the World Bank), but worsens it.

f) It entails the establishment of a national structure of interdependence between prices and sources of finance that is in conflict with the very principles of micro-economic profitability. In fact the autocentric industry, in order to meet popular needs, must accept the juxtaposition of highly unequal production units – modern industries, semi-mechanized manufactures, crafts factories. The unity of labour rewards and prices will lead to unequal surpluses. These must be redistributed to avoid the polarization of progress in the modern units; and on the contrary to finance the gradual modernization of the backward sectors with the surplus from the modern sectors. This is scarcely possible on a substantial scale without broad public ownership: the national private enterprise and a fortiori the subsidiary of the multinational will not agree to distance themselves from profitability to this extent. As we know, they have behaved in a totally opposite manner, and by destroying uncompetitive crafts have made unemployment worse and deprived the population of a useful product.

This schema shows that a surplus broadly sufficient to finance development is possible even in a 'poor' country. Obviously there are other sides to the issue, related to the size of the country, its natural resources potential, and so on, that have not been discussed here. The argument for an 'open door' rests on three considerations: (1) the need for a massive appeal for foreign capital and imported technology; (2) the comparative advantage of specialization; and (3) the question of size (for example, natural resources, markets). The first argument neglects the price to be paid for this importation of capital and technology, and encourages laziness. The second argument is based on a thesis of comparative advantage that ignores the concept of the unequal international division of labour, and hence the transfers of value inherent in the system of world prices. Only the third argument contains a vestige of truth.

Obstacles to popular national, autocentric and delinked development

The obstacles to the implementation of these principles are obvious. But are they unstoppable? What are the most serious obstacles? We can think of five.[4]

a) The obstacle of size, especially of the African countries, is evident. But it has much greater impact on industry than on agriculture. In fact many of the immediate problems facing agriculture could be solved by direct action at the base, and by the base. Undoubtedly, solution of these problems would require some materials to be imported if they cannot be supplied by local industry. The obstacle here is less the impossibility of supplying the means than the social framework imposed by the global strategy. If the role of agriculture is to provide a surplus for – at best – an unrelated industrialization or, more often, parasitic consumption, it is useless to expect rural mobilization, since an attempt is being made to smash the peasants' autarky not to improve their lot but to exploit them. The methods envisaged reveal this option: a preference for huge dams and enclosed settlements, plantations for the multinationals and the green revolution associated with modernized large and medium scale properties (driving the poor peasants off the land), state farms and co-operatives, imposing on the country the crops and techniques that produce an increasing surplus. These methods suit the agribusiness supplies of inputs; but they are extremely expensive and of dubious efficiency, owing to the very factor of peasant resistance. A diffused progress, based on thousands of small improvements – assured water supply for small holdings, intensive agriculture and livestock, among others, calls for an entirely different social framework and an overall strategy that does not aim at securing an increasing surplus from the peasants. Size is not much of an obstacle at this stage. And it can be seen that some of the large African countries, where this obstacle does not exist, do no better than the others.

This obstacle should not prevent the beginning of an autocentric industrialization, at least for the countries with a population of more than five million. Undoubtedly the industrialization for these countries would not be 'complete' and would not avoid fairly heavy dependence on imports. Moreover, the obstacle could be lessened by intra-African co-operation, founded on planned complementarities. But this co-operation is incompatible with the 'common market' formula that encourages rather than reduces inequalities.

b) The effort required of Africa to achieve the agricultural revolution is gigantic. The problem of the agricultural revolution in the contemporary Third World is in no way comparable with that Europe faced in centuries gone by. Development economists nearly always forget that the European agricultural revolution involved a vast movement of expulsion from the rural areas. At the time the migration had two trump cards to play: the industry of the day had jobs on offer out of all proportion to the jobs available in modern industry; and Europe had an outlet in overseas emigration that is closed nowadays to the Third World. It suffices to recall that the regions inhabited through European migration (the American continent, Australia and New Zealand, white South Africa . . .) have nowadays ten times the population of the regions of Europe where these populations originated to see the difficulties population pressures would have meant for Europe in the absence of the migration.

In today's Third World the agricultural revolution has to be made at the same time as the majority of the population must for some time to come be maintained in the countryside. This is still possible in South and South-East Asia, and in China, and in some regions of Africa. But already, as in the Arab and Latin American countries, urbanization is accelerating at such a rate that it will be too late to do it tomorrow.

c) Advanced, sometimes maniacal, urbanization is a new and additional obstacle. In this case, what has been said of relations between agriculture and industry is also true of relations between the modern urban activities and the so-called 'informal' sectors. In other words, forms of useful activity that show low productivity must be rediscovered to ensure the long transition. The latter must not be conceived as the source of financing for the other activities, as is the case in current capitalist relations, where the 'modern' sector benefits from super-exploitation of the 'informal' sector and it is the latter that supplies cheap components for reproduction of the labour force. The relation must be reversed.

d) Integration in the world system is of itself an obstacle. This integration benefits those centres that have peripheries – whether true colonies or not – to contribute to their own accumulation, while the peripheries – who are not in a position to exploit colonies in turn! – are expected to do the same. Undoubtedly the external obstacle would have been lessened if the demands the Third World formulated in the plan for a 'New International Economic Order' had been met. To be sure the NIEO was not in itself an autocentric strategy, since it was basically a revision of the international division of labour on terms beneficial to the South. But this improvement in the resources available to the South might have been put to use in making autocentric development less difficult. The NIEO plan was aimed at changing for the better the mode of Third World integration in the world system, by 'adjustment' of the North to the demands of the South's development. It is clear that the fight has to be fought on two grounds, the long-term strategy, which must be for delinking, and the medium-term strategy, which aims at reducing the damaging effects of the world system as it is.

e) If the internal factor is decisive, it is in the sense that in the final analysis the real obstacle is emphatically social, since autocentric development sacrifices the privileged growth of the middle classes. The adjustment policies proposed serve to reinforce these classes, through the liberalization of prices and transfers, for example. The aim is obviously political; it is a matter of reinforcing the class allies of international capital, of creating a 'comprador' state and society.

In the remaining chapters we shall return in greater detail to the conditions for national and popular development, the internal factors (popular alliance, democracy, new state, and so on, in Chapter 6) and the external factors (South–South co-operation, in Chapter 7; favourable international evolution, in Chapter 8).

Meanwhile, is there something positive to be done?

a) Returning to the example of the CILSS, it should be noted that the advantage of the position taken by the Arab Bank for the Development of African States (BADEA) is that it does not, in the ingenuous way of the World Bank, assume that the world environment is by definition 'favourable'. On the contrary BADEA seeks to define the relations between the (more or less favourable) modes of integration in the world system and the possible modes of agricultural development.

From this point of view it is easy to identify two approaches, each in its way extreme, and possibly a provisional compromise solution.

The first extreme approach: acceptance of the current forms of integration in the world system, depending on mining or oil royalties (when there are any!) or exporting tropical agriculture, and seeking to develop import substitution industry on this basis. This is ultimately the World Bank option. But it is a mediocre one, as history shows.

Moreover, this option is a dire prospect for the regions without mining or tropical agricultural potential. For the Sahel it means famine and beggary, with an effort to make them the least explosive possible by preserving the archaic structures of the rural universe and crowning them with a naturally despotic comprador state.

The second extreme approach: delinking through national and popular revolution, strengthened by regional, or African, unity. In the long run there is no other answer.

Meanwhile is it possible to imagine a better form of integration in the world system and agricultural development?

A better world integration is possible if one is able, in regard to:

i) *mining or oil royalties*, to impose a new negotiated, stable and 'acceptable' guaranteed level, with good popular management of this income to avoid the pure and simple waste that commonly occurs; ii) *agriculture*, to complement the effort to export specific tropical crops (with arrangements ensuring stable remunerative prices) through an effort to develop food and similar crops (dry-farmed and irrigated cereals, fruit and vegetables, extensive and intensive livestock, fish) for the local market and in the expectation of greater South–South trade, especially between the African and Arab countries; iii) *industries*, to move out of the narrow horizon of substitution light industry on small country scale to a complementary programme of machine tools and light industry on the scale of a group of associated countries. As an example, the iron mining in Mauritania could serve as the basis for ship construction giving Senegal, whose maritime role is obvious, a place in the establishment of West African merchant shipping and ensuring genuine industrialization of fishing.

Better agricultural development for a region such as the Sahel also requires relinquishment of archaic structures, without thinking that marginalizing them through the emergence of a kulak class would meet the challenge. The middle road is acceptance of some measure of 'inequality', but on a regional rather than social basis. Does common sense not suggest that it is easier to bring one million peasants from yields of one to ten tonnes than to bring five million people in the countryside from one to two tonnes? But this option implies a concentration on the 'best regions', those suitable for irrigation to ensure a constant supply of water, without prejudice as to the kind of irrigation (large, medium or small-scale hydraulic). The accent should be on policies to reduce social inequality in the areas of advance. As for the regional inequalities, could we not reduce their breadth by national policies of redistribution and by migration from one rural area to another?

There are, of course, many obstacles to the options proposed by BADEA. An enumeration of them would provide a snapshot of the current situation: (i) defence by the former colonial powers (who retain great influence in Africa) of the routine interests of the old colonization (commercial trading companies, for example); (ii) the fragility of states and corruption of the ruling classes (and hence waste . . .); (iii) micro-nationalism as an obstacle to regional co-operation; and (iv) financing difficulties, inherent in any strategy conceived within the framework of worldwide expansion but capable of being lessened through better use of income and South–South financial co-operation (which goes much further than 'aid' and includes financial associations).

b) It is also always possible to act, even in a medium size and exposed country, provided that great care is taken as to what can be achieved within modest bounds. In a first step no more can be expected than to reduce external vulnerability (by avoiding worsening the pressures of the double deficit in public expenditure and external commitments) and to reinforce national and popular support. A participatory democracy, direct involvement of the communities in preparing and managing small projects, denial by the state of seeking immediate profits from them (at this stage the profits must revert in their entirety to the communities at the base), reinforcement of an international policy of non-alignment and South–South co-operation, are undoubtedly the chapter headings of a viable programme. The late President of Burkina Faso, Thomas Sankara, chose this option. Is it surprising that he was assassinated in circumstances that left the blame for their authorship open to doubt?

Notes

1. Amin, Samir, 'Democracy and National strategy in the Periphery', *Third World Quarterly*, October 1987; 'Comments on Senghaas', (SUNY) *Review*, No. 1, 1988.

2. For the technical significance of Lorenz curves and the Gini coefficients see Chapter 3 of the original French text of *La déconnexion*, Paris, La Découverte, 1986, or an English version of the chapter published by the Research Foundation of the State University of New York as Amin, Samir, 'Income Distribution in the Capitalist System', *Review*, 8, 1, Summer 1984, 3–28.

3. Amin, Samir, *Delinking*, Zed Books 1989; Samir Amin's preface to Mansour, Fawzy, *The Third World Revolt*, in preparation; Amin, Samir, 'On the intelligentsia', *Qadaya Fikriyya*, 1988 (in Arabic).

4. See introduction to Amin, Samir, (ed.) *Modern Migrations in Western Africa*, BADEA, Rapport sur le Sahel, 1985.

6. Political and Social Conditions for Alternative Development in the Third World

The option for national and popular 'alternative development' cannot be reduced to a model of a particular macro-economic strategy. It entails the construction of a state other than the unachievable bourgeois national state (would it then be a 'socialist' state?); it entails a democratic operation of society, whose difficulties and problems must be identified; it entails an active historical subject taking charge of the crystallization of the popular coalition that is the precondition for its emergence.

Impossibility of the bourgeois national state in the peripheries of the world system[1]

The bourgeoisie is a complex social phenomenon that cannot be reduced to its economic aspect (ownership of the means of production). At this level moreover, the bourgeois is a class fragmented by competition and divergence of immediate interests among its component segments. During its emergence, its unification into a class for itself was produced primarily by its ideological struggle, which revolutionized European culture, then by the political construction of the nation-state it undertook. This ideology (along with the fundamental principles it inspires for the organization of political life: separation between the state and civil society, the foundation of modern democracy) became the dominant ideology in the central capitalist societies and the basis of a consensus that goes beyond class and political conflicts. In this emphatic meaning, the bourgeoisie is a phenomenon that is difficult to disentangle from its historical and cultural (European) substratum, and consequently a total social reality that is more or less slavishly imitated at the periphery of the system. Here, might it not be more appropriate to speak of the domination of capital, rather than domination of the bourgeoisie (which at the centre is really the synonym of domination of capital)? This would be an encouragement to stress the essential capitalist role fulfilled by the state, motivated and dominated by the ideology of capitalism. The state is basically a slavish imitation of forms (of administration, education, organization, and so on) or, when there is a greater degree of consciousness, seeks to incorporate into the reality the criteria of capitalist rationality (efficiency, productivity, profitability) regarded as rationality *per se*. It is then possible to understand why, when the real social base of this capitalist power is weak (or virtually non-existent), the capitalist power is unsure whom it is serving or should serve. In these circumstances it can slide under the prongs of compradorization, turning the local state into an extension of the dominant worldwide capitalist power. But, under popular and national pressure, it could also try to refuse this surrender and seek rather to build an autonomous state, bourgeois in the sense that it is founded on the ideology of capitalist rationality, but without the real bourgeois social support that transmits the rationality. There is a strong temptation for this kind of state to declare itself socialist.

The asymmetry between the domination of capital, founded at the centre on an entirely real bourgeois base, and the domination at the periphery based on its absence, or virtual absence, is one of the many aspects of the contrast between the centre and periphery. This asymmetry has vital consequences at all levels. Capital, through its expansion, unifies its domination going beyond the segmentary competition of bourgeoisies (in the plural), by virtue of the ideological hegemony it inspires and the system of states through which it operates (without, however, this unification negating contradictions between the central states, above all when none of them exercises global hegemony and the field is clear for conflict over access to the vacant hegemony). At the same time, capital breaks up the social force that is marked down as its burial party: it reduces the relative size of the working class at the centre, to the benefit of the middle classes whose expansion is based on the worldwide expansion of capitalism; it bases its domination of the periphery on multiform or amorphous societies constantly breaking up into extremes of a minority working class, highly differentiated peasantry, uneasy middle classes, landowners rather than capitalist entrepreneurs, and so on, and where the weakness of the real bourgeoisie does not allow the prospect of establishing a bourgeois national state. By way of a quip, the situation might be described in a reversal of the classic expression: it is bourgeois internationalism in the face of proletarian nationalism!

If the necessary recomposition of society at the periphery cannot be achieved by the bourgeoisie, it must be by other – ideological – popular social forces. It is, of course, a difficult operation: but, as history has shown, far from being impossible it has made possible (in Russia and China, then other countries) the only 'renaissances' we know that escape the catastrophic drift of the capitalist Third World. The whole problematic of delinking lies here. That this does not lead to 'socialism' but merely to a contradictory and complex 'post-capitalism' is an entirely different issue.

Inequality in the worldwide expansion of capitalism; the state's central role

To assert a central role for the state in the conduct of 'development' in the developed and underdeveloped capitalist countries implies a rejection of the 'anti-state' ideological propositions of conservative liberalism that are running before the wind in the West. For the bourgeois economic theory is based on the deliberate voiding of the state issue, overlooked in the analysis of 'economic mechanisms'. Such overlooking is of course ideological. Economic theory, even the best, has only limited application. At best it makes it possible to grasp the rationality of the conjunctural behaviour of economic actors and to forecast the short-term effects. It makes it possible to rationalize the eventual collective strategies of these agents of the state. But it is unable to take account of profound changes in societies, changes in structure, and it is furthermore unable to take account of unequal development in world capitalist expansion (the issue of 'development' and 'underdevelopment').

The inequality of nations challenges the theory of capitalism as a world system.[2] As Tamas Szentes puts it: from the outset capitalist development has been expressed in the dialectical and contradictory unity of the (internal) national factor and the (external) international factor; of its very nature, the capitalist system is incapable of overcoming this contradiction. Prevailing schools of thought (the non-Marxist analyses and the *de facto* main current in Marxism) attach too much importance to the internal factors; the common view casts doubt on the thesis of a trend towards polarization (as the debate on the semi-peripheries, within the same world system school, shows). As a result there are few takers for the view that the national versus world contradiction cannot be overcome within the capitalist framework. The answer given to that question determines the essence of the conception held of the nature of the options on the agenda of current history.

The fact that the worldwide expansion of capitalism has been and is unequal is not of itself denied by anyone. Our thesis goes further, since it argues that all the regions that were integrated in the world capitalist system with peripheral status have remained like that to the present. We make clear that according to this thesis, New England, Canada, Australia and New Zealand were never peripheral formations; by contrast, Latin America, the Caribbean, Africa and Asia – with the exception of Japan – were and have remained so. The thesis also distinguishes the areas integrated as peripheries from non-peripheralized backward countries that crystallized as centres, albeit later than the rest (Germany and Eastern Europe, Southern Europe, Japan). In addition, we are told that some Third World countries are on the path towards full capitalist development, of a central kind. This remains to be seen. Very much the same was said, with similar arguments, a century or two centuries ago, without subsequent events confirming the optimistic view of capitalist expansion playing a homogenizing role.

The decisive criterion whereby to classify societies of the world capitalist system as 'centres' and 'peripheries' is the character of their state. The societies of central capitalism are characterized by the crystallization of a bourgeois national state, whose central role (beyond the simple maintenance of the domination of capital) is to control the conditions of accumulation through the national control it exercises over reproduction of labour power, the market, centralization of surplus, natural resources and technology. The state here fulfils the conditions allowing 'autocentric accumulation', that is, subjection of (most frequently aggressive) external relations to the logic of accumulation. By contrast, the peripheral state (which like any state fulfils the role of maintaining the internal domination of classes) does not control local accumulation. It then becomes – objectively – the instrument of 'adjustment' of local society to the demands of worldwide accumulation, whose changing directions are determined by changes at the centres. This difference explains why the central state is a strong state (and when it becomes democratic in the bourgeois sense of the term, this is an additional sign of its strength), while the peripheral state is a weak state (and among other things this is why access to genuine bourgeois democratization is virtually barred and why the scale of the civil society is inevitably limited).

Why has the bourgeois national state been able to form in one instance and not the other? This raises the following three groups of questions.

First: how are the 'internal factors' and 'external factors' articulated in this differentiation? Which are decisive? Undoubtedly the internal conditions are always the decisive factor in the last resort. But that is only a platitude; and it is dangerous and ingenuous to halt the analysis at these internal conditions alone. To do so assumes – implicitly or even explicitly sometimes – that the external conditions (that is, those flowing from integration in the world system) are of themselves 'favourable', that is offer the possibility of a capitalist development as such and that it will be 'central' or 'peripheral' – in the sense of 'complete and developed' or 'incomplete and underdeveloped' – exclusively by virtue of the internal conditions. This supposition is totally false. In fact the 'external' conditions are unfavourable. In the sense that they are an obstacle not to capitalist development in general, but to the acquisition by this development of the characteristics of central capitalist development. In other words: the crystallization of the bourgeois national state for some excludes the crystallization for others. Alternatively: the 'underdevelopment' of some is the result of the 'development' of others. Again it must be made clear that this proposition is not symmetrical and reversible; we have not said that the converse is true ('the development of some is the result of the underdevelopment of others'). This observation, too often left unsaid, and the confusion between our proposition and the converse, give rise to serious misunderstandings and sterile polemic.

It must be understood that the destruction of the periphery by exploitation is massive and decisive. The destruction goes further than the purely economic and affects the political and cultural aspect too: it 'kills' local creativity, that is, the very possibility of responding to the historical challenge.

Second: why did this crystallization of the bourgeois national state occur early on in one place (Western Europe, then Central and Eastern Europe, New England and Japan) and not in another? The thesis we have put forward is one of unequal development in the birth of capitalism.

Third: are there not 'intermediate cases' in the central and peripheral situations, that might be described as 'semi-peripheries'? Might their existence show that peripheralization is not 'inevitable', and that when it does occur, it is for reasons mainly related to internal factors, and it might at the same time be possible – notwithstanding the 'external obstacle' – to be establishing a new centre? There is no doubt, in society as in life, that there are always 'intermediate cases' or some apparently so. This would be difficult to deny. But that is not the real issue. Our thesis is that the world capitalist system is motivated by a strong tendency to polarization. As in the capitalist mode of production, the tendency is to polarization between the two fundamental classes ('bourgeoisie and proletariat'). Crystallizations of centres at one pole and peripheralization at another, that is despite appearances increasingly pronounced, does not preclude at any given instant the emergence of 'semi-peripheries', by analogy with the 'middle classes' engendered by the dynamic of capitalist accumulation. For the exclusion of this constant emergence would imply an absurdly static view, as if the centre and periphery polarization were magically to appear fully blown at the outset, when it is the result of the movement in the world system. At the same time, the emergence of these 'semi-peripheries' does show the true nature of the dialectic governing this movement, the convergence, or conflict, between the (favourable or unfavourable internal factor and the (unfavourable) external factor. In any event history does show that 'semi-peripheries' are not 'centres in formation'. How many of the semi-peripheries identifiable in the history of the past four centuries have become centres? None to our knowledge. This fact alone would be enough to show to what extent the external conditions are unfavourable and strongly so, since even when the internal conditions are relatively favourable, the others prevent the attempts of the 'semi-peripheries' to hoist themselves up to the status of 'centres'. More than that, our thesis is that crystallization of new centres is more and more difficult; that is to say, the obstacle represented by the external factor is increasingly difficult to overcome. This is the case even when we consider the historical formation of new centres, constituted on the basis of 'backward' but non-peripheralized situations (Germany and Japan for example), and a fortiori when we consider the fate suffered by the societies described as 'semi-peripheries'. For example, it is obvious that Germany, despite its backwardness, succeeded in 'catching up and overtaking' Britain in a few decades of the 19th century. How much time will it take for Brazil to 'catch up and overtake' the United States? Is this prospect imaginable in the foreseeable future? The concept of a cut-off point established at the end of the 19th century by the formation of the imperialist system – in Lenin's sense of the term – seems to us entirely defensible from this standpoint. We have expressed its meaning as follows: before this cut-off point, there was no contradiction between the crystallization of a new centre (from the starting point of a backward but non-peripheralized situation, provided of course that internal conditions were favourable to this crystallization) and its integration in the world system; later there was a glaring contradiction (and for this reason, there are no more 'backward' societies that are not peripheralized). In other words, the imperialist cut-off point marks a qualitative change in the constitution of the world system.

In the light of this series of theses in the formation of the bourgeois national state, a 'counter-thesis' has emerged over some years that argues essentially that this is all in the past and that the 'centres–peripheries' polarization is disappearing, along with the prevailing form of the bourgeois national state, to the benefit of a new form of worldwide capitalism.

The arguments adduced are highly varied. The most common – and certainly most widespread – is one that drawing on capitalism's adaptive capacity urges that the 'North has an interest in the South's further development'; all the partners of capitalism would gain since this is not a zero sum game, where the advantage of one party is necessarily paid for by the detriment of another. This is ideological reasoning without scientific foundation; it is the modish language of states ('We are all in the same boat and have common long-term interests . . .'). The proposal for the New International Economic Order was exemplary from this point of view. The proposal in no way clashed with the long-term abstract logic of capitalism, in the sense that the proposed new order would have provided the basis for greater expansion in the North and South. The proposal was, however, rejected by the North. Why? Quite simply because capitalism was not motivated by a search for the strongest long-term growth for all, but for the maximum of short-term profit for the strongest. The argument of the ideology of a possible universal harmony ignores – or pretends to ignore – this reality. It does not mean that capitalism is insufficiently flexible to be able not only to adapt but even to make profits from the structural changes forced upon it by the social forces it exploits. Wage improvements in the West have created new markets for the expansion of capital; they were not the result of capital's strategies but of workers' struggles. In the same way improved growth in the South could create markets for the capitals of the North, but it must be fought for by the Third World countries against the West's strategies.

A second group of arguments stresses the – real – changes that, operating at the level of the expanding forces of production, seem to challenge autocentric accumulation and the role of the bourgeois national state at the very heart of the system. Does this mean that the phase of imperialism is finished? that we are going into an 'ultra-imperialism' unified through the interpenetration of capitals that have already lost their 'national' character? This does not appear to us to be the case. First and foremost since the essence of imperialism is not the conflict of imperialisms but the centre/periphery opposition reaching a stage making the crystallization of new capitalist centres impossible. This contradiction, far from being eased by the weakening of the conflict of imperialisms, is on the contrary sharpened by the North's 'common front' (against the South and the East). Further, since we are still very far from the time when a world state (albeit limited to the capitalist North of course) will have taken over from the national states. The national state has so far been the only framework in which the social and political conflicts can be fought out. This particular contradiction between capital – whose worldwide dimension is much more marked than half a century ago even though appropriation and control of capital have remained largely national – and the state – which has remained strictly 'national' – is typical of the crisis of our time. The contradiction, attenuated by United States hegemony allowing the American state partly to play the role of a 'world state' (or world policeman), has come to the surface with redoubled force now that the US has ceased to be the exclusive fount of innovation and to play that role of world policeman. The Reaganite counter-offensive did not affect this evolution in its essentials.

The third group of arguments remain, highlighting what is – or could be – new in the South. It has been suggested that new 'semi-peripheries' have emerged that are already on the way to constituting themselves as new capitalist centres (Brazil, India, South Korea, for example) and putting a decisive end to the existence of a Third World that would henceforth be fragmented. Without returning here to the diversity of the periphery – a commonplace of every age over the past four centuries – we should like merely to emphasize that it has not yet been established whether the 'semi-peripheries' in question can really succeed in building the bourgeois national state capable of controlling internal accumulation and subjecting their external relations to this accumulation, that is, to escape the heavy constraints of 'adjustment' to the demands of the expansion of central monopoly capital. But, we are told, this construction is useless now, as the national state is itself on the way to being dissolved in the centres themselves. It would then have to be shown that the society of the semi-peripheries under discussion was on the way to approximating to that of the already established centres, within the global prospect of this future homogenized capitalist world in the making.

Such a demonstration has not been made and is not feasible, as the social changes under way in the foreseeable future are such a mixed bag. Once again analysis of the real contradictions and their dynamic has been replaced by an a priori perception of a harmony that has overcome the former. This is supposed to resolve the problem, but that kind of reasoning is unacceptable.

The worldwide spread of value[3]

Polarization within the world system is not some kind of inevitable result of the implacable play of the economic laws of capitalism. It is a complex and total social phenomenon where economic laws do of course have their place, but subject to the conditioning of social forces (classes, nations, states, ideologies) governing the evolution of societies.

That being so, it goes without saying that the centres/peripheries dichotomy does have 'economic' effects (manifest in a transfer of value from the peripheries to the centres) and 'economic mechanisms' permitting their reproduction, and that the latter tend to shape the society in accordance with the needs of this reproduction. The 'economic' aspects of the changes and their political, social and ideological aspects are interlocked. It is worth recalling that direct political domination and 'pillage' precede the social and economic structures that later provide for the 'normal' exploitation of labour by capital. Undoubtedly the capitalist system has reached a state where 'economic' forms seem capable on their own of ensuring reproduction of the conditions of labour exploitation. When we describe the prevailing trend in the Third World bourgeoisies as 'comprador by nature' we are only illustrating this predominance of 'natural' (in fact economic) forms of exploitation. It is not enough to stop there, as the 'non-economic' forms also have their place in the operation of the system: political and military pressures and intervention, cultural alienation (the allure of the 'Western' pattern of consumption, for example), are also part of the system. In our view, this 'non-economic' shaping is the real obstacle, making any attempt to escape the system by 'delinking', refusing to accept capitalism as eternally destined, 'desire' for socialism, and so on, appear 'utopian'. In this sense, therefore, the political, social and ideological effects of the centres/periphery polarization are more significant than the strictly economic effects. For the societies of the periphery, accepting this dichotomy is the equivalent of an 'ethnocide' since it kills their creativity, their capacity to respond to the challenge they face. These effects are more damaging than the transfers of value indicative of the specific forms of exploitation. The effects of the polarization are no less in the societies of central capitalism: the ideological consensus on which their stability depends is much more than the consciousness – if there is any – of the 'material advantages' gained from exploitation of the periphery. This consensus has its own cultural aspect, manifest day by day in every way by Western-centred arrogance or sufficiency, or racism, or more modestly 'complacency' ('we're the best', 'We're the only ones to enjoy democracy' and so on).

The strictly 'economic' – and quantifiable – aspects of transfers of value reveal many forms that can in no case be reduced to a single mechanism. The multiplicity of these forms makes it impossible to separate absolutely those of 'economic' character from those constituting sheer 'pillage'. Pillage is not only a feature of the prehistory of the system. Contemporary ecology has rediscovered what Marx saw long ago, namely that the thirst for profit may also bring destruction of the natural basis on which the future depends. This destruction operates with peculiar crudeness in the peripheries. Some examples among many: (i) the contribution of oil at a derisory price to the West's great upsurge from 1950 to 1974 (to the detriment of the oil-producer countries' future); (ii) the irreversible destruction of the soil in Africa, caused by its extensive colonial exploitation for the benefit of export and which is at the root of the African disasters (it scarcely matters that the values extracted were only a negligible total in comparison with those produced in the metropolises, the effect of the destruction on the societies that suffered them is calamitous). How should one describe the – quantifiable – advantage of exploitation of labour of migrants, whose costs of upbringing and retirement have been borne by the societies of the periphery while the societies of the centre take all the benefit of their productivity?

Without losing sight of all sides of the problem – that anti-Third-Worldism in the West is quick to forget – it is worth taking a systematic look at the 'normal transfers' governed by the strictly economic operation of the system.

This world system has the following characteristics: (1) great international mobility of goods (and hence the non-specific character of the output that is traded); (2) strong mobility of capital (and hence the tendency to equalization of the rate of profit, with the limitations to this equalization brought by virtual monopolies); (3) relatively weak world mobility of labour.

These are the characteristics of the current system; it goes without saying that they were only embryonic in the past. It is, moreover, a matter of strong trends, rather than complete characteristics. In this sense it is always possible to modulate the expression, and agree that 'all the goods are not produced from all the goods', to use a turn of phrase in Sraffa's style, not even at the national level (where there is the qualitative significance of the distinction between wage goods and others, that do not affect the determination of the rate of profit), and a fortiori at the world level. It is also possible to modulate the description of the products exchanged as 'non-specific'. Evidently some products are relatively specific by their character (some agricultural or mining products, for example). Others are so by virtue of unequal development itself: the Third World countries are obliged to import machinery they do not produce, the countries of low industrialization manufactured goods in general, and so on.

If it were not a matter of trends but a complete process, the problem of the centres/peripheries inequality would be solved. With 'all production being the result of all production' and 'all regions producing some of everything', we should be dealing with a capitalist mode of production perfectly homogenized on a world scale. There is, therefore, a contradictory unity at local (national) and world level for local determination of value and its world determination.

The key issue is to know which of the two aspects of the contradiction is decisive, in the dominant position. In the current system, the world aspect directs the movement (this is the meaning of the fact that the trends in question are 'strong'). This dominance of the world aspect is the factor reproducing and magnifying the centres/peripheries qualitative dichotomy. The disarticulation of the dominated sub-systems, inequality in specialization – in other words the characteristics of 'underdevelopment' – are active in the reproduction of the centres/peripheries dichotomy.

In the current system too, the world aspect dominates the determination of value (hence the national aspect is dominated). This is obviously a historical about turn, for over a long period the values were determined primarily at local level.

Does the pre-eminence of worldwide values entail the generalization of wage employment as the form of labour and the equalization of labour productivities?

It is the correlation of the pre-eminence of worldwide values and non-wage forms of labour (of lower productivity) that reproduces the centres/peripheries dichotomy and makes it insurmountable within the framework of capitalism. Workers at the periphery are super-exploited, not because they have equal productivity and lower wages, but because the differential of wages (and incomes from non-wage labour in general) is much higher than the differential of productivities. Why do we also take into account the income from non-wage labour, since the non-proletarianized producers are no more autonomous in relation to the global system, but closely integrated in it? In turn, the fact that the differential of rewards for labour is greater than the differential of productivities implies a transfer of value. This transfer is manifested in unequal exchange; but it has its source in the conditions of production and exploitation of labour. The choice of the expression 'unequal exchange' was perhaps unfortunate, as it allowed anyone who did not bother to look beyond the words to think that the inequality had its source in the exchange and not in the conditions of upstream production. This choice of words is perhaps the origin of useless misunderstandings that could easily be cleared up for those who care to understand.

Does the transfer of value benefit the capital dominating the system or the wage-earners at the centre? The transfer is mainly to capital and raises the average rate of profit. But the transfer also facilitates wage rises at the centre (if the social organization of the working class can insist on them).

Global equilibrium, demanding that the level of reward for labour be in relationship with that of development of the forces of production, operates on the world scale. That is why for this purpose the unit of analysis must be the global system and value is a worldwide category. In each of the asymmetrical parts of the system (centre and periphery), the level of reward for labour depends on that of its productivity and the demands of equilibrium at the global level.

Is the pre-eminence of worldwide values a figment of the imagination unrelated to empirical reality? This is argued by those who believe that systems of prices and values are determined exclusively (or only mainly) by internal conditions (of productivity, exploitation of labour, equilibrium, and so on). But then the world system is nothing more than a juxtaposition of national systems, whose inequality of development is pegged only to causes internal to themselves.

In fact, it can be seen that the structural systems of prices of the countries of the periphery are largely governed by the worldwide system of values. The decisive evidence is that the table of distribution of value added per worker, which is close to the average for the economies of the centre, is widely dispersed for the economies of the periphery.

If the system of prices at the periphery was determined essentially by conditions internal to the periphery, the distribution would also be close, as it is in the centre. The dispersal, associated with the disarticulation of which it is cause and effect, is itself a significant ingredient in the reproduction of the centres/peripheries dichotomy. Furthermore, the worldwide expansion of values is manifest at the ideological level to an unchallengeable degree: is not the insistent language of 'international competitiveness' a sign of this? as is the World Bank's conformity with capitalist practice in purporting to base the 'rationality' of its recommendations on 'reference to world prices'.

This economic analysis is enough to give a flavour of the reproduction mechanisms of the centres/peripheries polarization. But it is insufficient if the question is raised whether the vicious circle of this reproduction can be broken. Why do the bourgeoisies of the periphery not seize the opportunity of the rate of super-exploitation of labour to keep the surplus for themselves and invest it, in order to accelerate the development of the forces of production and 'catch up' on their backwardness?

A return to the Third World?[4]

Is the national liberation movement of a stature to transform the asymmetrical centre/periphery relationship and force the world system to adjust to autocentric, national development of the periphery? In this case, imperialism will have been only a stage in the expansion of capitalism on a world scale, and not its 'highest stage' but simply an intermediate stage to ensure transition from a system marked by the centre/periphery asymmetry to a homogeneous global system of domination of capitalist relations.

Are the Third World bourgeoisies which have come to power against the old colonial alliances capable of setting their countries on a new step: after winning political independence can they win economic independence? The conjuncture of the period 1970–75 made it seem possible.

The growth from 1945 to 1970 created an illusion of the possibility of the construction of new centres, and established a definition of autonomy of national bourgeois hegemony (control of reproduction of the labour force, the market, the centralization of surplus, technology and natural resources). The illusion is the more remarkable for the fact that the phase is precisely defined by the political victory of the liberation movements in Asia and Africa, who seized independence, proceeded with the setting up of a local state and often embarked upon 'anti-feudal' reforms. This apparent progress in the constitution of autonomous bourgeois hegemonies does not call for strategies of delinking. On the contrary, almost throughout the globe, in Latin America, in Africa, the Arab world, and in Asia, this expansion is accompanied by a relative intensification of external exchanges, an increase in imports of technology and even of private capital (associated with the penetration of multinationals) and public capital (external public debt), despite the – normal – fact that re-export of profits cancels out or even exceeds the flow of financial inputs. The most radical advances in this direction – self-styled as 'socialist' – are based on a reinforcement of the state's role and frequently on Soviet support, for conjunctural reasons of the conflict with imperialism. But even there, one can scarcely speak of a strategy of delinking, even when conjuncturally the intensity of relations with the West has been diminished.

The crisis has revealed the extreme fragility of these attempts at the very moment when, on the 'anti-Third-World' helter-skelter, so many commentators were rushing to bury the concepts of centre and periphery, the analysis of unequal development, and so forth. With surprising ease, the 'socialist' experiences were dismantled, sometimes evidently through the mobilization of the West's policemen for the purpose. Through the Camp David agreements and the invasion of Lebanon, the surrender of the Front Line countries in Southern Africa, begun by Mozambique, the whole of the Arab world and Africa was brought into line. This is further confirmation of the schema we have put forward of attempts at autocentric development of the periphery looking like a long series of successive abortions, brutally arrested before term by an acute crisis in the external balance occasioned by the reflux of super-profits appropriated by dominant central capital. Is not the external debt – nowadays a conventional proof (but a total denial of the World Bank forecasts of development 'fuelled by external demand', forecasts that were quickly embraced by anti-Third-Worlders) – the contemporary form of this murderous drain of surplus?

It is clearly understood and nobody denies it that capitalist expansion in the Third World in the years 1945–70 has been unequal in the extreme and has taken multiple forms. In this sense, saying that the Third World does not exist since it is not homogeneous, is not a new discovery – since it never was uniform – nor an answer to the question whether, apart from its heterogeneity, it will cross the stepping stones to become 'analogous' to the centres of the system.

Those who urge that such is the case base their arguments on what might be called 'exceptions' in recent Third World development. It is fairly clear that the forms of development in eastern Asia (South Korea, Taiwan, Hong Kong and Singapore) reveal particular characteristics that distinguish them greatly from the rest of the Third World. At first, these developments, especially in Korea and Taiwan, were based on significant agrarian reforms (certainly for fear of contagion from the communist model) reinforced by the peculiarly egalitarian sensibility of Confucian ideology. Whereas in Latin America, Brazil in particular, the Arab countries and South and South-East Asia, the internal market has been extended by a comparatively higher income for the middle strata to the detriment of the mass of the people, here in a highly unusual way, wages as a whole (including those of the middle strata) have been maintained at a minimal level, allowing for substantial savings, largely public, and for peasant incomes to remain reasonable. In the Chinese states of Taiwan, Hong Kong and Singapore, a close collaboration has been established with what one might call the overseas Chinese bourgeoisie, spreading throughout the western Pacific and South-East Asia. In demographic aspects, Confucian Asia has reached modest growth levels that indicate greater social control and greater penetration of the ideology of individual and family enrichment. Finally, attempts at technical education have been much more systematic and effective. On the basis of a strong national reality, these developments come much closer than elsewhere to the emergence of a hegemonic national bourgeoisie, legitimated by a fairly broad social consensus, although the democratic expression of recent years casts some doubt on this supposed consensus.

For the rest, the crisis reveals the vulnerability of strategies based on deliberate integration in the international division of labour. Confucian Asia, more skilled than Latin America or the Arab world at social control of the readjustments imposed by the external crisis (notably the debt burden), is doubtless able, if necessary, to withdraw in upon itself. An intensification of the relations of the countries in question with China and Japan might provide a substitute that was profitable to all the partners and have a noticeable effect on world balances.

Brazil's spectacular growth, contrary to the erroneous ideological statements of the World Bank, was not 'fuelled by external demand' (Brazil's exports, which at their peak were 10% of GDP, fell to 5%). Transnationalization occurred essentially at the level of finance and not of trade. The foreign debt that resulted from this model of integration in the worldwide scheme was no less spectacular. But repudiation of the external debt would be fairly easy for Brazil, as the reprisals would be more costly to the partners than to Brazil. The obstacle to change is internal since growth was based upon increasing inequality. Could the popular and democratic forces reverse the trend here? But would that not be precisely the start of the supersession of the bourgeois national state by a national and popular evolution?

India's relation with the world system has been even less constringent. In fact the choice made by Pandit Nehru and Indira Gandhi was one of 'semi-delinking', not only through strict control of foreign trade, capital transfers and the technology on which it relied, but also in a more profound sense. Hence, for example, the internal structure of prices (and notably the internal terms of trade for the prices of basic foodstuffs and industrial prices) was semi-delinked from the world system, as has often been noted (and this delinking was often the subject of the most heated criticism by the World Bank). The Gandhian ideology, willingness to isolate the Indian elite from Western models, obviously played a not insubstantial part in this choice.

The results achieved for the development of India are fairly praiseworthy, but due to this semi-delinking and not its reverse – an 'open-door'! For the rest, the contradiction of the system lies in the social content of power, largely one of a bourgeois alliance (state bureaucracy, industrial and agrarian capitalists). These forces have always exerted pressure for a reduction of the 'delinked' dimension of the development strategies. It would appear that for several years the Indian Congress's use of power in crisis combined with the personality of Rajiv Gandhi has encouraged the 'comprador' aspirations of the middle classes, avid for immediate enjoyment. Will India thereby encounter a serious crisis? It does rather look like it.

Political analysis of 'exceptions', far from weakening the thesis that the national and popular option is a necessary objective, reinforces it. In the absence of such an option the countries under discussion are not 'semi-peripheries' hurrying to 'catch up', but real peripheries of the world capitalist system of today and tomorrow.

The consequences of unequal development

The thesis that unequal development cannot be overcome within the framework of capitalism entails fundamental consequences as to the identification of the issues that are really on the agenda of necessary and possible political changes in the modern world. In fact this thesis defines the 'system' not only by its attribute of 'capitalist' (an accurate but insufficient description), but also by its inequality and polarization in capitalist expansion.

All the key questions of our age must be situated within the overall problematic framework, including questions of 'socialist transition' (the East), the stability of central capitalist societies (the West), and the crisis peripheral capitalist societies (the South).

The unequal character of capitalist expansion, that cannot be overcome within the framework of capitalism, objectively requires that the world be remade on the basis of an alternative social system; and the peoples of the periphery are obliged to be aware of this and insist upon it, if they want to avoid the worst, that is, reaching the point of genocide, the real danger of which is amply shown by the history of capitalist expansion.

The form of challenge to the capitalist order from revolts at the periphery, obliges us to give serious reconsideration to the issue from 'socialist transition' to abolition of classes. Whatever one said, and whatever shading one gives, the Marxist tradition remains handicapped by its initial theoretical view of 'worker revolutions' initiating, on the basis of relatively more or less advanced forces of production, a relatively 'speedy' transition, characterized by democratic power of the popular masses. If it is described as 'dictatorship over the bourgeoisie' (through the means of a proletarian state of a new kind that should rapidly 'wither away'), it is nevertheless much more democratic than the most democratic of bourgeois states.

But this is evidently not the reality. All the revolutions so far that have sought to be anti-capitalist have taken place in the peripheries of the system: all have found themselves confronted by the problem of development of the forces of production and the hostility of the capitalist world; none of them has achieved any form of genuinely advanced democracy; all have reinforced the statist system. To the degree that, more and more frequently, doubt is cast on their claim to be 'socialist' and their prospects one day, however remote, of achieving genuine abolition of classes. On some views they are no better than particular forms of capitalist expansion.

The essential issue is clearly not that of 'describing' these systems, but of understanding their origin, problems and specific contradictions, the dynamic they initiate or foreclose. In taking this point of view we arrived at the thesis that it was a matter of national and popular states and societies; we say popular and not bourgeois or socialist advisedly. We also reached the conclusion that this national and popular 'phase' was inescapable, and imposed by the unequal character of capitalist development.

These systems, therefore, face the task of development of the forces of production and are founded on social groups who reject the thesis that this development can be attained by a simple 'adjustment' within the framework of world capitalist expansion. They are the product of revolutions led and supported by forces in revolt against the effects of the unequal development of capitalism. Hence these systems are contradictory and conflictive combinations of various forces, perhaps three in number. One, socialists or those potentially socialist, express the aspirations of the popular social forces that are the source of the new state. Another, the capitalists, express the fact that at the actual stage of development of the forces of production, capitalist relations of production are still necessary and that by this token they are called upon to locate the real social forces to support the maintenance of these relations. But the existence of these capitalist relations must not be confused with integration in the world capitalist system. The state is there precisely to isolate these relations from the effects of integration in the system dominated by central monopoly capital. The third category of real social forces operating here, which we describe as statist, has its own autonomy. It cannot be reduced to a disguised form of capitalist relations (as statism really is in the capitalist Third World), nor to a 'degenerate' form of socialism. Statism represents its own real and potential social forces.

The state here fulfils a specific role, different from that it fulfils in the centres and the capitalist peripheries. It is the means to national protection and assertion, the instrument of what we have called 'de-linking', in the sense of subjection of external relations to the logic of an internal development (one that it is not simply 'capitalist'). It is the pole of the – conflictive – articulation of the relations between the three 'tendencies' indicated.

Of course, this state is not analogous from one country to another of this world called 'socialist'. It is the product of specific concrete histories, in dynamic evolution, whereby combinations between the conflictive forces indicated are shown over time and space. But these are always strong states, precisely because they have 'de-linked'.

The question of 'democracy' must be viewed in this framework. For complex, special reasons related to the history of Marxism, these systems are not democratic, to say the least, despite their material achievements to the benefit of the popular masses and the varying degrees of support they may enjoy from the latter. The problems facing these societies cannot be overcome except by a development of democracy. This is so because democracy is an inescapable precondition, essential to ensure the effectiveness of a socialist social system. Social relations founded on workers' co-operation rather than their surrender to exploitation are unimaginable without a complete expression of democracy. Will the 'really existing socialist' countries, as they are described, reach this stage? Or will they remain stuck in the impasse of their rejection?

It is here that we find the basic issue of 'internal factors', not in the capitalist peripheries, where the internal factor, although an explanation of past history (peripheralization) has nowadays a very restricted autonomy under the burden of 'external' constraints. By comparison, the internal factor has become decisive in the national and popular states. In this sense we find again that there is no historical 'inevitability'. And by 'internal factor' we mean, of course, the dialectic of the triple contradiction described above.

The description 'national and popular' should then be attached to those societies of the East embarked upon a long historical phase whose essential task is to efface the heritage of unequal development – in the knowledge that this cannot be achieved by playing the 'adjustment' game within the world system, but on the contrary by taking the side of de-linking. The ideological description 'socialist societies' must be abandoned (as they are not such), and even the description as societies engaged in building socialism. Even though in the countries of the East they cling to this description of socialist, or at least of socialist construction (or transition). There are not only bad reasons for this attachment (intellectual laziness or dogmatic habit, or more seriously the desire to deny the real problems with the assertion that socialism 'has been achieved'); there are also the good intentions of those who merely want to say that the objective is socialism and that such an objective is possible and not utopian. The latter are quite ready to acknowledge that the historic task of effacing the effects of unequal development is far from being achieved, and that the 'transition' to socialism is and will be long, complex and even uncertain as to its outcome. Use of the expressions 'underdeveloped socialism' or even 'primitive socialism' is a mark of their courageous perception.

There is no great inconvenience in retaining the term 'socialist construction', provided that it accompanies a rejection of the ingenuousness – or false ingenuousness – of the prevailing official ideological portrayal of the issues facing these societies. In this portrayal the state is regarded as the very expression of the socialist forces; the capitalist trends operating in the society are alien to it; the 'line' it inspires is always more or less correct (except for a few 'flaws' to be cleared up some day or other). In the same ideological confusion, the issue of relations of production is grossly oversimplified, or taken out of the discussion: public ownership is no longer regarded as solely a necessary preliminary to the transformation of relations of production, but as a sufficient condition for these to become *ipso facto* 'socialist'. When 'capitalist forces' are mentioned, it is as 'vestiges' confined to a 'capitalist' (or 'commodity') sector, distinct from the 'socialist' sector and defined by continuation of private ownership.

The issue arises in a totally different way. The state is itself at the centre of the social conflict between the various trends in effect. In all sectors of activity the relations of production are ambivalent and retain the essential aspects of capitalism, in the technical handling of labour, hierarchical submission, and so on. These aspects are not merely 'vestiges' of the past; they correspond to objective needs with continuing effect. At the same time, abolition of private ownership, commitment of the state to 'serving' the people (this commitment inherited from the popular and anti-capitalist character of the revolution is not mere lip service: rejection of unemployment, aspiration for less inequality, fierce loyalty to national independence are real concepts), concern for society and these commitments, are factors that make the progressive reinforcement of the socialist forces possible. The outcome depends, therefore, on the complex issue of the genuinely advanced democracy these forces must insist upon.

This formulation of the 'transition' in terms of the national and popular society leads to an out and out rejection of the current thesis of 'socialist' construction and 'revolution by stages', whereby the so-called national democratic stage will be followed by that of socialist transformation.

The classless society, as the ultimate aim, demands by definition real control by the workers over the means of production, and all aspects of social life, that is, the practice of advanced democracy (or even the disappearance of the state).

The 'socialist transition', if it means anything at all, must include the characteristics of this aim and ensure progress towards them.

This is a different argument from the thesis of rapid supersession – within a few years – of the so-called national democratic phase by socialist transformation. In the first phase, the new authorities carry out great reforms that capitalism in its peripheral form has not accomplished, including a radical land reform. But then nationalization of the commanding heights of the economy (finance, transport, heavy industry), planning and control of external relations (de-linking in the sense of subjecting them to the logic of the internal plan) signal the move to a second phase, that of 'socialist' construction, marked by the abolition of forms of private ownership, including 'collectivization'. The move from the first stage to the second is, as can be seen, little more than substitution of forms of (state and co-operative) public ownership for mixed (public and private) ownership. The thesis stops there; it takes out of the discussion the content of the ownership in question. Public ownership is equated with socialism, whereas it is no more than a precondition for it; no consideration is given as to whether the actual operation of society permits control of the means of production by the producers (through an advanced social and political democracy constantly progressing).

The reality has undermined this thesis. The socialism that is supposed to be built is constantly confronted by a resurgence of commodity and capitalist relations of production, demanded to ensure greater efficiency in the necessary development of the forces of production. Fifty years after the 'victory of socialism' in the USSR (after the end to the NEP and collectivization) the issue of the 'market' came back on to the agenda. Twenty years after the Chinese Cultural Revolution was supposed to have solved the problem, the same – previously 'abolished' – relations had to be re-established.

These evolutions show that the long phase of transition cannot be regarded as having in the first round settled the issue of non-socialist social relations. this does not rule out the possibility of socialist construction. Still less that in these circumstances we must resign ourselves to accepting preliminary development of the forces of production through the means of capitalism. The latter, under the conditions of peripheral expansion, is intolerable by virtue of the contradictions it provokes. The anti-capitalist revolution is on the agenda of what is objectively necessary. But this initiates a longer period of 'post-revolutionary' conflict, very different from the ideological and mystical vision of 'socialist construction'.

Instead of hollow dogmatic incantations, we need to analyse the post-revolutionary experiences in the concrete terms of the tripartite conflicts (of socialism, capitalism and statism) that underlie the current evolutions. This concrete analysis prevents the acceptance of the notion of a more or less generally valid 'model', just as it prevents the various experiences from being treated as an expression of the gradual achievement of a 'general line'. We must rather stress the differences in the experiences, their advances and retreats, their impasses and the supersessions of these. In that spirit, we should note that Maoism did not reproduce the Soviet model in the essential area of relations between towns and countryside. In the same way Mao's call for an attack on the party–state, in marked contrast with the deification of the Soviet party–state, prevents us regarding Maoism as a reissue of Stalinism. The flexibility characteristic of the Chinese, Yugoslav and Hungarian systems seems from this point of view to indicate a potentially more promising future that the dogmatic statist rigidity that has enclosed the Soviet Union and some other countries in impasse. But the latter is not necessarily 'definitive', as recent evolutions of Gorbachev's USSR show.

Undoubtedly, the question of relations between the 'plan' and the 'market' (a cover for the tripartite socialism–capitalism–statism conflict) is not the only aspect of the inescapable contradictions of the post-revolutionary society. No less decisive is the conflict between 'statist authoritarianism', and democracy and popular control of the forces of production. Advanced democracy cannot be a spontaneous product of the 'market', as capitalist ideology supposed and as some self-management illusions have also suggested.

Some analysts propose treating the socialist countries (the USSR in particular) as semi-peripheries. This proposition assumes that the world system includes all the regions of the world, regardless of their political and social regime. It further supposes that external determination by the system is equally decisive for all in the same way. It therefore reduces the internal factor to virtually nothing, and as if it were the same everywhere. Our thesis stressing the so-called 'socialist' rupture (that I prefer to call national and popular de-linking of a socialist bent) restores the pre-eminence of the internal factor peculiar to these societies; it shows the limits of worldwide expansion of capitalism and rejection of it. The arguments adduced to 'prove' that the countries of the East are fully 'integrated' in the world system are always superficial. It is thought to be enough to say that these countries 'trade' with the West – increasingly; that they have never shown a desire for autarky (what they have was wished upon them); that they openly express the desire to increase their foreign trade (and that the West is the obstacle). The argument can be turned on its head. If the countries of the East want to increase their trade it is because they largely control how it is used and can use it to strengthen their independence, and they control it because they have de-linked. If the West is hesitant it is because it is aware of the 'danger' of reinforcing the socialist countries. The situation is quite different in West–South relations, where the peripheral societies (including semi-peripheries such as Brazil) have not de-linked and for that very reason do not control their relation to the world system.

A thesis that extrapolates to the utmost the trends in the 'socialist' countries for 'reintegration' in the world economy argues that the future will be one of a re-established single, world market. The thesis paints a broad historical sweep of oscillating movement. A single world market, constituted in the 19th century in the framework of British hegemony (a Sterling standard), threatened from the end of the century by the rise of rival imperialists, maintained more or less until 1914, ceased to exist during the German–US 30-years war (1914–45) for succession to Britain, to be re-established in the framework of United States hegemony. This market was threatened for a while by the rise of the countries of the East but is being rebuilt. This time the rate of oscillation would be quicker, as the distance separating the countries of the East and China from the West would not allow them to stand alone, especially in disunion. We should add that the attitude shown by the countries of the East to those of the South indicates the priority afforded by the former to the maintenance of a network of multilateral world exchanges. But this raises a series of side issues there is no space to discuss here.

Not long ago the received wisdom was that the Russian revolution, followed by China's, had irrevocably divided the earth into two – the capitalist system on the retreat, and the socialist system on the advance. Whether Russia's 'really existing socialism', as it is called, was perfect or perverted (the old Trotskyist thesis) is not the issue. Moreover, the so-called Maoist thesis substituted the socialism achieved in China for the 'restoration of capitalism' in Russia. The defeat of the Line of the Four and the triumph of Deng Xiaoping clearly struck a blow against this range of views on the capitalism–socialism conflict. China appeared to differ less and less from the Soviet Union in the essential structures of social and political organization, so that the former and the latter were regarded as variants of a perverted 'really existing socialism', of a new society of specific classes or of modalities of capitalism. Moreover, should it not be remembered that China and Russia alike seek further integration into a world system from which they had previously been isolated against their will?

The drift of the analyses could then gradually crystallize around the following theses: first, the so-called socialist revolutions are moments of constitution of social and political forces capable of bringing forward national strategies of modernization and development; second, the accomplishment of these tasks passes through a moment of 'separation', or isolation, from the world capitalist system; third, the development of the system gradually wipes out the original illusions about its 'socialist' character; and fourth, finally the system aspires to reintegration in the capitalist world order.

André Gunder Frank has gone furthest in this field in the most systematic way. Noting that Russia and China appear as 'semi-peripheries' (above all, I believe, if one takes account of the place and role of the state in their evolution rather than the simplistic development criteria of economism), that their revolutions come within a B cycle of contraction of capitalist expansion, between 1914 and 1945 (to adopt on his behalf Kondratieff's language on the succesion of A and B cycles of capitalist expansion), Frank propounds the thesis that in the B cycles some semi-peripheries (or 'peripheries') 'de-link' to emerge as centres (or semi-peripheries) reintegrated in the following A cycle, corresponding to a higher stage of capitalist development and thereby consolidating this development. This occurred before the 20th century and is still occurring; hence the so-called socialist revolutions are bringing nothing new.

The logic of this thesis must, we believe, be taken still further. If it is the case, that is if the aspects of global movement indicated are the most significant, the thesis means that it is nation-states that constitute the decisive historical subjects, and not the popular classes that enter their composition. Within this perspective the world expansion of capitalism should necessarily lead to the emergence of new ripe 'centres', taking their place in the global system of interdependence, and eventually challenging the hegemonies *in situ*, and so on. Undoubtedly this conclusion does not necessarily conflict with Marxism. For the thesis does not prevent the societies in question being class-based societies, giving rise to capitalist exploitation (including the statist form that purports to be 'socialist'). It does not prevent the ruling classes of the states in question being precisely those exploitative bourgeoisies. It does not necessarily adopt the nationalist ideology of the 'common good' of the various components (whether classes or not) of the national society. But it acknowledges – albeit sorrowfully – that the popular classes have not reached the maturity that will allow the autonomy of their plan for an eventual classless society. These classes are therefore manipulated and their intervention channelled and 'recuperated'. Everything happens as if they were ready to believe in the supremacy of common national interests, to the benefit of the classes that lead them. The 'nation' is, therefore, in the fullest sense, at the current stage of inadequate maturity of class consciousness, the decisive historical subject.

This thesis is not ours. We subject it to a double critique. First, the social systems of Russia and China cannot be reduced to capitalism (capitalism cannot exist without the competition among capitals) nor can the one be reduced to the other. Second, it is incorrect that in the previous B cycles certain backward formations should come to emerge through a phase of 'de-linking', such as Russia and China in the 20th century. The new centres that emerged one after the other until the end of the 19th century immediately integrated into the world system, and increased their active participation in it, without 'de-linking' in any way, at any time. But they are masters of their external relations, which is another matter. In other words, there was no contradiction then between the construction of new centres – new hegemonic national bourgeoisies – and the 'constraint of worldwide expansion'. This is a new contradiction and means that worldwide expansion has reached a qualitatively new level.

There are, admittedly, some apparent moments of 'de-linking' before our epoch. We prefer to call them moments of 'debilitation' of integration in the world system. Some peripheral societies in the 19th century withstood the effects of the crisis in this way. That some of these cases – notably in America – suggest, by the positive local reaction to this debilitation, that 'development is not synonymous with integration in the world system' is clear. The fact that none of these experiences is crowned with the emergence of new centres clearly illustrates the qualitative difference between the de-linking of our epoch and the debilitation of world integration in earlier epochs.

The 'de-linking' that follows the socialist revolution is in fact voluntary and positive, even if it is also imposed by a strategy of imperialist counter-attack that fails over the long term. This is the first difference in regard to the debilitations of integration withstanding the effects of crisis. In addition it is associated with strong social and ideological changes. And this factor is not without significance, even if the association is with a myth of socialist construction, a 'new', 'classless' society, a 'new man', a 'cultural revolution'. For it is precisely this association that allows of a criterion of rationality independent of that of world capitalism. This de-linking is also one of the indispensable aspects of the emergence of a new social mode – whether socialist or not. Its 'reintegration' in the world system therefore remains dubious. The eventual intensification of exchanges is not synonymous with integration.

A further step must certainly be made in making the analyses more concrete. One must distinguish the Soviet Union from Eastern Europe, China and other countries of the socialist Third World (Korea, Vietnam and Cuba). Without going into this complex subject, let us offer our broadly intuitive conclusions: first, the USSR would not accept a 'reintegration' that threatened its internal political system; second, China would not accept a 'reintegration' that threatened its pursuit of independent development; third, by contrast, the Eastern European countries might, if circumstances allowed, 'cross over to the West', but the risk would be reduced to the degree that a margin of autonomy (Hungarian and Yugoslav style) were allowed them, in conjunction with acceptable and accepted internal social changes.

In this framework, we support the view that, whether one likes it or not, de-linking is associated with a 'transition' – outside capitalism and over a long time – towards socialism. This raises a host of other questions: that this transition is not the one conceived by Marx perhaps, or by the Second International, or even by the ideology of the systems in question (Bolshevism, the current Sovietism, Maoism, Deng's ideology); that it is not linear; that its still distant point of arrival is largely unknown. After all, socialism has still to be built. As Silva Michelena aptly put it, if in 1500 one had been asked what capitalism would be, one would doubtless have furnished inadequate replies, even supposing one could then have imagined that what one was building was capitalism. How then will the USSR and China solve their problems, if they manage to do so? By evolution or by revolutions (those Mao expected)? How will these transformations articulate with other socialist break-throughs? So many questions that evidently are without a priori answers.

The problems facing the capitalist Third World countries in the aftermath of their political liberation were no different in character from those facing the so-called socialist countries. With the exception that here, the strategies were even more marked by the fact that, even in the cases of prior radicalization of the struggle for independence, the option in favour of popular content and de-linking was handicapped by bourgeois aspirations and the illusions the bourgeoisie had about their plan. So why has the Third World not yet embarked upon the path of building a national and popular state? Why does it stick to trying to build a bourgeois national state in imitation of the central capitalist state? Of course, this situation is not produced by ideas devoid of a social base; it is the expression of certain classes and social strata of bourgeois inclination, which dominated the national liberation movement (that is, the revolt against the effects of the unequal development of capitalism) and still dominate the state that emerged. History teaches us that the bourgeoisies of the periphery have attempted this construction at every stage of world capitalist expansion, although in the forms appropriate to the time. As history shows too, these attempts have always been brought down by a combination of external aggression and the internal limitations peculiar to each of the attempts.

The issue of democracy

The issue of democracy in the socialist countries and in those of the Third World must be seen in this framework.

Let us be clear: the critique Marx made of bourgeois democracy – in regard to its formal and limited character – is entirely correct. Meanwhile this democracy has not been offered by the bourgeoisie to its people, but conquered – belatedly – by workers' struggles. The capitalist mode of itself does not require democracy. The hold of its social dynamic lies elsewhere, in the competition of capitalists and individuals.

Capitalism separates economic and social management, governed by fundamentally non-democratic principles, from political management, governed nowadays by the principle of democratic election. We might add that this democracy operates only when its social impact is annihilated by the exploitation of dominant central positions in the world capitalist system, when the labour movement has renounced its own plan for a classless society and accepted the capitalist 'rules of the game'.

At the periphery, democracy is even more limited and is only the expression of the crisis of the normal despotic system of capitalism. Latin America, Korea, the Philippines and perhaps others in the future, provide glaring examples of the violent political contradictions that shake the Third World in crisis. Latin American *desarollismo* of the 1950s argued that 'industrialization' and 'modernization' (in bourgeois style and in the framework of closer integration in the world system) would of themselves bring democratic change. 'Dictatorship' was regarded as a hangover from a supposedly pre-capitalist past. The facts have shown that modernization in the framework of this bourgeois plan has merely 'modernized dictatorship' and replaced the old oligarchical and patriarchal systems with an 'efficient and modern' fascistic violence. But the bourgeois plan itself has not achieved its proposed results: the crisis has revealed the vulnerability of the construction and the impossible 'independence', that for some legitimized the dictatorship. But are not the democratic systems imposed in these circumstances confronted by a terrible dilemma? Either the democratic political system accepts subjection to the demands of world 'adjustment': it can then not envisage any significant social reform, and democracy will not be slow to become part of the crisis. Or the popular forces, seizing the channels of democracy, will impose these reforms: the system will then come into conflict with dominant world capitalism and glide from the bourgeois national plan to a national and popular plan. The dilemma of Brazil and the Philippines come within this conflict.

The popular option requires democracy. This is so because democracy is a necessary internal condition for socialism. Once the hold of capitalist competition is broken, social relations founded on workers' co-operation and not their surrender to exploitation become unimaginable without the complete expression of democracy.

In the socialist countries, despite national and social achievements and the support this wins from the popular masses, the rejection of political democracy reveals the preponderance of the statist dimension over the socialist tendencies. The situation is still worse in the radical Third World countries. Here, the absence of political democracy works in favour of private or state capitalism and drives the system down into a bureaucratic capitalism that, by definition, carries the further danger of compradorization. In the socialist countries this is not a real danger, as the national and popular state (although non-democratic) has solid historical foundations, so that either the situation will go on stagnating in the relative cul-de-sac in which statism has trapped it, or the society will resume its forward march. By comparison there is no shortage of failures by Third World radical states and their recompradorization.

In all cases, democracy is the sole means within the national and popular society of reinforcing the chances of socialism, isolating the internal capitalist relations of production from comprador integration in the world capitalist system, and reducing external vulnerability.

But what democracy are we talking about? This is not the place to disparage the heritage of Western bourgeois democracy: respect for rights and the rule of law, freedom of speech, institutionalization of electoral procedure and separation of powers, checks and balances, and so forth. But we should not stop there. Western democracy has no social dimension. The people's democracy at moments of revolutionary social change (the USSR in the 1920s, Maoist China, for example) have also taught us much about what 'people's power' should be, if we allow this much-abused expression its real meaning. To stop at Western democratic forms without taking into consideration the social transformations demanded by the anti-capitalist revolt of the periphery, is to remain with a caricature of bourgeois democracy and thereby condemned to alienation from the people and extreme vulnerability. For our democracy to take root it must at once take a position that goes beyond capitalism. In this, as in so many other domains, the law of unequal development operates.

This is the prospect that imperialism cannot accept. That is why the campaign on 'democracy' orchestrated by the West stresses some sides of the issues and ignores others. For example, it equates multi-party politics and democracy. Undoubtedly the 'single party' has in fact become the most frequent expression of statist domination. But it has also often been a product of the effective achievement of national and popular unity; this is the case of the Chinese Communist Party for example and some other organizations emerging from the liberation struggle. In these cases the creation of 'alternative parties' might be an artificial procedure that has no place on the agenda of the popular struggles. Democratization of the party, its separation from the state, a clear distinction between state and civil society, openness of the party and social institutions (genuinely independent trades unions, peasant co-operatives, and so on) to debate and confrontation, are the necessary reforms with which the Western false friends of the Third World peoples refuse to credit democracy.

The historical subject of the popular national option; the role of the intelligentsia

This is the exact point where the particular role of the intelligentsia in the national and popular transformation comes. We should say at once that this analysis is particular to the historical movement engendered by a bid to escape from the impasse of peripheral capitalism. This concept of intelligentsia is peculiar and specific to peripheral capitalist societies.

The intelligentsia is not synonymous with *petit bourgeoisie* in general or 'cultivated circles' (or 'intellectuals' and a fortiori 'graduates'). The *petit bourgeois* is a motley collection of social strata engendered in any capitalist development – central or peripheral. As a class – overall – it plays no decisive political role; the thesis that this class remains divided and vacillating between right and left seems to be fundamentally correct. In the capitalist centres it sometimes joins the capitalist camp and the right, and sometimes supports the working class in its reformist strategy, according to circumstances. But this vacillation, entirely within a structure where right and left accept the system's rules of play (that is, the fundamental criteria of capitalist management of the economy and electoral democracy), has no greater historical impact than the right–left cleavage typifying the life of the central capitalist societies. In the peripheries the *petit bourgeoisie* also vacillates between the camp of the local bourgeoisie (which can envisage power only within the bounds permitted by 'adjustment' to the demands of the worldwide capitalist system) and that of the popular classes (constantly required to revolt against the fate wished upon them by peripheralization). There, however, the right–left cleavage does have a decisive historical impact; it is this cleavage that lies at the heart of the really important changes in the modern world: the so-called socialist revolutions and national liberation in Third World countries.

The particular strata formed by intellectuals or graduates, bureaucrats and technocrats are little more than sub-groups of the *petit bourgeoisie*, along with others (petty producers, middle cadres, and so on). In this sense there is nothing special to say about these strata as such, other than the general rule of the vacillating character of the *petit bourgeoisie* and its non-decisive role in history.

In the centres, where the integrationist function of capitalist development has established a social consensus, as we have shown (rules of play accepted by right and left), the middle classes and the intellectuals are within the entity that is fully integrated in the global system. It is the classic *trahison des clercs*.

Gramsci, in arguing his well-known concept of the 'organic intellectual', supposed that every significant class in history – whether dominant (the bourgeoisie in capitalism), or aspiring to become so (the working class) – collectively produced its own ideology and culture, organizational forms and practices. The organic intellectual is the catalyst of this production to which he gives sufficient expression for the ideology of the class he represents to establish itself as the dominant ideology in society. Gramsci also supposed that the working class of the capitalist centres was revolutionary, and on this basis considered the conditions for the emergence of the organic intellectual of the social revolution (the avant garde party). If one believes that Gramsci's hypothesis was mistaken and that the working class of the capitalist centres also accepts the fundamental rules of play in the system, then one must infer that the working classes there are not, under the present state of things, able to produce their own socialist 'organic intellectual'. What they do produce is cadres who organize their struggles, but they are cadres which have relinquished the thought of an alternative plan for a classless society. There are within the societies some individuals who still dream of this. But as has already been said, 'Western Marxism' is a Marxism of cults and universities without social influence. There are also within these societies demands of a socialist character conveyed in various ways. But it is typical that these demands are not articulated within an overall plan (hence the Greens and the feminists, for example, formally refuse to go beyond their own specific issue), and do not produce the organic intellectual Gramsci expected.

The situation at the periphery is quite different: the popular classes have nothing to gain from the capitalist development as it appears to them. They are therefore potentially anti-capitalist. But their situation is not the same as that of the proletariat in the classical Marxist conception. It is that of a motley collection of victims of capitalism affected in highly diverse ways. On their own these classes are not in a position to draw up a plan for a classless society. They have constantly shown themselves capable of 'rejection' and even revolt, and more generally of active and passive resistance. In these circumstances there is historical scope for the constitution of a social force capable of fulfilling this objectively necessary and possible role: of catalyst to formulate an alternative social plan to capitalism, to organize the popular classes and lead their action against capitalism. This force is the intelligentsia.

The intelligentsia – or the revolutionary intelligentsia if we are to qualify it – is not as a class the *petit bourgeoisie* as a whole of these societies. The intelligentsia does largely recruit within this class – for fairly obvious reasons – but not exclusively so: personalities from the aristocracy and the people are often equally numerous. The intelligentsia is not defined by the class origin of its members. It is defined by: (i) its anti-capitalism; (ii) its openness to the universal dimension of the culture of our age, and thereby to locate itself in this world, to analyse its contradictions, understand its weakest links; and (iii) its ability to remain in lively and close contact with the popular classes, to share their history and cultural expression.

It remains to add the conditions conducive to the crystallization of such an intelligentsia, and the obstacles thereto. In my view, this question, to which too little thought has been given, is fundamental to the progressive movement of our day, the real question that history has placed on the agenda objectively. I shall not attempt a hasty answer. I shall merely say what seems to me evident at the level of the cultural conditions for this crystallization. No effective answer can come from a refusal to accept and grasp the universal dimension of culture that current worldwide expansion initiated by capitalism has already imposed (despite the contradictory character of this expansion of which the peoples of the periphery are victims), and from a withdrawal into a negative culturalist nationalism (purely and simply an often neurotic 'anti-Westernism'). Contrarily, Westernized alienation divorced from the popular reality will also lead to impasse.

I believe that Marxism is the only intellectual means that can possibly provide the necessary happy mean. There is of course a 'Western Marxism' that might more appropriately be described as Western-centred. This alienated Marxism is by its nature powerless, since it refuses to locate itself where action is possible. That is why in my book, *Delinking*, I wrote that Marxism had acquired an Asian and African vocation that might perhaps be its principal vocation. I know that by saying this I shall draw the fire of Western Marxists who will see it as no more than a commonplace 'nationalist deviation'.

I shall put forward the notion that, in the spirit of this analytical proposition, the Bolshevik Party and the Chinese Communist Party were perfect expressions of the crystallization of a revolutionary intelligentsia capable of organizing the popular classes and becoming their avant garde. Each of these histories has special characteristics and a particular context. Perhaps the Russian case has a particular advantage, as in a Russia as part of Europe, Marxism did not seem so much of an imported foreign body. Perhaps in China the civil (that is, non-religious) character of the traditional dominant ideology – Confucianism – was less of an obstacle in the sense that it did not offer any fierce resistance to cultural 'importation' – of Marxism in this instance (elsewhere, in Japan, a similar culture did not show any hostility to the importation of capitalism). In contrast perhaps, the totalitarian interpretation of religions (Hinduism and Islam) may have been a serious obstacle to the necessary effective universalist opening, to date at least.

National and popular transformation conducted successfully under these circumstances is at the origin of the problem of statism in post-capitalist societies. It is an essentially new problem. By that I mean that it cannot be reduced to a 'specific and transitory' form of capitalist construction. I mean, too, that it is not an expression of an inevitable linear development imposed by the increasing centralization of capital, itself in turn produced by the movement of capital. The first reduction, the implicit hypothesis of a theory whereby the revolutions in question are only capitalist revolutions, simply ignores that these revolutions are against the movement of capital, whose effect is to increase its worldwide expansion. The second reduction is also contrary to reality: if the centralization of capital imposes the possible emergence of statism (in the future, provided that nothing changes at the most essential level of class struggle) in response to the contradictions engendered by this centralization, the tendency should be manifest in the developed West and not at the periphery.

The national and popular new state is necessary for many reasons. First because, within the world system of states, the national and popular society established as a breach with worldwide capitalist expansion (the essence of de-linking) will confront the capitalist states whose aggressiveness has never been lacking. Then, because the national and popular society is not a 'dictatorship of the proletariat' (which is at best a tiny minority). It is an alliance of classes with partially convergent, and partially divergent, interests (there is, for example, a divergence of real short- and medium-term interests between peasants and the urban population). The state is the sole means of mediating these relations. Finally, because the relation between the intelligentsia (the avant garde 'Party') and the popular classes is not one-dimensional (the avant garde 'represents' the people) but complex and riddled with alliances and conflicts.

These conditions are the source of the fetishism of power so apparent in the post-revolutionary societies. A fetishism that harbours serious illusions, including that it is possible to 'control' the capitalist, and the socialist tendencies affecting society. History shows that power can 'control' the capitalist tendencies only by suppressing them at the cost of the economic difficulties of which we are well aware. As for 'control' of workers, through a combination of state paternalism (real material achievements to the benefit of workers), manipulation (the instrumentalization of official Marxism and repression) history shows, too, that it weakens economic development and has severe limitations. We are brought back here to the fundamental issue of democracy.

Whatever the case, in this analytical schema, statism seems to constitute a third autonomous component. It is not a mere cover for capitalism under construction. No more is it, as the ideological discourse of the authorities pleads, a form whose content will, by definition and without question, be socialist.

I shall not say it is the same for the initial responses to the challenge of capitalism as shown in the Third World, where there has been radicalization of the national liberation movement.

There are, however, similarities between the two kinds of modern experience. Both are responses to the challenge of capitalist expansion and the refusal to accept the peripheralization it entails. The radical national liberation movement is also the expression of a broad social alliance including the popular classes. If, in some cases, bourgeois leadership is in evidence, it is less so in others. The bourgeoisie is often found in the camp of ready compromise with imperialism. It seems to me that, in the radical national liberation movements we find the intelligentsia fulfilling the role as catalyst of the popular forces, whose role – underestimated in formal analysis – has been more decisive than that of the *petit bourgeoisie* generally (and wrongly) regarded as the main actor.

It would, in my view, be more interesting to take a closer look at this radical nationalist intelligentsia and its ideological and cultural perception of the challenge of modern times. As always, it would be necessary to avoid hasty generalizations and to examine concrete instances case by case. In Egypt's case I suggest that the entire modern history of this ancient country is largely determined by its intelligentsia. This intelligentsia, is, however, divided into three strands without their managing to converge or one of them taking a decisive lead. The 'modernist' strand has remained largely culturally alienated from the popular masses, whether we are speaking of the 'Westernized' liberal bourgeois branch in decline, or the radical branch that was receptive to communism in the 1920s, long before the other countries of the Orient. The Islamist strand, present from the Nahda to the Muslim Brothers and fundamentalism, has always thrown up intellectuals who found a ready response in the people, but has never formed a social force able to lead the people and has, therefore, always found itself in the end manipulated by more powerful forces (local and regional reaction and behind this imperialism). It serves above all as a barrier to the spread of the ideas of the radical left.

In these circumstances, it is a third strand of 'modernism', represented in recent history by the Free Officers groups, that has seized the historic opportunity. I regard the Free Officers organization, along with communist organizations, essentially as kernels of the intelligentsia that have been unable, in the circumstances, to organize the masses and unite the anti-capitalist forces behind them. This branch of the intelligentsia – which gave rise to Nasserism – is not an overall expression of the *petit bourgeois* ideology, despite some superficial signs of this. It has proved itself modernist, thoroughly anti-imperialist and nationalist, ready to discard the rich classes and appeal to the people, but nonetheless 'pragmatic', as Nasser himself acknowledged. This characterization, in our view, masks the society's overall cultural bankruptcy, and the failure to provoke a creative synthesis of the universalist dimension of modern culture and the particular style of the people's historical heritage.

The movement going 'beyond capitalism' and initiated by the radicalization of national liberation, constantly finds itself trapped by its ambivalent character and uncertain 'plans' or by objective obstacles within society. The two are mutually reinforcing and in the end, in combination with constant imperialist aggression, they abort the hope of a national and popular revolution. Here, therefore, statism is not the product of the national and popular revolution, but indicates the backsliding that confrontation with imperialism imposes. It has operated on a society where the component of internal capitalist forces has remained preponderant in the face of a component of still merely embryonic socialist aspirations. The model of Nasserist construction has remained a model of 'bureaucratic capitalist' adaptations to the crisis of peripheral capitalism, to use a terminology corresponding to the typology offered by Fawzy Mansour, one I find highly persuasive. Along with Fawzy, I note that the model is unstable, constantly threatened by 'recompradorization', as has already occurred in the Egyptian case.[5]

Without going into too precipitate a generalization, I should say that all attempts to go 'beyond capitalism' from the starting point of radicalization of national liberation have encountered the same limitations and have therefore displayed the same frailty. But this story may be only just beginning, and it is perhaps because we are in a hurry that we lose sight of the future potential lurking in the radicalization of the refusal to accept compradorization.

Notes

1. See Samir Amin's preface to Anyang' Nyong'o, Peter (ed.), *Popular Struggles for Democracy in Africa*, London, Zed Books, 1987, and cf. notes 1 and 3 to Chapter 5 above.

2. See Szentes, Tamas, *Theories of World Capitalist Economy*, Budapest, 1985, and cf. Amin, Samir, 'Etat et développement', *Socialism in the World*, No. 58, 1987.

3. On worldwide value, see Amin, Samir, *The Law of Value and Historical Materialism*, New York, Monthly Review Press, 1978; and cf. Amin, Samir *Delinking*, London, Zed Books, 1989.

4. See Amin, Samir, 'Democracy and National strategy in the Periphery'; 'Etat et développement'; contribution to *Dynamics of Global Crisis*; 'Les perspectives du socialisme', *Socialism in the World*, No. 54, 1986.

5. See articles by Fawzy Mansour and Samir Amin (in Arabic) in the Egyptian journal *Qadaya Fikriyya*, 1987.

7. Inter-African and South–South Co-operation

There is a fair amount of truth in the argument that the Balkanization of Africa and the Arab region is an additional obstacle to any form of development, a fortiori development to match the challenges of our time, and leaving integration in worldwide development without any alternative and hence making de-linking impossible. Although such an argument is often put forward as an excuse, co-operation – or integration with the outlook of constructing vast autonomous areas, if not great unitary states – is no substitute for the preliminary internal changes required, even of small and medium size countries, to begin autocentric national and popular development.

Africa – even in its existing states – is not unaware of the fact that for small states the impasse is real. In the continent as a whole there is no shortage of institutions, attempts and plans for co-operation. Alongside the national efforts to escape from the rut, shown earlier, efforts at mutual support and co-operation have been undertaken even before the 'South–South' theme took over from the failure of the NIEO. Moreover, these attempts at co-operation are based on solid historical and ideological foundations: pan-Africanism and pan-Arabism. The Organization of African Unity (OAU) and the Arab League have taken the initiative in creating numerous institutions, established sub-regional confederation schemes (based, it is true, on 'common market' principles, such as ECOWAS in West Africa), organized common fronts for the struggle against their adversaries (such as the SADCC in the face of South Africa), systematized Afro-Arab co-operation (which by volume is the largest South–South co-operation plan).

The results, so far, have been meagre and below the minimum required to launch an 'alternative development'. The reasons must be analysed: micro-nationalisms and an inappropriate ideology of nation? Colonial inheritance? Drift in the system of international relations?

Pan-Africanism in the light of the colonial inheritance[1]

Despite appearances colonialism did not unify the countries and regions it conquered. It fragmented them.

The colonial development, to which the whole of the African continent was subjected, did not create economically integrated areas anywhere in Africa. But within the geographically vast colonial empires, unification in the liberal – capitalist – meaning of the word was perfectly achieved in the threefold sense of unified markets for commodities, capital and labour.

The goods in question that circulated freely were, however, products of metropolitan industry, and the capital too was from the metropolis. This space was organized as the periphery of another system; it was not organized in terms of itself. It cannot, therefore, be called an economic area as this can exist only if it is organized in terms of itself. Here the flow of exchange of goods and capital of internal origin was negligible, sometimes even in comparison with what it had been before colonization. Integration in the space dominated by the metropolises disaggregated the embryonic organization of the national space.

There is no analogy between the gradual establishment of a national economic space, in the framework of the European nation states during the development of capitalism gradually integrating provinces in a space organized in terms of itself, and the kind of formal space colonization constituted in its empires. In fact the colonial spaces were a series of micro-regions bundled together and unequally developed according to the needs of the metropolises at successive stages of the latter's evolution. The result is that some regions developed at one stage of development were later abandoned because they were no longer of interest. The imperial geographic area was a patchwork of these micro-regions integrated in the light of the needs of metropolitan capital at various stages of evolution; some were 'prosperous' and others – exploited at an earlier stage and then abandoned – devastated.

Since the colonial development brought no integration of the space, this geographical area could, at independence, be chopped up quite arbitrarily. There was no economic need to prevent this arbitrary chopping-up of the space. The empire might be chopped-up and each piece survive, if not develop, without creating any great difficulty for the colonial and neo-colonial economy. In these circumstances further break-up is always possible at the periphery of the system. It is easy to blame it on local, political, ideological or ethnic forces with centrifugal effect. It is often suggested that, for example, Africa broke up thanks to micro-local interests, wrongly designated as tribalism here, or micro-nationalism there. The explanation is false, since it overlooks that it was this organizational form of the geographical area dominated by the metropolises that created these centrifugal forces. In this geographical area, the micro-regions enjoying 'prosperity' at a stage of colonial development have no interest in dragging in their wake the areas devastated and those as yet undeveloped. It is not surprising in these circumstances that it is the 'prosperous' micro-regions who have been the source of the break-up, Côte d'Ivoire for example in what had been French West Africa. Elsewhere this kind of colonial development set up embryonic social forces that would become the bureaucratic bourgeoisies in the administrative capitals. These bureaucratic bourgeoisies had an interest in shutting themselves up into tiny states of which they would be masters. It is often said that the Africans are sympathetic to large economic units, but that external forces are opposed to them. This is incorrect, since with the exception of the most backward segments of foreign capital, corresponding to primitive stages of colonization, big international capital is not hostile – on the contrary – to the organization of large economic 'units', as long as they are conceived in its style. This does not mean that we should renounce the objective of economic unity, but that we must see it differently. Certainly, colonization of Africa was as a whole primitive colonization, entrusted to the most backward segments of capital (especially in regard to the French colonial empire) such as colonial trading companies descended from the mercantilist era and the slave trade. For the operation of such a system, it was of little account whether or not there were organized economic units, as there was no industry at this stage of colonial development there was no problem of markets. The centre of gravity of dominant capital is, however, shifting from these backward segments to the multinationals who do have an interest in the organization of large units in order to establish viable industries benefiting from the opening of more extensive markets.

The large space that we must conceive in the prospect of autocentric development has nothing to do with this kind of economic unit. The classic approach, in terms of monetary and customs unions and African common markets, does not meet the demands of a development policy since it accentuates regional inequalities within Africa and social inequalities within each region. Obviously, the most deprived countries are naturally opposed to this kind of neo-colonial integration. It is understandable that, in West Africa for example, the interior savannah countries have no interest in sacrificing their own development to this kind of so-called African unity.

Any analogy between the European common market and any possible common markets in Africa is quite meaningless. The European common market is organized between countries that have already reached the same stage of development and are able to compete. For these countries it is a matter of organizing a unit that already virtually existed, whereas for the African countries it is a matter of creating a unit that has no existence at all. It is a totally different problem. On this issue we have no more than the embryo of a theory, that of the handling of space around transport routes through the simultaneous and complementary installation of basic industries, for example.

From this angle, the great autocentric space is a precondition for Africa's advanced development: a necessary but not sufficient condition, since if this space is differently organized, as the periphery of a space dominated by foreign capital, it will have no developmental effect of itself but will, on the contrary, have the effect of accentuating the inequalities. What are the achievements and plans under way for African integration? We have first what was maintained of the colonial system, particularly the monetary unions in the Franc zone. These monetary unions are often defended on the grounds of being 'better than nothing'. But these are not units that will permit autocentric development of the monetary zone. As conceived by the metropolitan power, these units merely alleviate the management costs to the dominant metropolis by balancing the deficits of some components with the surplus of others. This is no more than a modality of management by the imperial system as has been shown.

As for the customs unions inherited from colonization, they are breaking up one by one for the obvious reasons indicated.

The assessment of positive achievements is unpromising. There are some tentative beginnings here and there, not through industrial integration, still a long way away, but more modestly through a minimum of collaboration in the installation of industries. It is very far from the demands of the creation and organization of an integrated economic space.

At the same time, note must be taken that significant discussions on the creation of monetary unions with autonomy in regard to the exterior, and of payment unions that might begin a genuine process of integration, have gradually been dropped since the 1970s. This is an example of the drift considered above.

The conclusion is that it is impossible to conceive of the creation of an economic space in Africa in a liberal framework, founded only on rules of competitiveness and profitability. Such a space would serve only to maintain and heighten the inequalities of underdevelopment. The alternative lies in planned organization of the space in terms of the prospects for long-term autocentric development.

The problematic of the Arab nation[2]

If the Third World peoples are to meet the challenges of our time they have no option but to establish relatively broad solidarity groupings, well equipped in natural resources, able to prevent the subordination that their economic and financial vulnerability encourages, and even to give pause to a possible military aggressor. But their history and heritage in ethnic, cultural and linguistic terms, and their inheritance of frontiers and statist institutions, could serve as serious handicaps to this reconstruction. The Arab world embraces a vast geographical space that enjoys all these favourable conditions. Provided of course that what the Arabs call the 'Arab nation' becomes a reality. Aspirations for Arab unity – if there is an aspiration and whose? (of the peoples? of states and governments? of bourgeoisies? of intellecutals?) – are, in general, badly received in the West, whether they are regarded as utopian, unrealistic, or ludicrous, or whether they are regarded as a 'threat', the revenge of 'Muslim fanatics' on 'European Christianity'. Despite such prejudices, the achievement of Arab national unity is not only possible and desirable, but even objectively necessary in the interest of the Arab peoples. This 'historical necessity' is, however, no more inescapable than another, and more serious fact: that the Arab peoples are not currently embarked upon this path.

We shall not again go over the ground of the roots of the Arab question, discussed in its historical dimension in *The Arab Nation*, nor the issues arising from the theory of nation, discussed above. We shall say only: (i) that Arab unification in its heady early days rests on a material base, the centralization and circulation of surplus effected by the hegemonic state-class of 'merchant warriors'; (ii) that the subsequent fragmentation and decline were precisely the results of the disappearance of this system of centralization and circulation of surplus; (iii) that this contradictory heritage results in a 'nation' in two stages: a real potential of building a unified Arab nation (in Arabic *qawmiya*) already in possession of an essential instrument in common language and culture, and the parallel need at the inferior stage to recognize the reality of 'sub-nations' (in Arabic, *watan*), broadly corresponding to the main states of today.

There are serious obstacles to the achievement of this aim of unification. First, the interests of the hegemonic blocs constituted on the basis of existing states, which, as elsewhere in the peripheralized Third World, have no other ambition that that of attempting to 'adjust' individually to the demands of the world system. These 'adjustments' provoke inter-state rivalries and underlie some of the regional hegemonic aspirations. The relative and unequally distributed financial prosperity brought by oil exacerbates these negative trends. But there is also the obstacle of the Euro-American Western geo-strategic concern to prevent by all possible means the emergence of this strong nation on Europe's southern flank. To the extent that Egypt is the kernel of the potential Arab construct, there has been a constant in Western policy – from Mohamed Ali at the beginning of the 19th century to Sadat: to smash any attempt to build a strong Egypt. The West did not create a full-fledged State of Israel for any other reason.

In the face of this challenge, two modern Arab ideological currents have looked towards unity. The Ba'athist current put forward the thesis of the priority of unity over social transformation (socialism in principle). History has shown that bourgeois nationalism (for this is what it boils down to) cannot under the circumstances of the contemporary challenges replicate what was possible in another age and other circumstances (in Germany or Italy). The Nasserist current from a neighbouring stance drew the lessons of the failure of the only real attempt at unification (the United Arab Republic of Egypt and Syria from 1958 to 1961), and began then to understand that the only social classes capable of carrying forward a unitary plan were the popular classes. But for complex reasons peculiar to the history of Egypt and of Nasserism, it did not succeed in overcoming the obstacles along the path to socialist construction and a strategy of de-linking from the world system, the only viable alternative to the impossible 'adjustments'. Meanwhile, imperialist aggression, through the Israeli attack of 1967, put an end to the experiment before it could make further progress and become irreversible.

The popular ideological reaction following this failure, and the recom-pradorization underway in the Arab world, is not currently part of a prospect of socialist and unitary supersession. We come back to our analysis of the 'Islamic renaissance', the form this reaction takes. Here for the sake of brevity let us recall only: (i) that the Muslim religion, like any religion, is susceptible to various interpretations, reactionary, conservative, progressive and revolutionary; it has in the past been able to adapt to social evolution and nothing prevents it from continuing to do so; it might even adapt to a secularization of society; (ii) the medley of contradictory tendencies within the global current dominated by fundamentalism is simultaneously evidence of a rejection of the prospect of compradorization that is all capitalism can offer and of the historical crisis of the socialist alternative; and (iii) that in the state, the current of Islamic revival, far from strengthening the prospect of Arab unity, works against it and offers nothing but sterile escapism.

The people do make their own history, but sometimes they do it badly. The challenge the Arab peoples must take on lies right in front of them.

Afro-Arab co-operation[3]

When the United Nations was founded in the aftermath of the Second World War, the decolonization process had not yet begun and the African and Asian states represented there could be counted on one's fingers. But within a mere five years, the Asian and Arab states with formal independence constituted an 'Arab–Asiatic' group that aimed to speed up decolonization, of Africa in particular, through support to the liberation movements. At Bandung in 1955 the principles of the solidarity of the peoples and states of the Third World were systematically formulated. The Asian–African conference declared its full support of the principle of self-determination of peoples and nations. It rejected the 'anti-communist' blackmail of the United States that, in the name of 'Atlantic' solidarity in the first cold war, tolerated colonial wars and/or systematic repression on the part of the old colonial powers, Britain and France in particular. The Asian–African conference also refused to subject their independence to the conditionality of arrangements of collective defence to serve the particular interests of any of the big powers (of the kind the United States was actively promoting against the Soviet Union and China). The conference was in favour of 'positive neutrality' that precluded going further into a Soviet sphere of influence as the price of freedom. On these foundations various formal and informal organizations for Afro-Asian co-operation were established – the Afro-Asian People's Solidarity Organization in Cairo and the All-African Peoples Organization in Accra – in 1958.

The decade of 1955 to 1965 saw the great years of Afro-Asian co-operation in general and Arab–African in particular. It was a question of mutual political support, where independent states and national liberation movements took their place side by side. This decade was the period of the great 'wind of change' that obliged colonialist Europe to yield: after an attempt to lop off one of the heads of the movement, through the tripartite Anglo-French–Israeli aggression against Egypt in 1956, it tried to limit concessions in North Africa to independence for Tunisia and Morocco (1956) and deny it to Algeria, which, therefore, was ravaged by colonial war for eight years (1954 to 1962), gave way to the United States to take over from France in Vietnam (from 1954) and finally, in 1960, Europe chose to accelerate the accession of sub-Saharan Africa to an independence that was steered into the hands of its 'friends'.

The conflict between the radical nationalist political forces and those that emerged from European concessions, from 1960 to 1963 divided Africa into the

Casablanca group and the Monrovia group, particularly on the issue of the former Belgian Congo. As we know, the fusion of the two groups in 1963 was the origin of the OAU, whose members went on to decide to accept the colonial boundaries and the Balkanization of the continent, and non-interference in each other's 'internal' affairs, and to support only the liberation movements of the colonies not yet freed (the Portuguese colonies, Rhodesia, Namibia and South Africa).

It was in this atmosphere that the first plans for intra-African, intra-Arab and Arab–African co-operation took shape. It was a matter of extending the political solidarity of the liberation movements into a new economic co-operation between the states liberated from colonialism, and refusing the surrender to the neo-colonialist prospects offered by the West. The co-operation was highly selective and involved only the radical nationalist states: Nasserist Egypt, promoter of the movement had a crucial place, alongside independent Algeria (from 1962), Nkrumah's Ghana, Sekou Touré's Guinea, Modibo Keita's Mali, and Nyerere's Tanzania. As for the neo-colonial regimes, they were not interested in principle, as they regarded 'Western aid' as satisfactory and spurned co-operation 'between the poor' who, in their view, had nothing to give each other.

By contrast, the radical nationalist states nurtured a vision of the total liberation of Africa and the Middle East that would pave the way to overcoming the handicaps inherited from the past and colonization, 'underdevelopment' (understood as dependence on imperialism and not as 'backwardness and poverty'), and the break-up into more or less artificial states, vulnerable by virtue of their inadequate size. Nasser's pan-Arab language and Nkrumah's pan-African language, far from being absurdly utopian, were rather evidence of the perceptiveness of these historic leaders. The co-operation envisaged was not limited to 'financial aid' to one another. In view of the general poverty of the states in question such aid played only a secondary role in the strategies, policies and co-operation programmes.

Two sides of this overall co-operation strategy were envisaged: the constitution of a common front against the imperialist West, in order to strengthen the negotiating position of the partners and reduce their vulnerability; the gradual construction of a regional society better integrated through the development of its internal complementarities and leading at least to partially overcoming the asymmetrical and unequal North–South relations.

Undoubtedly, the plans for 'common fronts' against the West rarely went beyond the embryonic stage: exchange of views did not lead to the founding of effective producers' associations (only OPEC was to emerge later, at a different conjuncture). Likewise, the shared plans for technological exchange and exploitation of (mining, agricultural and industrial) resources, such as those for integrated transport systems, rarely went further than the drawing board. The conjunctural circumstances were not promising: it was still a time of easy growth and to some it seemed a softer option to follow the line of least resistance, to promote the traditional exports to the West and to import from it the means to launch industrialization. But this shows the limitations of the radical nationalist regimes of the time.

Some positive achievements were initiated at the time in many areas. The exchange of students and specialists, popular congresses and conferences of professional associations, encouraged an Afro-Asian internationalism whose significance it would be wrong to underestimate. Political and military consultation gave this co-operation a sense of direction. In terms of economic results – construction of industry and infrastructure, increase of trade – a great many positive steps were taken. The partner states were largely influenced by the models of co-operation offered by both the USSR and China: long-term credits on soft terms, repayment in kind from the output of completed projects, and so on.

This co-operation cannot be isolated from the context of the internal politics of the radical nationalist partners, or escape a judgement that includes the limitations and contradictions of these systems. The latter may be characterized by a latent internal conflict between the trend towards evolution in a progressive social manner and the trend towards reinforcement of conservative social forces hankering after a bourgeois national state. For the components of the national liberation movement from which the radical nationalist state had emerged had not yet come into direct confrontation. The indecisive and contradictory content of the development policies pursued under these circumstances reflected this latent internal conflict. In fact, as we have said above, what we have called the 'Bandung plan' was essentially geared to the construction of a bourgeois national state, in the sense that on the one hand it sought control over internal accumulation and on the other it conceived of this within a 'global interdependence' (in fact the pursuit of integration in the world capitalist system) freed of the inequalities inherited from colonization. This plan was in opposition to the tendency towards a more or less well-defined national and popular plan that would have entailed a genuine de-linking in the way we have defined it, and opened the long chapter of the history of a transition capable of bolstering the gradual trend to socialism. The subsequent events confirmed the thesis that in our age the crystallization of new capitalist centres (the definition of the content of the bourgeois national plan) was impossible in the Third World in general, and the Afro-Arab region in particular. Even before the global crisis brought the dismantling of national bourgeois attempts, the drift, from the mid-1960s, had already doomed these experiments hastily dubbed as 'socialist'. With the fall of Modibo Keita and Nkrumah and the Egyptian defeat of 1967, the first wave of this Afro-Arab co-operation was played out.

The bourgeois national plan was, in fact, in operation for only a brief period. Even before the opening of the crisis of the early 1970s its historical limitations were fairly apparent.

With the signature of the Treaty of Rome in 1957 and the beginning of the European construction, the neo-colonialist pressure of the Common Market took over from the old colonialisms. African states, only freshly independent, became 'associated' with the community, and subjected their vision of development to the imperatives of European strategy. The African radical nationalist states themselves accepted the terms of the Yaoundé Convention (followed by the Lomé Convention) without too much bother; those in the Maghreb tried to extend the 'advantages' of the opening-up of the French market to their traditional products or to those of their new industry (especially textile sub-contracting). At the same time, this new European 'friend' pursued its policy of open or concealed support to the old Portuguese colonialism, the apartheid regimes in South Africa, Rhodesia and Namibia, and Zionist expansion.

Africa, in the OAU, also continued its support to the liberation movements of Portuguese and southern Africa. But the results of these liberation struggles did not appear until later (1974: independence of the Portuguese colonies; 1980: independence of Zimbabwe) and in incomplete form as, South Africa to this day maintains its destabilizing intervention without Europe gainsaying . . . As for Israel, it pursued its intervention south of the Sahara on behalf of the United States; it took the 1967 war to see it provisionally and partially hounded out of the region. In Asia, neo-colonial dependence was less strongly felt, although the Vietnam war dragged on to 1975 and the countries to the south and east of the Arabian peninsula did not achieve independent status until the end of the 1960s.

The gradual gaining ground by the dominant conservative forces in Africa, the Arab world and Asia, alongside the collapse of radical national experiences, would at the same time encourage new currents attaching more significance to North–South relations than to South–South co-operation.

The overt crisis in the system from the 1970s accelerated the process of decomposition of the bourgeois national plan of Bandung. A global realignment of the West behind the United States was detectable and – on the excuse of debt and through the IMF and World Bank – this intervention proposed imposing on the Third World countries the now familiar 'readjustments'; the latter have no room for the demands of autocentric development at national, regional or collective level. Simultaneously the Soviet Union was subjected to the arms race imposed by the United States in the latter's strategy of counter-attack to re-establish its hegemony and to impose an Atlantic pact realignment on Europe and Japan through the blackmail of East–West conflict. For this reason perhaps, the Soviet Union appears to have gone generally on the defensive. The penetration they achieved by providing defence for Angola and Mozambique threatened by South African destabilization, and by intervening in the conflicts of the Horn of Africa, from 1975, is rather limited and possibly provisional. In the Middle East, obviously, its presence has been largely marginalized by Egypt's about-turn since 1973.

In turn, the general retreat of the Bandung spirit encouraged the resurgence of various ideological and political currents and ambivalent and even dubious strategies. For example, it enabled Saudi Arabia to give the 'Pan-Islamic' current an airing it could not have achieved while Nasser was on guard, as he would not allow it to counter militant, unitary pan-Arabism. The current would give rise to such institutions as the Islamic Bank that would really take off a while later. It also permitted illusions as to a 'common front' of the Third World countries, regardless of their regimes and internal options, that would be able to force upon the West a revision of the terms of operation of the world economic system. This illusion was no doubt fuelled by the victory gained by OPEC in 1973. This was indeed a victory for the Third World: for the first time in history, the countries of the periphery were able to intervene effectively – and collectively – in setting the price of a significant raw material. It was of no great consequence from this point of view that the regimes principally benefiting by this victory were conservative. It was of no great consequence too, that OPEC reached this conclusion by able exploitation of a conjuncture of internal conflict in the Western world (the United States discovering that readjustment of the oil price could serve their interests in competition with Europe and Japan).

The limitations and ambivalence of what would be built in this framework were too often lost sight of, in the light of a euphoria that subsequent events would show to be unfounded. The regrouping of the non-aligned and Third World countries in 1975 to present an overall plan of reform of North–South relations, under the name of New International Economic Order, is a sign of these illusions. The West's predictably implacable opposition to the attempt hastened the later decomposition of the Third World.

As was to be expected, this decomposition accentuated the internal conflicts within the Third World. Some of these are of longstanding and not necessarily the exclusive product of the colonial heritage and great power manoeuvres. But it is not by chance that it is in the African and Arab region – the weakest and most exposed of the Third World – that we find a huge number of these conflicts: the Horn of Africa, Chad, Western Sahara, Iran–Iraq, civil war in Lebanon, rivalry of the two Yemens, amongst others.

Expansion of Arab–African co-operation comes exactly within this period of ambivalence, from 1973. The connection between this blossoming of co-operation and 'oil prosperity' — from 1973 to 1985 ending, perhaps, in the crumbling of OPEC underway – is an obvious factor. A study of this co-operation brings out its general characteristics, perhaps three in all.

First, it is a matter of substantial programmes, by far the most impressive throughout the Third World.

Second, it is all-round co-operation, meaning that it embraces all the African and Arab countries, regardless of their political regimes and internal and international ideological and social options. The financial institutions established within the framework of overall co-operation between the OAU and the Arab League (BADEA among others) are evidence of this all-round conception of the co-operation. It is distinct from the selective co-operation of the 1960s.

Third, it is programmes essentially with access to substantial funds derived in the main from the 'oil surpluses' of the 1970s. This 'advantage', however, also has its negative side. It has contributed to distorting the outlook on genuinely alternative South–South demands, rather than complementary to North–

South demands, just as it has encouraged well- or ill-founded expectations of boundless financial 'wealth' from the oil-producer countries. It is hardly surprising to note that little attention has been given to the sharing of non-financial resources (expertize, possibilities of technological research) and to increasing trade within the group of countries concerned (with priority for development of agricultural, mining and industrial complementarities, loan repayment through increased trade).

There are varying opinions on the positive features and shortcomings of these programmes for Afro-Arab co-operation. The analyses available, whether global or by sector and country, allow room for this. Our personal opinion is that the principle of South–South co-operation is always positive of itself, whatever the limitations and shortcomings in any particular example. It is, nonetheless, necessary to bring out the concrete characteristics of the projects implemented through the co-operation in question, and on this basis to assess the significance of this development for a liberation we see as synonymous with autocentric development for the states concerned, individually and as wholes or part-wholes. The battle for genuine South–South co-operation requires this.

From a formalist point of view, it is acceptable that the choice of projects put forward for financing by Afro-Arab co-operation is of concern only to the beneficiary states. This choice is bound to depend on the character of the internal development strategies. The latter are often questionable, that is, from our point of view, not leading as systematically as possible to an autocentric structure. But it is accepted that the Third World countries have the right to determine their own options and, on principle, interference by the agencies of the North is ruled out; although they do, in fact interfere, as we can see from the constant statements by the World Bank. It should be said then that mutual aid between Third World countries should follow the same principle of scrupulous regard for sovereignties. But putting the issue in these terms removes from the discussion the real terms of the alternative: all-round, or selective co-operation between countries embarked upon economic liberation from their dependence on the North? We are not entirely convinced that the all-round choice of Afro-Arab co-operation is the best. Perhaps a more judicious recourse to choices (if possible) would have avoided certain disappointments. The bottomless pit of Zaire is a good example of the waste that international co-operation sometimes accepts. Some circles want it for particular political reasons (the cynical view, for example, that the stability of the regime is more important than improving the living standards of the people affected . . .). In principle, this kind of reasoning should not be used by leaderships in Third World countries, on the assumption that they do not have an unwarranted hankering after imperialism. Some Third World countries may share Western views and follow the same guidelines. But then it is hard to believe they can imagine a South–South link other than one intended to reinforce the North–South link.

If South–South ties are still as they are (and the same is so of Afro-Arab co-operation and of other forms of regional Arab and African interaction), there are numerous factors on both sides of the divide: the countries (mostly of OPEC) financing this co-operation and its beneficiaries (the 'poorer' African and Arab countries). So far, the co-operation has not brought any appreciable increase in complementary trade flows. The explanation is that neither side is engaged on policies of de-linking in the sense we have given the term. Neither side envisages reference systems of internal prices (and a profitability measure of options intended to strengthen the autocentric character of their development) as distinct from those governing the 'rationality' of the world capitalist system. This shortcoming is manifest in the respect shown for 'World Bank strategies' that they try to reproduce in the imitative detail of co-operation conventions. It was shown above how Arab aid to the countries of the African Sahel financed projects largely drafted by the 'donors' (the 'friends of the Sahel': the West, with the World Bank at its head) and playing no part in the prospect of autocentric development for the region. In these circumstances the increase in financial flows from the Arabs was matched by a reduction in those coming from the OECD countries and institutions. A fine example of the implementation of the currently fashionable Euro-Arab–African 'trialogue': carrying on doing with the money of others (the OPEC countries) what you had been doing with your own (from the OECD)!

Afro-Arab co-operation is, however, a major objective necessity for the economic liberation of this region of the Third World. The reason is that the African and Arab region is, as has been shown, the weakest and most exposed of any in the modern Third World.

The bourgeois national plan – still dominant on the African political scene and in the Arab world – is, therefore, from the start doomed to lead to nowhere except permanent failure. If, in Asia and Latin America the margin of possible adjustment to world development is still broad enough to contain the expectation (or illusion) of bourgeois national crystallization, in Africa and the Arab world there is almost no such scope. More than elsewhere there is a stark alternative: going forward quickly to a national and popular plan or perishing (sometimes in the literal sense, through famine).

The fragmentation of the region into tiny states (as compared to Asia and Latin America) heightens the vulnerability and lessens the chance for any of them in isolation to escape. There are, however, objective elements to strengthen Arab–African unity, with origins in history (the objective foundations of pan-Arabism and pan-Africanism) and in the fact that the region as whole is dealt with in a similar manner by a common adversary, at an economic and strategic level and with the same instruments of intervention (South Africa and Israel).

The challenge is easily defined, although difficult to overcome. Kwame Nkrumah and Gamal Abdel Nasser will remain prophets of our age for having initiated this consciousness. Unfortunately, Afro-Arab co-operation began to peak after the two of them had gone.

Prospects for South–South co-operation[4]

The idea that solidarity of the peoples of Asia and Arica would lead from mutual support in anti-imperialist struggles to positive economic collaboration in alternative moulds to 'dependence' and unequal North–South exchange, dates back to the Bandung conference (1955). The Non-Aligned Movement also adopted as one of its constant themes of word and deed the promotion of South–South relations. After the failure of the North–South negotiations over the plan for the NIEO, the South–South theme had a new burst of life, tinged – since the end of the 1970s – with a certain ambivalence, as Faysal Yachir has noted, since co-operation between Third World countries had the same role as that previously belonging to the NIEO, such as transfer of technology, opening of new industrial markets and availability of financial resources, leading to the adoption by the '77' of an agenda reproducing all the topics of North–South relations.

The sum of recent developments in South–South economic relations is far from insignificant. The facts are well-known and we borrow the essence of conclusions in Yachir's excellent study (*La coopération Sud–Sud, une alternative?*, Dakar, FTM, 1983).

At the level of international trade, the salient fact of the past two decades or so is certainly the emergence of new countries as exporters of manufactured goods. Nowadays, the share of these countries – the so-called 'newly industrializing' – accounts for more than 10% of world trade in industrial goods. These exports are sent to the South and to the North (where they compete successfully against some well-established industries, such as textiles, and even some new industries, such as electronics, provoking neo-protectionist responses, despite the liberal language). The annual rate of growth in South–South trade – 15% since the mid-1970s – is far and away the clearest indicator of all the rates of growth in international trade. This not insubstantial change in the structure of world trade, reflecting the evolution of the new international division of labour, is, however, a factor for only a restricted number of countries, as 80% is accounted for by five countries of East and South-East Asia (a 'gang of four' – Korea, Taiwan, Hong Kong and Singapore – and then to a lesser degree, Malaysia) and four large Third World countries (India and Brazil and to a lesser extent Mexico and Argentina).

A close examination of the new factors will show that they differ from both the 'old' South–South trade or some other new phenomena related to the strategy of relocation by the multinationals.

There were some South–South exchanges as part of the former division of colonial labour. In Africa, for example, the Sahel region, as a 'second-rank' periphery, traditionally supplied food exports (livestock and cereals) to the first-rank periphery in the adjacent coastal areas. These flows were accompanied by massive migrations from the interior to the coast that, in the space of half a century (1930–70), changed the proportion between interior and coastal population from two-thirds and one-third to half-and-half. But this kind of complementarity belonging to colonial and neo-colonial spatial arrangements is declining, as we have noted.

There are further South–South exchanges that are expanding and entirely due to the multinationals' strategies of relocation. In addition to an import substitution role, the small industries controlled by foreign capital in such countries as Côte d'Ivoire, Nigeria, Kenya, and so on, in Africa, Colombia and Costa Rica in Latin America, the Philippines and Pakistan in Asia, now export their surplus output to neighbouring territories. The explosion of the processing industry based on cheap manpower in the 'free zones' (of which Tunisia is a good example in the Arab region) is also part of this 'controlled relocation'.

The boundary between this second kind of South–South exchange and that originating in the 'nine powers' mentioned above is difficult to trace. A high proportion of the export of manufactured goods from the nine countries is, in fact, by subsidiaries of multinationals of the North. This is mainly the case for motor cars, electronics, and pharmaceuticals, 60% to 90% controlled by foreign multinationals in Latin America (including Brazil) and to a lesser extent in Asia (expecially in regard to Korea and India).

In the mid-1970s, the latter factor inspired a thesis of 'sub-imperialism'. This was to some extent an expansion of phenomena that were not entirely new. In Africa the volume of exchange between South Africa and the countries of Southern Africa was of the same kind.

If this factor of the emergence of the 'nine' in world trade deserves special attention, it is perhaps precisely because it reveals new trends in the international division of labour. More than 40% of the manufactured goods of the 'nine' are producer goods, vectors, as we know, of technology transfer. Most of these exports come from three countries – India, Korea and Brazil – which are also in the forefront of Third World exporters of engineering, sometimes more appropriate to Third World markets than the goods of their competitors in the North, just as these three countries are in the forefront of the emergence of 'Third World transnationals'. This phenomenon cannot be reduced to the simple effect of relocation controlled by the North's monopoly capital. There is some conflict – albeit at the mercantile stage – between capitals from North and South. It is a conflict that fuels the thesis of qualitative diversification within the Third World.

By contrast, South–South capital flows have not so far opened up any really new prospects. Direct investments of capital are still negligible despite the combined efforts of the OAU and Arab League to encourage direct investment by the oil-producer countries in other countries of the Arab–African region. The investments represent a substantial portfolio. But they are almost entirely the sole concern of the OPEC countries and are entirely placed on the financial markets of the North. The only South–South financial flow of any consequence is represented by aid from the oil-producer countries – principally the Arabs – to African partners. This flow accounts for 80% of South–South capital transfers and has already reached a level, for certain beneficiary countries, comparable in order of magnitude with the flow of traditional aid supplied by the OECD countries.

The South–South migration of unskilled workers or brain drain of skilled workers is also limited to the impact of the oil boom, while the old migratory flows, linked to the colonial division of labour, are exhausted.

What conclusions can be drawn from these facts?

The economic relations between the newly industrializing, and the other Third World countries resemble in some ways the North–South relations. In the nature of things, the former's exports have to be competitive and hence operate within the structure of the world capitalist system's prices. If there is unequal exchange in North–South relations the same thing will occur in South–South relations. But the same could be said of interventions by countries of the East on the world market. Despite the restructuring there is some advantage in the new developments, if only to the extent that the NICs, unlike the Western countries, cannot fit their trade into global economic and political imperialist strategies. The emergence of this kind of exchange between NICs and other Third World countries is, in any case, one of the favourite arguments of the proponents of the theory whereby the concepts of centre and periphery should be abandoned once and for all, as it has been proven that the Third World countries can develop within the framework of worldwide expansion and even compete successfully against the countries with the longest tradition of industrialization. Other Third World countries' failure to do so would reflect not the imperatives of the world system but unfavourable internal factors for which they are themselves to blame. The sharp differentiation within the Third World would provide evidence of the mistakes in the theory of international polarization implicit in capitalist expansion.

This takes us rather quickly to the conclusions we have already discussed above. The South–South link as it is, in fact extends the unequal North–South relations, without the beneficiaries of change among the countries of the Third World having real access to the closed club of the imperialist centres. There is an enormous amount of evidence in support of this conclusion. The surplus of the NICs on exchange with the Third World compensates for the deficit on their trade with the North and allows a speeding-up of import of equipment by the NICs. These imports carry a technological dependence behind which – as the debt experience has shown – stands a financial dependence that the NICs cannot escape. The NICs as exporters of technology to the rest of the Third World are intermediaries, unable to innovate but only to absorb. Beyond these purely economic considerations, the impact on the character of the state in the NICs and the social effects of their development are part of the worldwide expansion (these effects are, as we have seen, heightening and not reducing internal social inequalities). This impact strengthens rather than denies the thesis of polarization reproduced by world capitalist expansion. That is why I have suggested regarding the NICs as the true periphery of tomorrow, and not as 'semi-peripheries' on the way to crystallization into new centres, while the rest of the Third World countries – especially the fourth world, in a more recent coinage – are the areas laid waste by this expansion.

There are variations and shades of meaning within this overall schema. Relocation is not necessarily and entirely 'controlled' by the monopolies of the centre, according to a simplistic schema of 'redeployment', as it would be if the multinationals' strategies could be operated without any hindrance. But the industrialization of the NICs as it is, is closer to this form of relocation than to that foreseen by the NIEO. The latter aimed to establish autocentric industrialized national economies and to breathe new life into world trade. Within the framework of relocation without autocentric national and popular crystallization there are various strategies, each with its particular characteristics. Brazil is an example of relocation without progressive social transformations (so far at least, and it is the tragedy its young democracy is facing); Korea an example of relocation from a more socially balanced starting point; India an example of relocation grafted on to a strategy with some elements of de-linking (and hence led into a new contradiction between the path of further de-linking and that of relocation and incorporation into the worldwide expansion). In all three cases a strong and interventionist state gives the lie to the 'World Bank' language of liberalization.

We are brought back at this point to what we have been saying about de-linking, as the central axis of national and popular autocentric thrust. As long as we operate within the framework of the structure of world prices (and the South–South link has yet to escape), as long as the strategies internalize this structure (through the criteria of profitability in force), industrialization in our time can only be a relocation incapable of effacing the structural characteristics of peripheral capitalism (that is, an increasingly unequal internal social distribution, in contrast to that typifying the societies of central capitalism where the distribution is stable). To change direction it is essential to adopt alternative criteria of economic rationality, de-linked from those that operate in the worldwide framework. A South–South link that would support autocentric national and popular policies and give them more scope demands this de-linking. It is still a long way off.

Notes

1. Amin, Samir, 'Le commerce interafricain', *Revue Française d'Etudes Politiques Africaines*, No. 4, 1967; 'Quelques aspects économiques de l'unité africaine', Algiers, SNED, 1972; introduction to Amin, Samir, (ed.) *Modern Migrations in Western Africa*.

2. Amin, Samir, *The Arab Nation*.

3. Zarour, Charbel, *La coopération afro-arabe*, Paris, Harmattan, 1989; Amin, Samir, Founou-Tchuigoua, Bernard, and Zarour, Charbel, *Afro-Arab Cooperation, Africa Development*, 1986.

4. Yachir, Faysal, 'La coopération Sud–Sud, une alternative?', *Bulletin du FTM*, No. 2, 1983.

8. A Polycentric World Favourable to Development: A Possibility?

Like it or not, Africa's development, like that of other Third World regions sensitive to its peoples, will depend in great measure on the economic, political and cultural evolution of the world system. Accordingly as East–West and North–South relations are favourable or unfavourable (the variation depends on internal evolutions in West, East and South) the chances for such development will be the greater or the lesser and the difficulties more or less surmountable.

The current overall crisis of the world economic and political system is such as to provoke an immediate response of gloom. But beyond the short term, is there not a challenge to be conquered by humankind with a resolute commitment to a polycentric world, more conducive to peace and progress for all peoples? These are some of the issues we shall tackle in this closing chapter.

The scope and stakes of the global crisis

For more than 15 years the world economic system has been in an enduring structural crisis quite different from a conjunctural 'recession' in a phase of expansion.[1] This is a world crisis, marked by the collapse of growth in productive investment, a notable fall in profitability (very unequally distributed in sectors and companies), persistent disorder in international economic relations.

Without reopening the debate on 'long cycles' in capitalist expansion, we start from the view that any crisis in the capitalist system is an expression of a malfunctioning of the law of value under the effects of class and national struggles in the broad sense. It is expressed by imbalances that make realization of the value impossible and consequently cause a fall in the rate of profit. This general proposition is not enough to describe a particular crisis at a given state of the system's evolution. In fact, for example, in the 19th century, when the law of value was still operating mainly on the basis of national contexts, the crisis was national, although it could be communicated from the hegemonic centre of the time (Great Britain) to other countries. If nowadays the law of value operates throughout the world system, the crisis must be grasped at a similar level, that is, as an expression of the impossibility of ensuring world circulation of capital and world realization of value. The current crisis is, therefore, most apparent in the field of world relations; from an examination of the latter it may be possible to identify what is really at stake in the crisis and what the outcomes may be.

North–South relations and the conflicts around them constitute the central axis of the current crisis. Why?

There are various explanations for the crisis. Is it a matter of deficient demand? Is it, on the contrary, a fall in the rate of profit due to loss of flexibility in the system stemming precisely from the stiffening of the system in the previous period of prosperity? The crisis of 1930 came after a series of defeats of the working classes in the West – when the Russian Revolution did not spread throughout Europe. In these circumstances, the redistribution of income through the Keynesian policies of the 1930s might have been a solution to the crisis. By contrast, our crisis comes after a long period of full employment, the rule of the welfare state, with wages rising along with the rate of labour productivity. Today's deficient demand is essentially deficient demand in the peripheries by virtue of the super-exploitation from which their workers suffer. In other words, only a redistribution of income at the international level, in favour of the South, would permit a fresh start for the world. The obvious question is 'under whose aegis' will this reconversion of the international division of labour be carried out? Will it take the form of redeployment of the capital of the US and European imperialist monopolies? Or will it rather be carried out for the benefit of the peoples of the South under the direction of national powers with popular backing?

But it is also a crisis for US hegemony, whose decline has begun, since post-war expansion has restored to Europe and Japan a competitiveness they lost in the course of the Second World War. Will Europe, in these circumstances, revert to being an autonomous imperialist force in regard to the United States? A close look at this highly complex issue will shed light on the ambiguities of Europe's relations with the Third World, the United States and the USSR.

The crisis is a normal consequence of the changes in economic and political relations of force accumulated in the growth of the 1945–70 period. The main changes are to be found along the 40th parallel and affect: (i) intra-West economic relations, marked by the end of US hegemony and the emergence on the one hand of Japan and of Europe (Germany in particular) on the other as partners that would henceforth be competitive, or even capable of taking over from the United States some at least of its dominant positions; (ii) West–East military relations, marked by equality of the two superpowers from 1960; and (iii) West–East–China political relations, marked by the emergence of China as an autonomous nation able to subject its international strategy to the imperatives of its development options. By contrast North–South relations were only marginally affected: the Third World, as a victim of extraverted development pursued and intensified in the 1945–1970 period, joined the crisis as a weak partner who suffered its full effects.

Our comment that North–South relations constitute the central axis of the crisis does not in any way imply a simplification leaving out other aspects of the crisis: intra-West competition, the crisis of Fordism as a mode of exploitation of industrial labour, the crisis of the welfare state, the articulation of the crisis with the East–West conflict, the Atlantic pact and the crisis of United States hegemony, and so on. It merely implies that these various aspects of the crisis are deliberately treated in relation to what is essentially at stake in the light of the worldwide spread of value.

The prevailing analyses on this range of questions are particularly arid. They focus on various aspects of the crisis of capitalism in the West (crisis in labour organization, contradictory prospects of the new technology, intra-West competition, among others) as if this were of the essence, and the (peripheral) South and (socialist) East mere spectators condemned to adjust to the demands of the West. The evidently underlying hypothesis is that the backward East and South are condemned to further integration in the world systems as their sole lifebelt. The opposite is true: the West is stable despite the crisis, while qualitative change is occurring elsewhere, in the East and South.

It is a crisis of the capitalist system inasmuch as the world system is in effect largely governed by the fundamental rules of this mode of production. But the crisis also affects the countries of the East (usually described as socialist, with all the reservations we have as to this description) inasmuch as they participate in the world system (through commercial and technological exchanges and capital borrowings). But these countries also suffer another crisis, peculiar to them: the difficulty of moving from extensive accumulation to intensive accumulation. This crisis for the regime has, of course, obvious political implications.

The current crisis, like any deep crisis, is manifest in 'ungovernability of the system'. This is identifiable at three levels by: (i) the resistance of the peoples at the periphery to the demands of the logic of the transnationals; (ii) resistance of the working classes at the centre (rejection of Fordism) and the resistance of the peoples at the centre to the lifestyle (inter-class movements); (iii) the conflict between the strategies of worldwide capital and the national policies of states. In the absence of hegemony (that of the United States is in decline) to play the role of a world state, the national states have less and less hold on the strategies of capital ('You nationalize, we internationalize', it might be put). The crisis is a global challenge for the forces of progress. Will the latter be able to devise a credible and articulate programme, susceptible of effective implementation and offering an alternative to the policies of the capital offensive whose aim is to exploit the weakness of the worker and popular forces, to impose a global, national and worldwide, restructuring governed by the only criterion capitalism knows: financial profitability of investment?

They are ill-prepared. For the general economic upsurge of the quarter of a century after the Second World War encouraged many illusions. In the West, the Keynesian remedy was believed to have shown a definitive solution to the problem of crises and unemployment. It was thought that an era of eternal prosperity and definitive control over events had begun. In the so-called socialist model, a formula was believed to have been found for even stronger growth that allowed Khruschev to declare triumphantly that by 1980 the USSR would have caught up with the United States in all areas. In the Afro-Asian Third World, the national liberation movement that had seized political independence also had its share of cures that with the appropriate mix of capitalist and socialist ingredients would, it was thought, make it possible to overcome 'underdevelopment' within 'interdependence'. In Latin America, the thesis of 'modernization' (known as *desarrollismo*) played the same role. It was, therefore, the belief that the world economic order could gradually be changed in favour of the Third World.

Undoubtedly the real performance of the 'great prosperity' was more modest than is generally supposed: alongside the 'miraculous' growth of the European periphery and Japan came the British decline, while the ideological malaise of the consumer society was taking shape; the denunciation of Stalinism was not followed by the expected leap forward; in the Third World the social effects accompanying the development in question were often tragic (increasing inequality of income distribution, rural and urban marginalization, to name but a few). The rediscovery of the 'external limits' of growth (the planet's limited resources) was also a reminder of the fragility of the optimistic hopes of the 1950s and 1960s.

The global crisis opening in the 1970s should have put a complete stop to such illusions. But we are asked if the crisis offers a new chance (that of reassessing the dominant post-war thinking?) or is a further constraint. The disarray follows the fact that the illusions have not yet been swept away. In the West, the left has largely shared in the consensus based on unlimited growth and what the consensus assumes in the international order underlying the growth. In the countries of the East the ice of dogmatism has been broken, but it has to be observed that progress in the liberation of thought and deed are slow. In the Third World, the 'recompradorization' underway on the ruins of the radical nationalism of Bandung tends more to bring nostalgic regrets for the past – if it does not unleash new illusions of obsolete culturalism (in the form of religious and other 'fundamentalisms') – than to move on in the critique of the limitations and weaknesses of that past.

Conservative forces' offensive

The logic of the immediate conservative response to the crisis entails: (i) submission through the compradorization of the South and crystallization of a Northern bloc against the South; (ii) grinding down the labour movement at the centre through unemployment and the inter-class movements through inflation; (iii) surrender to the US counter-attack aimed at re-establishing its hegemony whose decline was initiated by the very fact of European and Japanese advance.

a) The offensive on the South is at the heart of the conflicts opened up by the crisis.

The relatively favourable conditions flowing from the worldwide expansion of capitalism in the preceding phase (1945–70) had sometimes allowed the Third World bourgeoisies to push the imperialist system into making concessions. The radical wing of these bourgeoisies, emerging from a powerful national liberation movement with a popular element, had founded and legitimized its national leadership through social (mainly agrarian) reforms, the development of a public sector and the implementation of a policy of speedy industrialization. An alliance with the Soviet Union sometimes contributed to broadening the space for manoeuvre of these new bourgeoisies. But these national policies, by virtue of their class base, internal alliances and ideologies, never considered 'de-linking' from the international division of labour or a 'popular strategy'.

These limitations are the source of the fragility of these attempts, a fragility revealed by the crisis in economic terms (foreign deficits and indebtedness) and political terms (disaffection of popular support). The current phase of the crisis provides favourable conditions to destroy the 'impossible' aspirations of the bourgeoisies of the South and to force them to capitulate. Everything possible is done for the purpose: financial aggression (through the IMF and the Club of Ten), economic aggression (shown in the rejection of the claims of the NIEO), and even military aggression (Zionist expansion, South African destabilization exercises, and so on). The West has so far lined up behind the United States, despite a few contrary statements here and there. The global attack on the South would, if successful, end up 'recompradorizing' the bourgeoisies of the South and making their further growth part of the strict logic of the transnationalization strategies of monopoly capital.

This vast movement of flow and reflow in the national plan in the South is evidence that national liberation is still on the agenda, that it cannot be achieved by the bourgeoisie at the periphery, that a popular alliance here is the only way to overcome social contradictions that are only aggravated by the development of capitalism, that a national and popular objective entails 'de-linking' and that this may begin a 'socialist transition'. The least that can be said is that this necessary evolution is an aspect of the problematic of socialism and the only effective aspect as the option for an 'alternative' national and world development has not been initiated in the developed centres of the system.

In the short term the offensive for recompradorization is gaining ground. But so is the response, in the initial form of violent popular rejection (for example: Iran, Nicaragua, El Salvador, Ethiopia, Ghana). Can this 'populist' response mobilized around an ideology of rejection (Islam for example) go further and allow the crystallization of a new national and popular stage? It is, of course, an open question. The answer will in part depend on the answer to another significant question: can external forces (in Europe for example) break away from capital's offensive against the South, play the 'non-alignment' game (of real and equal opposition to the two superpowers) and support a national and popular outcome for the South?

If we put the attack on the South at the head of what is at stake in the crisis, it is because it can readily be seen that the Western bloc has been reconstituted on this basis. The alignment behind the United States has provisionally outweighed the potential conflicts between the Western partners (United States, Europe, Japan) just as it has blocked the way to peaceful settlement of East–West disputes.

b) In the developed capitalist countries, the offensive of capital is built on three principles: (i) re-establishment of a pool of unemployed permitting industrial restructuring at the expense of the weakened and divided working class (steady jobs and unskilled labour, women, youth and immigrants, and so on); (ii) priority for options reinforcing international competitiveness, heightened by the crisis; and (iii) priority for the struggle against inflation, itself a means of avoiding falling back in international competitiveness.

In these countries, response to the previous crisis was Keynesian, that is, redistribution of income and increase of overall demand through public spending with strict regard for the rules of financial profitability. It is debatable if this response was really effective in the 1930s or if it was only an illusion, and if the 'imperial withdrawals' that accompanied it were not rather an ingredient in the crystallization of blocs leading, for example, to the war; the fact is, that this kind of response is quite impossible nowadays.

Is the working class of the developed capitalist countries doomed to defeat, that is, to accepting 'restructuring' in terms only of the demands of the profitability of capital?

Such an outcome is inevitable if we accept the sacrosanct 'international competitiveness' as the final criterion for immediate options. The only way to avoid surrender to the demands of capital is to relate the immediate option to two complementary perspectives, in favour of 'alternative development' and in favour of support for the national and popular plan in the South. Defeat is also inevitable if we accept the rallying to the Atlantic pact entailing the subjection of North–South and intra-West relations to the East–West confrontation.

Undoubtedly, too, the hegemonic centres and the other centres do not behave exactly the same way in the phases of the crisis. The hegemonic power of the moment is the only one that can play the game of worldwide expansion to the limit. The rest are obliged either to keep their distance (imperial protectionism, and so on) or to submit. Nowadays, the United States makes the decisions, and Europe with good or bad grace rallies round and accepts them. This asymmetry suggested to André Frank that there is a single 'national' bourgeoisie, that of the hegemonic power, and all the others are to varying degrees subordinate. It seems a strained conclusion. First since hegemony is characteristic only of moments of capitalist history, Great Britain's from 1815 to 1880, the United States's from 1945 to 1970. The hegemony has never prevented the rise of adversaries and an eventual challenge to itself. If worldwide expansion at the current stage no longer permits the emergence of new centres, the centres established at an earlier stage are not susceptible to being 'disintegrated' and 'compradorized' as the peripheries are. The prior national construction has created an irreversible reality.

c) The crisis of the world system is multidimensional. By this token the strategies of East–West relations are articulated in the internal strategies of capital.

The attitude of the West in this regard is somewhat ambivalent. On the one hand there is an effort to 'reintegrate the East' in the world system, in the hope that this reintegration might offer new prospects for the expansion of capital. It must be stressed that capital here is obliged to respect the political autonomy of the countries of the East, despite the deep crisis in the economies of the Communist world (difficulties of moving to intensive accumulation with respect for the statist modalities of the system, foreign indebtedness, among others). On the other hand the Reaganite counter-offensive recruited the West into the arms race it wanted ('Star Wars', and so on) which obviously reduced the possibilities of 'reintegrating' the USSR into the world economic system.

The question to consider is not the character of the USSR or its outlook, but the empirical one of the tactical military balance. At this level is the USSR the main threat today? Why does it not use its supposed military superiority to attack the West today instead of waiting until it has lost that superiority? Is there not really a disinformation campaign aimed at winning acceptance for the re-establishment of the hegemony of the United States? The European gamble that yielding to American demands on this would allow the negotiation of economic concessions has turned out to be a trap. The opposite has occurred: rallying to the Atlantic pact has reduced the scope of Europe's economic autonomy.

In such case, the East, whether or not it is regarded as 'socialist', is no more incapable of becoming potentially expansionist, or adventurist in order to overcome its internal crisis. Its internal crisis is deep and specific. But it is doubtful if it can be overcome by gradual integration of the East in the world system. This option strikes significant obstacles: the threat of loss of control through too much integration . . . the East would back-track whenever it felt threatened. This is the lesson of the failure of Khruschev's illusions, followed by a return to the conservatism of Brezhnev. It is true that Gorbachev now seems ready to take these reforms further. These reforms, like those under way in China (that are in part their inspiration) cannot, however, be reduced to a 'readiness for reintegration in the world system'. Their political, democratic and popular aspect gives new heart to the socialist forces in the society. By restoring greater balance between the three components of the post-capitalist society (socialist, capitalist and statist components) – and putting an end to the hegemony of the statist trends – the reform may unblock the situation and open new ground for the dialectic of social progress. Of course, have not the conservative forces in the West, fearful of progress and proponents of a 'socialist menace', for this very reason chosen to reheat the atmosphere through the arms race?

The difficulties of forecasting

Capital's global offensive does not lessen conflicts between the states (super-powers, Europe–Japan–United States, conflicts with Third World countries . . .) but aggravates their violence. The crisis will continue and probably worsen, since the forces in play as they are cannot impose a solution.

Since the beginning of the 1970s, each recession is worse than the previous one, each recovery a more uneasy convalescence leading to relapse. The new market opened by OPEC and the semi-industrialized countries (through recycling) has closed down. The response is artificial and based solely on galloping inflation, in the United States' external and internal debt, without genuine investment, and turning capitalism into a roulette wheel ever more threatened with financial crash. A relaunch through dollar devaluation no longer works for the United States and a relaunch through the German and Japanese engines is refused.

Undoubtedly, in this situation the ruling classes will become aware of the solidarity that links their fate. A solidarity that extends in part to the leadership of the countries of the East.

Can the conclusion be drawn from this that solidarity is worth more than competition and that, 'all in the same boat', the ruling classes of the West will agree to wipe off the Third World debt, if only to prevent the debtors who must serve the debt being forced to export more, at the cost of increasing unemployment among the Western creditors? Will a united Europe agree to be the starting motor for a compassionate relaunch based on a common social policy?

It is very doubtful, simply because capitalism is not governed by the pursuit of common long-term interests (even those of capital) but by competition of capitals and capitalist countries. It is obvious that unemployment in the short term is not the problem of the capitalist, but of the unemployed. The search for immediate profit is paramount, and without it the supremacy of financial speculation over investment would be inexplicable, and the alignment of the entire West behind the IMF to impose a further round of pillage on the Third World would be incomprehensible. Could the 'workers' of the West jointly impose upon their states an intelligent capitalist solidarity (through advanced common social policy and a moratorium on Third World debt, for example) that the capitalists themselves refuse?

Is the financial crash inevitable? It is not absolutely clear, although the possibility is by no means ruled out. There are nowadays 'financial techniques' that may prevent a formal crash, techniques unknown in 1929. But these tricks do not eliminate the problem. In the absence of a crash, the crisis may drag on, slowly worsening. This is what some believe the most likely, with the further conclusion that the European electors will continue to oscillate between liberal conservative and flabby social democracy. Really there is nothing new in the West.

In the longer term, anything may happen . . .

'Forecasting' in the cycles of long crisis of the capitalist system, the periods of 'wars and revolutions', is therefore a hostage to fortune. Who in 1910 would have been capable of imagining the world of 1945, just 35 years later: the Russian and Chinese revolutions, the independence of Asia and Africa, US hegemony and the end to inter-imperialist conflicts? The year 2020 remains unpredictable, and almost any scenario may be sustained. Are we looking at the 'desirable' future (from whose point of view?), or probable or possible? on what time scale: short term, that is, with existing political and social forces, or longer term, when the balance of forces may have changed, or new forces have emerged? If politics is the art of the possible, it is not only the art of the possible in the current relation of forces (that art is at best of the tactical, and most frequently opportunist policy) but is also the art of changing the relation of forces.

A further difficulty: what is the real extent of the scientific and technical mutation under way? Does it exempt the less advanced societies from acquiring control of 'routine techniques' to rush straight towards the future? This argument is so frequently invoked that it provokes in us a reflex to discount it. Is this a new and additional form of blackmail? It seems that the 'underdeveloped' society that managed to master what is still the essence of productive systems would also be able to move to the higher level more easily than is often supposed, and that without the initial mastery, its effort to go beyond it first may not be very successful.

Furthermore, is there a necessary relationship between this mutation and the constraint of worldwide expansion? Here again the prevailing view is that the constraint is 'inescapable' for everyone, capitalists and socialists. In this instance the current crisis would be of a 'new kind'. We should add that military technology – the real possibility of global destruction of humankind – must of necessity affect the strategies and tactics of the forces in play. A 'collapse' that would have been taken positively in other times is now frightening because of the danger it could bring of a slide into nuclear war. But we roll all these arguments into an 'absolute technical, military and cultural world-embracing constraint'. They have a fair measure of blackmail that gives us pause.

The real options for the peoples of the West

We were satisfied with saying above: 'Really there is nothing new in the West'. It is a phrase that needs to be expanded if we are to avoid misunderstandings. Obviously the West is the centre of countless evolutions of significance for the overall future of the world. It is, for example, the centre that drives the development of the forces of production on a world scale, the inventor of new technologies. In some aspects of social life it is also the locus of the most advanced breakthroughs (consider the impact of feminism on day to day social relations . . .). What the phrase we are considering means, is that the stability of Western society is such that the relations of production are modulated and adjusted to the demands of the development of the forces of production without occasioning serious political schism.

We might cite a living example. Fordism as a form of capitalist relations of production corresponds to a given phase in development of the forces of production (mass production, assembly line working, mass consumption, the welfare state, and so on). Fordism is nowadays in acknowledged crisis: productivity of labour can no longer advance on this basis and sometimes falls. New technologies (informatics and robotization, genetic engineering, space exploration, among others) force other forms of labour organization. But everything leads us to suppose that this crisis in Fordist labour will not bring revolutionary political fractures. At most it will lead to a reclassification in the hierarchy of centres, accelerating the decline of some (Britain, France?) and the rise of others (Japan?). To take the argument further, it might be said that there is less and less that is new in the West. A comparison between the social reactions to the current crisis and those of the 1930s is highly instructive. The crisis of the 1930s led to serious political polarizations: fascisms or popular fronts. In our crisis we see on the contrary left and right (in the electoral sense of the terms) drawing together in the conception of how to manage the passage to a higher stage of development of the forces of production. Is this not a clear political effect of the increasing and deepening polarization within the world system? In the West the capitalist relations of production adjust to the demands of the development of the forces of production without bringing a pronounced political and social crisis.

But if the underlying crisis continues over a long term, with or without a financial crash, are some as yet unexpected upheavals likely to occur?

It is not hard to see that, in the event of a crash, the mercantile conflict would prevail over any other consideration in the first instance; and the EEC would probably not survive as an institution. But even without a crash, would not a continuance and worsening of the crisis lead to the same result? Must chilling responses, bolstered by the shock of chronic unemployment, and taking on a fascistic hue perhaps, be excluded?

It is in any event striking that in the discussions on this outlook one question is not often asked: what will happen to the United States? Perhaps this is because the answers are either too frightening (a slide into war) or utopian, in present circumstances (a new 'New Deal'!). This vacuum is accompanied by an additional threefold vacuum: there is not much new in the East (a slow and controlled evolution or return to cold storage seem the only probabilities); nor in the South (the people will accept the fate the West deals out, even at the cost of sporadic, unimportant revolts); and in Japan still less change is expected.

So attention is focused on European reactions. Then all the imagination that is so cruelly lacking about the others has full range. In this spirit three scenarios are envisaged. First: break-up of the EEC, and internecine struggle of narrow nationalisms. Second: rallying to the Atlantic pact and East–West confrontation. Third: a change of direction and rapprochement of the two Europes.

These three hypotheses, if they are quantifiable, are all equally probable. The first might be said to lead to absurd attitudes that would entirely marginalize

Europe. But history has its share of collective suicides. The second might be said to lead to militarization of West and East (and a turning inward that the option would impose on the Soviet bloc) that would be appallingly costly for the two Europes and emphatically increase the danger of the slide into militarism. Is the risk being avoided? After all, is not anti-Sovietism, which does exist in Europe (and on the left), the best argument of the Atlantic pact? And has the Atlantic pact not had the last word on the mercantile conflicts between Europe and the United States? The third hypothesis is no less probable. There are some who doubt it, since the EEC will become an 'economic giant' unable to pursue a policy independent of US strategy: it cannot escape the dollar nor the American nuclear umbrella. There are others who believe that Europe will manage it sooner or later. For Europe cannot operate (that is escape the crisis) by accepting the dollar and the US nuclear umbrella. Just as the United States would be more and more drawn to the Pacific and a Washington–Tokyo–Peking axis would become inevitable (especially as Japan would have no option but to join with the United States and China, on the argument that it went on regarding the USSR as the 'principal danger') then, almost inevitably, the only safeguard for Western Europe would be a rapprochement with Eastern Europe.

Again, what is striking in these suppositions is the implicit hypothesis that the East would remain passive and would accept the European overtures without being able to change the modalities, and that the South would remain even more passive (nothing new would happen . . . after the Chinese and Russian experiences, revolution has come to an end . . .).

What is also striking is the confusion between probability, possibility and desirability. East–West European rapprochement is certainly possible (even if it is not possible to assess its probability in comparison with the other hypotheses), but above all desirable. Not in the ingenuous sense that it would 'solve the European problem' (the crisis in West Europe), but in the sense that it would offer more opportunities for social progress (in West Europe and East Europe and in the peripheries of the South). For – something that makes this prospect seem difficult – such rapprochement implies a dynamic new West–East–South relationship that must take into consideration the objectives of the peoples of the East and South.

Before considering more or less realistic or chimerical long-term projects, it is useful to examine what Western Europe is and what social and political forces operate there, and what are their practices and views.

In this framework it is easy to carry out the process for the EEC as an institution of a common European economic policy and of Europe as an ensemble of national political societies of central capital. It is obvious that the EEC has not been a means of resistance to the United States, but on the contrary the channel for an acceleration of Atlantic transnationalization (the EEC being a sub-unit of the worldwide unit) which does not preclude mercantile conflicts between partners. Europe is an active partner in the imperialist domination of the Third World, and in particular the senior partner in the domination of Africa. In some aspects of economic policy to the Third

World, and Africa in particular, Europe is no less harmful than the United States; and there is an image of the 'ugly European' no less ugly than that of the 'ugly American' in Latin America, as has been shown (cf. Chapter 4).

At the political level, European attitudes so far have scarcely been any more attractive. The alignment of Europe with the strategy of the United States (since Europe is not only the EEC but NATO too) has aggravated East–West conflict. The aim of this common strategy is not the defence of Europe but, if not driving the USSR out of Eastern Europe, at least a pressure on the USSR through the arms race in the hope that this pressure will trap the countries of the East in positions that prevent their democratic and social evolution. Unconditional support for Zionism, the plan to split the Arab world, connect the Maghreb with Europe on the Turkish model and 'Lebanonize' the Mashreq, are part of this negative perspective, as are many of the interventions in Africa (cf. Chapter 4).

Does this mean that the EEC is the institution responsible for all these tribulations? That without it the forces of socialism would have been reinforced in some if not all the European countries, in their mutual isolation? This view, recently held by some European Communist parties and, curiously, adopted by the British Labour Party, and argued by Johan Galtung seems totally illusory to me. Unfortunately the roots of the dominance of capitalist forces, on which the social consensus in Europe is based, are much deeper. That is why 'pro-imperialist', anti-Soviet, anti-Third World options have a very strong following among the electorally strong forces, of right and left, with or without the EEC.

It is still the case that outside the common institutions of the EEC, Europe as an ensemble of nations – albeit capitalist – forms to some extent one of the 'weakest links' in the system. This is not the 'weakest link' in the sense Lenin gave the term, meaning a maturing of contradictions giving rise to a socialist rupture; it is a 'weakest link' in the sense that it might be brought to smash the current tightly knit Atlantic pact. Why? Simply because, in the long term, the system marginalizes Europe in its strategy and the world economy. This is a motive that might (but need not necessarily) lead to a rupture in the Atlantic bloc. The more so as the forces of European capitalism might justifiably feel that this overture would not threaten either their external security (the USSR would not seize the opportunity to invade Western Europe!) or their internal security (the 'socialist rupture' would not be an 'automatic' consequence).

Whether we like it or not we are back to square one. The future of the European peoples will not necessarily be hostage to the dominant view of the political forces at present on stage, views that are in the end limited. The option of 'alternative development' is the sole objective around which the forces of progress can be mobilized.

We shall not revert to the discussions as to what this 'alternative development' could mean in the circumstances of the developed West. The options have been formulated, in embryo at least, by still marginal movements, in statements by the Greens and feminists, in the programme of the Swedish social-democratic left for gradual transfer of social ownership of capital, in Italy's talk in favour of non-commodity opportunities, in the programme of Pasok in Greece in favour of support for national and popular projects in the Third World and so forth.

These positions are as yet no more than embryo, but an embryo essential for the renaissance of a socialist perspective in the new conditions, very different from those imagined by Marx in his day. The gradual effective crystallization of an alternative development could pave the way for an extension of social ownership. Of course this evolution has still to be found and must devise solutions for the real problems it poses, especially as regards the relations between the state and democratic socialization. Evidently the start of an evolution in this direction entails the relinquishment of neo-Keynesian illusions and a counter-attack on the fashionable ideology of the right ('anti-statism', restoration of elitism and inequality, and so on). No doubt, too, this prospect would have more chance if it were possible for the forces of the left in Europe to band together to insist upon a 'social' (and political) Europe going beyond the limited horizons of the Europe of the 'common market'.

Options for socialist societies and East–West relations

A progressive outcome of the crisis suggests a discussion on East–West relations and the prospects for evolution of the 'socialist' societies.

As we have said, the offensive by capital is based on blackmail putting East–West relations (US–USSR in fact) at the centre of the strategy and subjecting intra-West and West–South relations to this military logic. The rallying to the Atlantic pact leaves little scope for an autonomous European policy, towards the South (as the Middle East, African and other conflicts show) and towards the East. It sees North–South relations as a complement of those of East–West confrontation and by the same token contributes to making the South the battle-ground of this confrontation. It also removes any hope for opening up space for reform in Eastern Europe and thus edges the situation even closer to apocalyptic confrontation.

The arguments to justify the Atlantic pact are made as if the East (of the Soviet and Chinese East) were incapable of their own initiatives and could only 'respond' to those of the West, Europe in this instance. This hypothesis stems from another more fundamental hypothesis, that the societies in question (the peoples and authorities) yearn to become 'like' those of the West. Their development is necessarily part of the worldwide expansion of capitalism, and they accept this necessary 'constraint'. Under various 'socialist' labels (Marxist or not) these societies would produce nothing but variations of capitalist development.

The argument is based on a series of narrowly 'economistic' or 'mercantilist' reasonings. This is the case for example of commentaries on the triangular (West–East–South) trade, or quadrangular (West–USSR–East Europe–South) trade. Too much significance is given to these commercial relations by regarding them as determining behaviour, without any regard to the internal social dynamic of the various partners. On the basis of this hasty judgement it is argued that the socialist countries 'form an integral part of the world capitalist system'. These countries are fully 'de-linked' in the sense that they have broad control of their external relations and subject them to the logic of their internal development, whereas the underdeveloped capitalist partners do the opposite: they 'adjust' their internal development to the constraints of accumulation on a world scale. This qualitative difference affects in turn the differing nature of the social systems.

It is true that the countries of the East want to step up economic relations with the West; but the West raises obstacles precisely because it knows that this stepping up, under the control of the socialist states, would strengthen them in their autonomous progress; and the West fears this strengthened autonomy more than anything else. The relative 'stagnation' of the socialist countries is seen to be one of the fundamental causes of the 'viability' of capitalism and that enhanced external economic relations could help the socialist countries to overcome this relative stagnation.

Assimilation of socialist countries to mere variants of capitalism leads to misleading simplifications. For example, people talk about an 'economic crisis' in the East and in the West as if it were the same phenomenon. It is highly inaccurate. The crisis in the countries in the East is one of the passage from extensive accumulation to intensive accumulation. It is independent of the crisis of world capitalism, even if the latter has conjuncturally made the performance of the Eastern world more difficult. The origin of the 'stagnation' is once again to be found in the specific social character of these societies.

In our analysis we describe the societies in question as 'national and popular' rather than 'socialist', meaning that these systems, products of an 'anti-capitalist' revolution (a revolt against the peripheralization imposed upon them by worldwide capitalist expansion), open a long transition where capitalist, socialist and statist forces and tendencies (with the statist forces enjoying a large degree of autonomy in comparison with the two others) are composed in unstable conflictive combinations. Analysis of the internal dynamic of this conflict is therefore essential, not only to an understanding of the societies, but also for an understanding of our modern world as a whole. The opinion that the – real or potential – socialist forces would be more powerful in France or Germany than in the USSR, China, Yugoslavia or Hungary seems quite unfounded, and bordering on the absurd.

It is in this framework that we must consider the three possible different futures for East–West relations:

(i) the rallying of Europe to the Atlantic pact and surrender to the aggressive attitude taken by the United States. The war envisaged here would, at least in the first stage, be waged on European terrain;
(ii) contrarily, a deepening of the divergence between Europe and the United States as regards East–West relations. Immanuel Wallerstein envisages here a possible consolidation of a Paris–Moscow axis against the Washington–

Toyko–Peking axis. It is a possibility that surfaced some years ago, and whose persistence is shown in the 'gas pipeline' affair. It is perhaps the most likely option if the currents of the most 'realistic' and least subjective in their ideological judgements about the USSR win their way in Europe. Certain currents of the European left, subjective in this ideological judgement, could fall into the trap set by Reaganism. Clearly, on this outlook, North–South relations are seen from a strictly 'imperialist' point of view but one where the Europe–US competition is maximized (a 'Gaullist' view) while the pro-Atlantic currents – of right and left – envisage a division of tasks between the United States and Europe (with Europe dealing with Africa); the rallying to the Altantic pact has not made revision of North–South relations entirely meaningless, as was shown in the astonishing retreat in the European stand on the Palestine issue and in Africa (for example, on support to Zaire and South Africa).

(iii) an 'alternative European policy' (or leftist) that was both anti-hegemonist (directed against the two hegemonisms), non-Atlantic and pro-Third World. In a word, rallying to 'non-alignment'. This option would reduce the risks of war and strengthen the scope for autonomy for workers in the West and the peoples of the South. It might, moreover, allow room for 'reformist transformation' of the East, blocked by the other policies. Evidently this option is out for the foreseeable future. A wavering Europe, where the left does not always grasp that you cannot go on wanting the privileges of imperialist domination and rejecting the restructuring that its expansion demands, is not ready to face up to it. China, from 1960 to 1970, chose this path, probably the wisest and best suited to the long-term interests of the peoples and of socialism. Isolated in its struggle 'against the two hegemonies', it renounced active non-alignment. The responsibility of Europe and of its left, which finally preferred to rally to the Reaganite Atlantic pact, is significant here.

In these circumstances, the thesis whereby an eventual rapprochement of the two Europes would constitute an even tougher front against the South than the current conflict is open to quesiton. This hypothesis, which Wallerstein takes to be a virtual certainty in the long term (in 50 years' time, he suggests) is based on two erroneous foundations: that the societies of the East will be less and less different from those of the West; that the South will have to submit to the dictates that the reconciled North will impose. At the least, according to Wallerstein, the ideological language will itself be toned down and if it does not become a mere hollow rhetoric, will at least betoken only minor amendments, like the opposition between the language of right and left in the West.

Even if it is admitted that all the so-called socialist societies are 'de-linked national and popular systems', there is room at the political level to distinguish the 'Easts' from one another. The USSR is both a global superpower and a European power, and this entails an internal conflict peculiar to its strategic and military aims that are not matters of blame but must be taken into account. This factor in no way justifies that, on the hypothesis of a political will for rapprochement between the two Europes, the USSR should be ostracized.

Meanwhile, it would probably be foolish and dangerous to set the aim of 'detaching' Eastern Europe from the Soviet alliance. Unfortunately this is the thinking of too many politicians of Western Europe, of left and right, sharing the same 'anti-Soviet' or 'Russophobic' position. The dangerous aspiration may find an echo here and there in Eastern Europe, with a fatal attraction by virtue of Europeanness to a West that must be described as capitalist. The aspiration does not serve the socialist forces and tendencies within these national and popular societies, but rather the capitalist and reactionary forces that operate there. The slide towards anti-Russian nationalism – notwithstanding the justifications that the 'big brother' provides – as it occurs in Poland, is a reminder of the limitations of this 'revolt', that, despite its worker element in some regards, is also fed on religious fundamentalism. Many Europeans irrationally applaud here what they condemn in Iran. In both cases, however, it is the same impasse. As for China, there is nothing to say that it must inevitably accept an extension of the Washington–Tokyo axis to Peking. It will do so to the degree that the USSR continues to be its principal danger. This was the case in the 1960s. It will no longer necessarily be so, especially if the Gorbachev era unfreezing goes deeper.

In East–West (or Easts–Wests) relations, the East is neither stagnant nor static, with initiative reserved for the West. The reality is rather the reverse. In the sense that the internal dynamic of the national and popular societies, the advances and retreats of the forces of socialism operating in these societies is in the forefront and largely shapes East–West relations.

Is an autonomous and progressive European initiative worthy of the name an illusory utopia? Perhaps it is in the short term, but in the long term it is an objective necessity.

This initiative obviously entails abandoning alignment with the anti-Soviet strategy of the United States. Does this mean that Europe should opt for vulgar 'pacifism' and leave it to Soviet whim to respect its 'disarmament'? Not at all. Europe must be able to defend itself on its own, without the American umbrella, and it has the capability. Without going into a complex topic that provokes prolonged discussion, we should say only that European atomic weapons are not an answer to the question. These would probably be inferior to Soviet weaponry in any event. The reconstruction of a modernized people's army (while the atomic options strengthen the professionals, who in European circumstances are almost necessarily reactionary) in the style of Yugoslavia and Sweden is probably the best answer.

Then the illusory prospect of 'economic domination' over East Europe must be relinquished, along with the even more illusory prospect of 'annexing' Eastern Europe and driving out the USSR.

Finally the 'neo-imperial' prospect of a unified Europe (under the aegis of its Western half) aggressive towards the Third World must be relinquished. Without this rupture, without the deliberate option of supporting the national and popular forms in Asia, Africa and Latin America, even to the detriment of (imperialist) advantages, talk of 'co-development' will remain hollow. It is impossible to carry out 'co-development' with a compradorized partner.

These are tough conditions. But is there not a beginning in Europe, in the frontier countries of the two Europes: Sweden, Finland, Austria, Hungary, Yugoslavia and Greece? Is not each of these countries in its own way, in its own framework (EEC or Comecon, or outside; NATO or Warsaw Pact, or outside; advanced or poor capitalism, or outside), and in this particular field (the social achievements of Sweden or Yugoslavia, or the armed neutrality of both countries) and with the modest means at its disposal, engaged in using as much as possible the narrow scope for manoeuvre that polarization on both sides has been unable to suppress?

This option is desirable since it opens up eventual (but not immediate) prospects to the forces of progress (socialist, popular or what you will) in the West and East of Europe, and may encourage their deployment on a wider stage. This is the way to contribute to a European 'cultural plan' in the best sense of the term, to a plan for a society whose history, after all, produced the Enlightenment and socialism, and thereby to play an active role – but with the others and not against them if without them – in the movement seeking to go far beyond the narrow limits of capitalist society.

The motivating forces on which such a plan could currently rely are certainly not substantial. They are not to be found in the working class as a whole, nor in the various alternatives (the Greens, and so on). But gradual deployment of these motivating forces is the only way to restore to the left the historical dimension it has lost.

The genuine long-term option: transnationalization or a polycentric world and broad autocentric regions

The offensive by capital shows the inexorable force with which it incorporates its strategies in the logic of worldwide expansion, as interdependence and interpenetration of economies has reached a much higher level than on the eve of the Second World War. This surrender to the law of worldwide expansion deprives the peoples and labouring classes of any possible autonomy and reduces their scope for choice to nil. It is also accompanied by an unprecedented ideological offensive: the objective of socialism is declared to be defunct, the dreams of 1968 absurd, and so forth.

It must urgently be recognized that submission to the demands of economic transnationalization is incompatible with a policy for a progressive outcome to the crisis. This is as true for the North as for the South.

There are two ways of envisaging evolution of the world political system towards polycentrism. The first reduces the centres of decision to five 'great powers' – United States, Europe, USSR, China and Japan – and leaves the Third World marginalized. The second envisages, in addition to these five centres, the crystallization of new forces organized at various regional levels of the Third World (Latin America, the Arab world, Africa, India and South-East Asia). This second perspective is the only one acceptable.

For the first question on the agenda of humankind is the solution to the problem of 'underdevelopment' affecting the majority of human beings. This situation will, in the future, as it does in the present, demand that we go 'beyond capitalism'. In this sense the Third World will be a storm zone for a long time to come.

In this perspective we can certainly start from the hypothesis that it is possible to act against the spontaneous laws of capitalism. There are bound to be some who think it impossible to act against the demands of worldwide expansion through which the absolute constraint is manifest today. But is that not a renunciation of the freedom that is perhaps the common denominator of the left presenting itself as a force for transformation as distinct from the force of conservation on the right?

The building of polycentrism entails significant transformations in the internal policies of the nations of North and South and in international political and economic relations.

It entails the beginning of 'alternative development' by the developed capitalist societies. Here, expansion of the social sector to the detriment of that governed only by value and in contradiction with the maximum pursuit of external competitiveness. It entails a selective protectionism without with the programmes indicated would be void of content. Of course European construction could contribute to a positive evolution in this direction, provided that a socially and politically conscious Europe was gradually established.

The last battle is far from won, since it has not even begun yet. If response to capital's offensive is sometimes marked by an electoral return to the left, it is as often a pronounced slide to the right, whose fascistic touches preclude a positive evolution of the European construct. It is true that European society is no longer what it was in the 1930s. Then the middle classes of the old kind (petty producers, and so on) could be the allies of the working class in popular fronts provided that these, without aiming for profound social changes, could unify them, in defence of democracy for example (against the fascism that was appealing to the same middle-class victims of the crisis). Today, greater steps have to be taken in the direction of satisfying the incipient 'post-capitalist' social aspirations.

Polycentrism obviously entails a start on evolutions towards autocentric national and popular constructions. As in Europe, regional co-operation is essential here to provide a sufficiently broad scope for these constructions. Some of the Third World bourgeoisies may still believe themselves strong enough to play the game of worldwide expansion as it is; but the failures of attempts at integration in the world financial system by OPEC for example – and the stifling of the model of industrialization by the NICs – should be enough to destroy these illusions.

Alternative North–South relations should be possible on this dual basis. The progressive governments of the North cannot ignore the South and line up with the strategies of the complex linking the United States, the World Bank, the IMF and the consortium of banks representing financial capital on a world scale, even if the alignment is larded with 'Third-Worldist' rhetoric as has sometimes been the case. The popular governments of the South will have difficulty in envisaging a withdrawal into virtual national autarky, and they can no longer rely, as they have rightly or wrongly believed possible, on the alternative of the Soviet alliance.

There is, therefore, a common interest in envisaging a new North–South co-operation on a selective basis that, if it is in conflict with worldwide expansion under the aegis of financial capital, could reinforce the supersessions of capitalism and the popular constructions in this or that place. The content, aims and modalities of this new co-operation must be discussed and envisaged in a creative spirit. For it is clear that development strategies cannot be identical from one region to another of our world, a world that is too diversified at all levels for this to make sense. The theological formulas that propose to make the 'market' – or the state – the pass-key to the happiness of everyone are today the main ideological obstacle to polycentrism.

Responses to the crisis challenge founded on this perspective of polycentric construction would certainly open up: (i) scope for popular autonomy to begin a supersession of capitalism in the North; (ii) scope for autonomy to progress with national and popular construction in the South; and (iii) scope perhaps to facilitate reformist advances in the East (on the basis of this might we hope to see a gradual annulment of the great schism that has since 1917 broken the world labour and socialist movement?).

Can we ask for more? Is there anything on the agenda more urgent than an internationalist revival.

Where does socialism fit into this perspective? I do not know much about that. But where does socialism fit into the developed West, the countries of the East, the nationalist or compradorized Third World? Socialism is surely still before us, if, as we suggest, we accept that the national and popular transition is not yet over.

The fracture of the world manifest in the centres/peripheries polarization inherent in capitalism obliges us to review the schema for construction of socialism produced in the 19th century. The fracture has put on the agenda of history the national and popular revolution at the periphery of the system and not the socialist revolution in its centres.

Is the conclusion that we must entirely accept all the consequences of this major fact?

Must we accept the fracture between the Western labour movement (which has abandoned the notion of a classless society to become a player in the capitalist rules of the game, and consequently a follower of the ideology and imperialist practice of dominant capital) and the popular movement of the backward countries (whether 'socialist' or not), stuck on a long, difficult and tortuous path that drives them into many compromises and retreats?

To refuse to accept this fracture as 'definitive' courts the risk of being described by some as 'voluntarist'. This does not prevent us believing that European détente, permitting a return to dialogue of peoples beyond states and even perhaps parties, could begin the long process of rebuilding popular internationalism. It does not prevent us believing that on the same condition a dialogue between the peoples of North and South (the two Norths and all the

South) could reach an unsuspected pitch.

Should we, in conclusion, return to the theme of 'de-linking'? This global perspective is precisely one of general de-linking, that is subjection of the external relations of each of the various parties in the world to the logic of the demands of popular development, demands that are necessarily varying and specific by virtue of the heterogeneities of the starting point. De-linking is neither commercial autarky, nor chauvinistic culturalist nationalism. If there is a positive side to the universalism begun by capitalism, it is not to be found at the level of economic development (since this by nature remains unequal), but definitely at the level of a popular, cultural and ideological universalism, boding for the 'post-capitalist' stage, a genuine socialist outlook.

What is at stake in the conflict is not capitalism or socialism in the abstract, as systems of social organization. The real alternative is worldwide development, which in the current phase supposes a return to subjection to the hegemony of the United States over the whole of the Western system, or the rejection of this prospect to the advantage of maximum autonomy. Accepting worldwide expansion means accepting the dual crystallization around the two superpowers, in an atmosphere of cold war tempered with hot wars and with all that the cold and hot wars may bring in terms of slide towards mass destruction. The alternative is: acceptance of worldwide development as it is with all this entails, or an attempt to implement autocentric national and popular development strategies that will operate as forces to reshape both the national societies and the world system. The latter is, after all, only a reflection of its components in the national societies. The alternative therefore is: worldwide expansion or greater scope for autonomy for peoples, states and nations, that is to the benefit of the popular classes. To surrender or to de-link to the utmost the fate and future of the peoples, states and nations from the implacable demands of gross, capitalist expansion worldwide.

A new internationalism of the peoples could be rebuilt on these bases. It is the only humanistic and civilized option for our age.

Conclusion: A crisis of transnationalization, ideology and development theory

The considerations we offer by way of conclusion encourage further discussion in four directions that seem to us of particular significance: (1) the character of the transnationalization typifying our epoch; (2) the new elements called into consideration by its crisis; (3) the dangers of the situation; and (4) the character of the crisis of ideology and the social considerations that flow from it.

Terms such as transnationalization (beyond nation) and worldwide expansion (that by-passes the concept of nation) that have come into common parlance are, like everything in the social science vocabulary, necessarily ambiguous, with positive and negative implications. They indicate in fact the existence of powerful trends in the economic, cultural and social life of all peoples, driving them beyond the limits of conditioning by forces operating solely within the nation and into acceptance of interaction with others. Worldwide expansion, the potential bearer of a humanist universalism, is given a positive value in all systems of modern thought. At the same time, transnationalization in a narrower but more precise sense defines one of the key characteristics of the system in which we live, one we prefer to describe as 'really existing capitalism'. It would require an acceptance of all the distortion that Western-centred ideology has imposed on the 'social sciences' to put an 'equals' sign between the two concepts. For the system is also, in economic and political terms, polarized between the centres that determine the direction of global evolution and the peripheries that more or less passively endure the worldwide expansion in question. Cultural universalism produced under such circumstances is truncated; it is a bogus universalism, an illusion.

Realistically speaking, transnationalization is nothing more than the expression of the subjection of the various segments constituting 'really existing' world capitalism to the worldwide law of value. Not that such subjection operates uniformly, ironing out specific local characteristics of the societies where it is implemented, and thereby bringing an eventual 'homogenization'. In contrast to such a vision, it must be understood that these specific characteristics are reproduced by a common subjection to the worldwide law of value. Certainly, the world system has varying productive systems, in a hierarchy. To some extent these systems, or the most evolved among them, correspond to the area of state government. Just as national productive systems are beginning to collapse and to re-emerge within the world scope. A plurality of productive systems in no way contradicts that values of one cannot be compared with values of another. Here the economy is running ahead of institutionalized politics. We are still living in an inter-state system where each state is in principle sovereign. There is no world state, nor world currency, nor common world legal system, still less common political, economic and social systems. Despite this fact, the world economy is based on comparability of values, whose reality is shown in talk about 'competitiveness'. The keystone currency of the hegemonic centre is imposed as a world currency; in the absence of an alternative, it goes on being imposed as such when the hegemony in question is declining and under challenge.

This worldwide system is no novelty. It is as old as capitalism. It has not had a linear development without 'ups and downs', but through a succession of long cycles through the centuries with alternations of relative stability of the hierarchies and the rules of the game and challenges to such hierarchies. We are currently at the peak of one of the latter and so we must ask ourselves what is new and in embryo and what, therefore, will be the structures of the future.

It might hypothetically be argued that the most significant qualitatively new feature is precisely the beginning of the rupture of the concomitance between the individual productive system and the established national bourgeois state.

This rupture – and not by chance – is operating within the framework of a triple 'revolution': cybernetic, cultural and military. The extent of the first, technological, dimension is still little known, and often obscured by the technological catch-phrase, whether in the rather childishly scientific style ('Science will solve the problems of humankind'), or in the discouraging doomsday style ('The peoples who do not join in this scientific revolution are irretrievably damned'). The extent of the universalization of the messages – the world is a global village where people overlook what these messages bring as supposedly universal values – is no less ambiguous: its strength is obvious, just as the frustrations it entails are. As for the extent of military technology, it is far too apparent for there to be any doubt as to its decisive influence on politics: for the first time in the history of humankind the earth's self-destruction has become a real possibility.

The dangers presented by our epoch are gigantic. The play of economic, political and cultural forces operating within national plans and the global system will, it seems, determine evolution in one of three possible directions: (1) pursuit in new patterns of the worldwide expansion dictated by the narrow demands of capital; (2) collapse of the system; (3) its reconstitution on a polycentric regionalized basis.

Only lack of imagination makes the economic technocrats consider only the first hypothesis. The institutions of world capitalism operate in this direction specifically. They argue that the inter-state regulation corresponding to the concomitance of productive systems and states can be replaced by 'private' regulation adapted to the rupture of this concomitance. As this is the fashionable ideology it commits the grossest blunder possible in social thought: it puts economics (reduced to the dominant productive system) at the helm, without regard to the political and cultural dimensions that are supposed to adapt to it without difficulty! It also pays little heed to the victims of the 'adjustment': the peoples of the Third World condemned to super-exploitation, and those of the fourth world doomed to extinction. It cannot conceive of their revolt against the system.

Sticking stubbornly to this line of thought and action is the sure way of maximizing the dangers of collapse that will then come as no surprise, except to the idiots who did not want to think about its mechanisms. The rush into speculation in response to the crisis worsens the dangers of financial collapse. The desperate political responses – whose potential is already clearly signalled – may cause the abortion of a still fragile construction such as that of Europe. The neo-imperial rush to North–South conflict or the 'hotting up' of the East–West conflict will turn these skids into directions whose result can be imagined!

The only remaining hope is for wisdom. Acceptance of a plurality of productive systems, political visions and cultures requires reconstitution within a polycentric, regionalized perspective along the lines sketched out in this book.

The analytical instrument available for an understanding of the mechanisms of social choice and a fortiori for effective action is far from meeting the scale of the challenges – to the extent that we prefer to speak of social thought and avoid the term social science, as the status of this discipline is in no way analogous to that of the physical sciences. The collapse of social thought along the lines of the various academic 'disciplines' sometimes leads to a belief that the economic dimension of the reality does follow laws similar to those sought in other fields of scientific research. But as has been indicated, it is obviously not the same when it comes to a possible 'theory' of power or 'theory' of culture. Their interaction in the explanation of contemporary history must remain subject to the hypotheses of 'schools of thought' and not to 'scientific' theories (where the adjectives 'true' or 'false' may legitimately be applied). That is why social thought remains a perpetual battleground of the models of opposing schools of thought, whereas in the physical sciences new more accurate and complex models displace the ancient and obsolete theories.

In these circumstances, prevailing social 'theories', that form this or that majority view, are inadequate. They are subject to a dual distortion. Its first facet is their 'economistic' character, in the sense that they are based on the notion that 'economics' rules the world and everything else must adjust to its demands. An economic conception that is often very threadbare is doubly limited by the belief that 'market laws' operate like natural laws (and that the former laws are known!), and by the belief that technological progress operates as an autonomous external force. Hence, Progess is analogous to Providence in the replacement of the ancient metaphysical alienation of former societies by the economistic and technological alienation peculiar to capitalism.

The second facet of the distortion in question arises from the view that worldwide expansion is 'ineluctable' and must therefore be accepted as it is. Eurocentrism lurks behind this distortion. In three books of the series that this book completes these issues have been tackled head on. Faysal Yachir stresses the shortcomings of the various theories offered to 'explain' recent evolutions in the world economic system, Samir Amin stresses the shortcomings of social thought as regards the economics–power–culture articulation and the western-centred distortion of the prevailing schools, while Bernard Founou-Tchuigoua synthesizes the discussions on the theme of transnationalization or national construction indicated in the title of his book.[2]

Periods of crisis such as ours exacerbate the conflicts between the schools. As is apparent every day and in the face of the challenge, the schools in question slide gracefully into theology; whether that in vogue of the market with the argument that market laws under a *laissez faire* policy can achieve what they have failed to achieve over four centuries (homogenization of the world and material happiness for all!) or that of the state willing to proclaim that it can effectively replace the shortcomings of the market. Rather than such largely sterile debates we prefer the path of 'critical thought', meaning by that a consideration that challenges all schools of thought.

The debate on the failure of development made us highlight several of the essential issues that critical thought must examine: the character and extent of the economic constraints of transnationalization and the worldwide expansion of the law of value, the character and extent of state power and the crisis of the nation-state, historical agents of social change and evolution of forms of expression in the social movement, the character of inter-state conflict in the East–West, North–South and South–South context, the evolving content of the capitalism versus socialism debate, the rigidities and flexibilities of cultures, and so on. As the reader will obviously have noted, the hypotheses put forward in these fields go beyond the single issues of 'development', although world polarization as the number one problem for all humankind is a privileged terrain of critical thought.

Notes

1. Amin, Samir, 'A. G. Frank and the Crisis', *Monthly Review*, No. 6, 1983; 'La crise, les relations Nord–Sud et Est–Ouest', *Nouvelle Revue Socialiste*, Sept.–Oct. 1983; *Une autre configuration des relations internationales est-elle possible?*, Delphes, in preparation; and cf. references to the study of the crisis in *La crise de l'impérialisme* and *Dynamics of Global Crisis*.

2. Amin, Samir, *L'eurocentrisme*, Paris, Economica, 1988, in English, *Eurocentrism*, New York, Monthly Review Press, 1989 and London, Zed Books, 1989; Yachir, Faysal, *La transnationalisation et la crise de la théorie et de l'idéologie du développement*, in preparation; Founou-Tchuigoua, Bernard, *Transnationalisation ou construction nationale: l'expérience africaine*, in preparation.

Index